THIS IS ANCIENT PHILOSOPHY

THIS IS PHILOSOPHY
Series editor: Steven D. Hales

Reading philosophy can be like trying to ride a bucking bronco—you hold on for dear life while "transcendental deduction" twists you to one side, "causa sui" throws you to the other, and a 300-word, 300-year-old sentence comes down on you like an ironshod hoof the size of a dinner plate. *This Is Philosophy* is the riding academy that solves these problems. Each book in the series is written by an expert who knows how to gently guide students into the subject regardless of the reader's ability or previous level of knowledge. Their reader-friendly prose is designed to help students find their way into the fascinating, challenging ideas that compose philosophy without simply sticking the hapless novice on the back of the bronco, as so many texts do. All the books in the series provide ample pedagogical aids, including links to free online primary sources. When students are ready to take the next step in their philosophical education, *This Is Philosophy* is right there with them to help them along the way.

This Is Philosophy, Second edition
Steven D. Hales

This Is Philosophy of Mind
Pete Mandik

This Is Ethics
Jussi Suikkanen

This Is Political Philosophy
Alex Tuckness and Clark Wolf

This Is Business Ethics
Tobey Scharding

This Is Metaphysics
Kris McDaniel

This Is Bioethics
Ruth F. Chadwick and Udo Schuklenk

This Is Epistemology
J. Adam Carter and Clayton Littlejohn

This Is Philosophy of Religion
Neil Manson

This Is Ancient Philosophy
Kirk Fitzpatrick

This Is Philosophy of Mind, 2nd edition
Pete Mandik

This Is Philosophy of Science
Franz-Peter Griesmaier and Jeffrey A. Lockwood

Forthcoming:

This Is Feminist Philosophy
Roxana Baiasu

THIS IS
ANCIENT
PHILOSOPHY
AN INTRODUCTION

KIRK FITZPATRICK

WILEY Blackwell

Published by John Wiley & Sons, Inc., Hoboken, New Jersey.
Published simultaneously in Canada.

For general information on our other products and services or for technical support, please
contact our Customer Care Department within the United States at (800) 762-2974, outside the
United States at (317) 572-3993 or fax (317) 572-4002.

Wiley also publishes its books in a variety of electronic formats. Some content that appears in
print may not be available in electronic formats. For more information about Wiley products, visit
our web site at www.wiley.com.

Library of Congress Cataloging-in-Publication Data
Names: Fitzpatrick, Kirk, author.
Title: This is ancient philosophy : an introduction / Kirk Fitzpatrick.
Description: Hoboken, New Jersey : Wiley-Blackwell, [2024] | Series: This
  is philosophy | Includes index.
Identifiers: LCCN 2023047959 (print) | LCCN 2023047960 (ebook) | ISBN
  9781119879404 (paperback) | ISBN 9781119879411 (adobe pdf) | ISBN
  9781119879428 (epub)
Subjects: LCSH: Philosophy, Ancient.
Classification: LCC B171 .F68 2024 (print) | LCC B171 (ebook) | DDC
  180–dc23/eng/20240112
LC record available at https://lccn.loc.gov/2023047959
LC ebook record available at https://lccn.loc.gov/2023047960

Cover design: Wiley

Set in 10.5/13pt Minion by Straive, Pondicherry, India

For Elizabeth and Forrest

CONTENTS

ACKNOWLEDGMENTS

I want to acknowledge the excellent team at Wiley-Blackwell. I am especially grateful to Steven D. Hales and Will Croft for their patience, support, and valuable advice. I am also thankful to the anonymous reviewers for their candid critiques. I am forever in debt to Charles M. Young, Richard D. McKirahan, and Daniel W. Graham for their pedagogy and mentorship through the decades. I could not have written this book without them. The book benefited greatly from multiple critiques by Kurt Smith and Lee Trepanier. Thank you also to Aubrey M. Bodine for making the map. I am grateful to Southern Utah University for granting me a sabbatical leave to aid this project. Finally, I want to thank all of my students through the last 31 years.

MAP

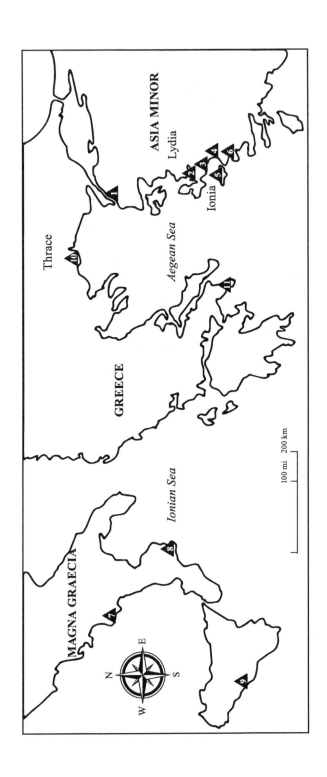

ASIA MINOR

1. Troy
2. Miletus—Thales, Aniximander, Aniximenes
3. Colophon—Xenophanes
4. Ephesus—Heraclitus
5. Clazomenae—Anaxgoras
6. Samos—Melissus

MAGNA GRAECIA

7. Elea—Parmenides, Zeno
8. Crotone—Pythagoras
9. Acragas—Empedocles

GREECE

10. Abdera—Leucippus, Democritus, Protagoras
11. Athens—Socrates, Plato, Aristotle, Antisthenes, Diogenes of Sinope, Epicurus, Zeno of Citium, Pyrrho, Arcesilaus of Pitane, Carneades

INTRODUCTION

The Precursors of Philosophy: Homer and Hesiod

Before Greek philosophy, there was Homer (c. 750 BCE), the cornerstone of all early Greek writings. He offers two epic poems, the *Iliad* and the *Odyssey*.[1] The *Iliad* is a story about rage, courage, and honor. The *Odyssey* is a story for training in leadership and excellence (*arete*). Athena mentors Telemachus until Odysseus returns. The epic poems employ the gods as anthropomorphic and immortal beings. The gods meddle in natural and human events. They have demigod children with humans, and they suffer the same emotions as humans. Homer employs a worldview that he inherits and weaves into his epic poems. He mentions the heavens, the gods, and the underworld. He treats natural phenomena, such as rivers, as gods. He puts gods on the battlefield. When Ares gets wounded in battle, he wails like a baby and runs back up to Olympus.[2] What he does not offer is an account of the heavens, the earth, the underworld, or gods in their own right. Still, for the early Greek philosophers and Plato, these are essential readings. The philosophers do not adopt the teachings. They critique the stories and propose alternative views. Any student of ancient Greek philosophy should read these works carefully.

---

[1] Homer's *Iliad* and *Odyssey* are available online at the Perseus Digital Library. The Iliad is here: https://www.perseus.tufts.edu/hopper/text?doc=Perseus:text:1999.01. 0134:book=1:card=1. The Odyssey is here: https://www.perseus.tufts.edu/hopper/ text?doc=Perseus:text:1999.01.0136.

[2] *Iliad* V.860.

This Is Ancient Philosophy: An Introduction, First Edition. Kirk Fitzpatrick.
© 2024 John Wiley & Sons, Inc. Published 2024 by John Wiley & Sons, Inc.

It might seem that Homer's works were the Bible of the ancient Greek world. This accurately places Homer at the center of Greek thought, but it ignores certain important points. There are two main differences between Homer's texts and the Bible. The Bible is sacrosanct; it excludes any alternative view. Its stories cannot be altered or varied without heresy. The ancients took Homer's stories as more fluid. A poet could claim, for instance, that Helen was not to blame for the war on Troy since the Helen in Troy was a specter. Helen all the while was somewhere else. Modern religions do not allow reinterpretation of their scripture. Historically, every Christian who wrote a book to distinguish all the heretics eventually became a heretic. Heretics did not fare well. Good luck for the Greeks, since they did not interpret Homer as sacrosanct.

Hesiod (c. 700 BCE) offers an importantly different approach to the archaic Greek perspective. Though he inherits the worldview, Hesiod is concerned to offer a more detailed and systematic treatment of the heavens, the earth, the gods, and human beings. *Theogony* and *Works and Days* offer an account of the topics. "Theogony" means the coming to be of the gods, or the birth of the gods.[3] The story that Hesiod tells connects the birth of the gods with the birth of the *Kosmos*, the ordered world. *Works and Days* tells of the cycles in the agricultural calendar, the regular cycles of the seasons, and the cycles in the many different ages of mankind.[4] In this work, we get the story of Prometheus and Pandora. We also get the five ages of man.

According to Hesiod, the god Khaos (chaos) came into being first or has always been. This god is the space between heaven and earth. Next come the goddess Gaia (earth) and the god Ouranos (heaven). Then came the gods Tartaros (underworld) and Eros (love). Khaos begets Erebos (night). Erebos begets the gods Aether (topmost air) and Hemera (day). Gaia begets starry Ouranos (heaven) and makes him equal to her size. Heaven is so nice that it is begotten twice, according to Hesiod. She also begets mountains and nymphs. Gaia and Ouranos beget the twelve Titans. First comes Oceanos (sea); it encircles the earth and flows around it. Then they beget Kronos (time), Tethys (rivers), and Themis (justice). Oceanus and

---

[3] Hesiod's *Theogony* is available here: https://www.perseus.tufts.edu/hopper/text?doc=Perseus:text:1999.01.0130.

[4] Hesiod's *Works and Days* is available here: https://www.perseus.tufts.edu/hopper/text?doc=Perseus:text:1999.01.0132.

Tethys beget Metis (wisdom). In the beginning, Ouranos ruled all the gods and nature. Ouranos ruled as the father of the other gods. One of Ouranos' Titans, Kronos, overthrew him and forced his way to rule. Time, then, comes to rule the gods and nature. Through time, Kronos and the Titaness Rhea (mother) beget six children. Hestia, Demeter, Hera, Poseidon, and Hades were her first five children. Kronos ruled through power. He was warned that his offspring would overthrow him, just as he had done to his father. So, Kronos swallowed his first five children whole. There, the five swallowed immortal gods were contained in him. Eating the children seems odd, but there are not many options for containing and controlling an immortal being. Zeus was the sixth offspring. Rhea saved Zeus by giving Kronos a rock to swallow, instead of her child. She hid Zeus in Gaia. Over time and by might, Zeus challenged and overthrew Kronos by giving him a potion that made him vomit. Thereby, he freed all his siblings that had been swallowed by Kronos. Zeus did not take kingship straightaway after freeing his siblings and overthrowing Kronos. After overthrowing Kronos, the gods voted to elect a ruler. Zeus won the election. He then swallowed Metis (wisdom), who was his first wife, and Themis (justice). Zeus rules through wisdom and justice. He provides rational and moral order to the *Kosmos*.

Hesiod adds curious features to his account. He says that heaven is the same size as earth. Possibly, though we do not know, he holds that the underworld is the same size as earth and heaven. He says that the distance between heaven and earth is calculated by the amount of time it would take for an iron anvil to fall for ten days and nine nights. The same calculation is used for the distance between the earth and the underworld. So, the earth is equidistant between heaven and the underworld. Hesiod offers a rational proportion among the top, the bottom, and the between of what is. In Hesiod's cosmology, an account of the *Kosmos*, the *Kosmos* is intelligible. Human beings can use reason to understand it and language (*logos*) to account for it. The *Kosmos* is guided by wisdom and ordered through justice.

Suppose we ask Homer or Hesiod how they learned such marvelous things. How might I discover such things? From the texts that we have, we can see that neither Homer nor Hesiod would have a justification that went beyond an appeal to tradition and an appeal to authority. They could say, "Believe me because we Greeks have always believed this or have believed it for a very long time." They might say, "Believe me because I am an authoritative source." As philosophers today, we can say that believing something because it has been believed for a long time or believing something because of who said it are instances of the informal fallacies of appeal to tradition and appeal to authority. Homer and Hesiod had popular accounts of the *Kosmos*, and there was no comparable rival. The philosophers would change this by offering a different sort or kind of explanation.

This Is Ancient Greek Philosophy

The sources that we have for conveying information about the early Greek philosophers are far removed from the original texts. Manuscripts from the era were disseminated by scribes, making copies of a text. The text that formed the basis for the scribe was more likely than not a copy of a copy of a copy. Scribes are imperfect conduits of information. In addition to the challenges faced in ascertaining the accuracy of the base text, there are errors that often occur in the transcription of the base text. There are errors of omission: *Homeoteleuton* occurs when a transcription skips words because a subsequent word has the same or a similar ending. *Homeoarchy* occurs when the transcriber skips lines because of the similarity of the beginnings of the lines. *Haplography* occurs when the transcriber copies a term that appears twice in the base text. There are errors in addition. *Dittography* occurs when the transcriber writes a term twice that appears only once in the base text. *Contamination* occurs when a transcriber inserts text that is not in the base text. There are errors in transposition. *Metathesis* occurs when a transcriber reverses letters, words, or phrases from the base text. Finally, but not exhaustively, there are errors of alteration. These errors occur when a transcriber attempts, deliberately or not, to make sense of the base text in the transcription.

We would be fortunate if we had confidence that our sources were copies of copies that could trace their preceding texts straight through to the original text. We are not so fortunate. Instead, we encounter the ideas of the early Greek philosophers through subsequent texts that offer information that is drawn from original texts or copies of original texts. Since we do not have the original texts, we cannot determine what sort the base text was for the author recounting the thoughts of his predecessors. Our sources offer information of two sorts. *Testimonia* offers paraphrases of a focal author's text, of a transcription of the focal author's text, or of the focal author's ideas or reputed ideas. *Fragments* offer a quotation from the focal author's text or a transcription at some remove from the author's text. The fragments might be a quotation of a word, phrase, or selection of varying length from a base text. We are fortunate today to have valuable collections of reference texts. This book makes use of certain standard sources.[5]

Ancient philosophy is distant in time and distant linguistically from us today. The manuscripts that we have often conflict with each other or only partially preserve the text. The expanse of time resulted in many works being partially or entirely lost to us. The ancient Greek language presents challenges of its own, since many of its terms cannot be directly translated into English. In this text, I have retained some of the central Greek terms. I offer the Greek terms in a non-technical phonetic form so that English readers can easily hear an approximation of the original terms.[6] The phonetic rendition of the Greek terms fulfills another goal. It stresses that we are discussing the Greek ideas and not their English translations. For instance, the book uses and examines the Greek concept of *Kosmos* and not the English term "cosmos."

It is common for texts on ancient philosophy to adopt one of two approaches, either focusing on certain philosophers or on certain themes. The following text adopts a hybrid approach by examining both philosophers and themes. There are three parts in this book and three chapters in each part. The three parts are organized in the same way. They start with two chapters on particular authors and conclude with a chapter on a theme. Part I of the book is Early Greek Philosophy. These

---

[5] The Early Greeks: Richard D. McKirahan, *Philosophy Before Socrates* (Indianapolis: Hackett Publishing, 1994). Daniel W. Graham, *The Texts of Early Greek Philosophy, The Complete Fragments and Selected Testimonies of the Major Presocratics,* Part I and II (Cambridge: Cambridge University Press, 2010). The titles in the Loeb Classical Library collection are here: https://www.loebclassics.com/view/LCL524/2016/volume.xml. The Golden Age: John M. Cooper, *Plato: Complete Works,* (Indianapolis: Hackett Publishing, 1997). Jonathan Barnes, *The Complete Works of Aristotle* in two volumes (Princeton: Princeton University Press, 1991). Hellenistic Philosophy: Long and Sedley, *The Hellenistic Philosophers* (New York: Cambridge University Press, 1987). A.A. Long, *Hellenistic Philosophy, Stoic, Epicureans, and Sceptics* 2nd ed., (Berkeley: University of California Press, 1986). Diogenes Laertius, *Lives of Eminent Philosophers,* R.D. Hicks trans. (Cambridge: Harvard University Press, 1931) refers to philosophers in all three periods. Digital Libraries: Massachusetts Institute of Technology Classics (MIT): http://classics.mit.edu/index.html. Project Guttenberg: https://www.gutenberg.org. Perseus Digital Library at Tufts University has Greek and English texts here: http://www.perseus.tufts.edu/hopper.

[6] To read the Greek words, pronounce the letter "c" as an English "k" and pronounce the letter "y" as a "u."

philosophers turn from the mythological and theological explanation of the *Kosmos* to rational and material explanations. Thales holds that water is the basic stuff; Anaximenes holds that it is air; Anaximander holds that it is the unlimited (*apeiron*); and Empedocles holds that it is earth, air, fire, and water. Democritus holds that it is atoms. Some hold that the explanation of the *Kosmos* is more abstract. Empedocles holds that it is Mind (*nous*) and seeds. Xenophanes is skeptical about almost all that we think we know. Part I concludes with a chapter called "The Philosophical Turn." This chapter examines the development of rational and material explanations through a comparative analysis of the early Greeks. We cannot overstate the importance of the early Greek philosophers. We continue to investigate and explain the world through rational and material explanations. Though science as we know it today did not sprout fully from the early Greeks, they turned us toward models and methods that continue to develop and guide us today.

Part II is The Golden Age. This part examines Plato and Aristotle's texts. Plato offers an account of Socrates and the Sophists. He also offers his own philosophical system in the theory of forms. The Plato chapter concludes by examining the implications of the theory of forms for ethics and politics. These implications show that one form of government is just and all others are unjust, in varying degrees. Aristotle innovates the subject of formal logic. He also offers his own philosophical system, in his theory of Hylomorphism. Through the implications of his theory, Aristotle gives an account of ethics and politics. His theory of ethics argues that virtue is a mean between two extremes, one of excess and one of deficiency. The chapter on Aristotle concludes with his account of politics and justice in the state. Part II concludes with the theme of The Subjects of Philosophy, offering the distinctions among the subjects of philosophy as employed in the golden age and today.

Part III is Hellenistic Philosophy. This period of philosophy begins with the death of Alexander the Great in 323 BCE. Aristotle died a year later. Under Alexander, the Hellenic world had expanded and unified in a way unmatched in western history. At the time of his death, Alexander's empire spread from Greece, Egypt and North Africa to the western part of India. During the fragmentation of the Alexandrian empire and the civil wars, Hellenistic philosophy developed and flourished. There were four philosophies in the period: Cynicism, Epicureanism, Stoicism, and Skepticism. The Cynics reject conventional values and live a life according to nature. They live without possessions in a hand-to-mouth existence on the streets. They strive for happiness through minimalist living and control over their desires. Epicurus adopts atomism, but he focuses on mental and physical quietude. He aims to embody imperturbability (*ataraxia*). Stoicism develops innovations in logic, by going beyond Aristotle's syllogistic logic and by offering an account of propositional logic. Despite this historically significant innovation, the Stoics are squarely concerned to develop a disciplined mind and body. They aim to control desires, passions, and assent to judgments. They consider it their duty to live according to nature. This disciplined life according to nature results in imperturbability and a happy life (*eudaimonia*). The Sceptics are the inheritors of Plato's Academy. They develop an account of argument that critiques the claims of other philosophers by opposing a thesis argument with an antithesis argument. They hold that any thesis can be opposed by an equally credible antithesis. So, they withhold assent (*epoche*) and suspend judgment. In this way, they avoid dogmatism (*dogmatikos*) to achieve both imperturbability and apathy (*apatheia*).

The theme of Part III is the focal concern of Hellenistic philosophy, the good life. Each movement aims at happiness. They find it through various means: imperturbability, apathy, and the suspension of judgment. They all agree that to live the good life, one must engage in purposeful voluntary action. They inherit accounts of voluntary action from Plato and Aristotle. These two golden age figures develop their accounts of voluntary action in the light of Socrates' claim that one cannot voluntarily act against one's better judgment. He denied that there are acts of moral weakness. This leads Plato and Aristotle to develop accounts of voluntary action and explain action against one's better judgment. The Hellenistic philosophers inherit the accounts of voluntary action, and they establish commitments in the early Greek philosophers. The materialism of the early Greek philosophers, especially the atomists, implies a fated outcome in the *Kosmos*. There is psychological determinism in Socrates' denial of moral weakness, in addition to the materialists' *Kosmic* determinism. Attempts to account for voluntary action against better judgment become attempts to account for voluntary action in contrapose to the necessity of the fated *Kosmos*. Each of the Hellenistic philosophers attempts to reconcile these conflicting concerns. This difficulty remains today as the question of the freedom of will.

Part I

EARLY GREEK PHILOSOPHY

1

MILETUS AND ELEA

1.1 Miletus

1.1.1 Thales

Thales of Miletus lived in the late seventh century BCE and early sixth century BCE. Apollodorus of Athens claimed that Thales was born in about 625 BCE. According to Herodotus, he predicted a solar eclipse that occurred on 28 May, 585 BCE. Diogenes Laertius tells us that he died at the fifty-eighth Olympiad (548–545 BCE) at the age of 78. His family history is reported as going back to the Phoenicians. Thales is cited as the only early Greek philosopher among the seven sages.

Thales is the subject of numerous anecdotes, which function historically to commend or malign philosophers. Thales is credited with devising a brilliant way to cross a river. Rather than cross the river, have the river cross you. The story goes that an army needed to cross a river, but the river was too strong to cross. So, he found a pronounced curve in the river, advanced into the bulge, and once the army advanced into the bulge, he rerouted a portion of the river behind them. With the river split, they could cross to the other side. Though many particulars of this story are dubitable, the engineering is not improbable. There are some stories about him that have become stereotypes of philosophers. When he was asked why he had little money, but was supposed to be wise, he invested in olives and made great profits. This story was meant to show that philosophy teaches practical skills, but philosophers are not preoccupied with employing them. Along similar lines, Aristotle tells us that Thales was criticized for seeming to be

This Is Ancient Philosophy: An Introduction, First Edition. Kirk Fitzpatrick.
© 2024 John Wiley & Sons, Inc. Published 2024 by John Wiley & Sons, Inc.

wise but being poor. As the story goes, Thales studied the heavens and predicted a bumper crop in olives the next year. He put deposits on the olive presses. In modern economics, he bought all the futures contracts for olive presses. He subsequently made a large profit. This anecdote was to show that though philosophers seem practically useless for studying the heavens, they are not. The philosophers do not go after money, but wisdom instead.

In another anecdote, when Thales was walking along, looking to the heavens and examining the stars, he fell into a well. This story portrays philosophers as practically useless stargazers.[1] Plato returns to the negative conception of the philosophers in the *Republic*, when he tells us that the majority of people (*hoi polloi*) call the philosophers "useless stargazers."[2] In everyday life, the philosopher is not worried about the peculiarities of what is proximate; instead, the philosopher wonders about what is universal. Thales does not know his neighbor, but he is keenly interested in humankind. Thales of Miletus was credited as the first to develop natural philosophy. He did not take payment from his associates or students.

Thales brought geometry and mathematics to Greece. Proclus mentions that Thales learned mathematics from knowledge handed down from the Phoenicians, whereas the Greeks learned geometry from the Egyptians. Thales traveled to Egypt and learned other science, both general and empirical. He theorized about math and geometry in the abstract, but he also applied his theories to empirical observations. In the abstract, he was the first Greek to identify the diameter of a circle. He divided the year into 365 days. He showed that an isosceles triangle has two equal angles. In Egypt, he measured the height of the pyramids by their shadows. By establishing the relation between an upright stick and its shadow, he calculated the height of the pyramids.

We have conflicting reports of Thales' writings. One work that he possibly authored was called the *Nautical Star Guide*. Alternatively, he is said to have written only two major treatises: *On the Solstice* and *On the Equinox*. Some sources tell us that he wrote nothing, and to date we cannot verify that Thales wrote any works. The works that are spuriously attributed to Thales are indicative of an interest that he had in the sky. Thales claims that

---

[1] Plato's *Theaetetus*, 174a. Plato's works are available online at MIT Classics: http://classics.mit.edu/Browse/browse-Plato.html. His works are also at Project Guttenberg: https://www.gutenberg.org/ebooks/search/?query=plato&submit_search=Go%21, and at The Perseus Project: http://www.perseus.tufts.edu/hopper/searchresults?q=plato.

[2] *Republic*, 489c.

the stars are composed of the earth and fire. This claim makes the unknown (the stars) like the known (earth and fire). The move is essential to reasoning that extrapolates known things and extends them to unknown things. We saw this move in measuring the pyramids; the known is the ratio of height to shadow as determined by a stick of known height in relation to a shadow of known length. This information is then applied to the unknown, the height of the pyramid. He is credited with predicting a solar eclipse, but it is more likely that Thales explained a solar eclipse. He argued that the moon passes in front of the sun to causes an eclipse. Here we have a natural explanation of a solar eclipse.

There is a singular innovation that Thales made to establish his place as an early Greek philosopher. He tried to find a principle of all things and a theory of all things in matter. This move is indicative of many early Greek philosophers, but it is important to note that it is not true of all of them. Since he was reputedly the first to develop a theory of all things in a material substratum, he is hailed as the first Greek philosopher. In the following passage, Aristotle offers a general account of the early Greek philosophers who found a material substratum that persists through change. All things come from this substratum and return to it.[3] Aristotle notes that this is a revolutionary innovation. The early Greek philosophers claimed that the substratum underlies and is the principle of everything. There is a wide variety of stuff, such as plants, animals, wood, mud, etc. These thinkers, Aristotle tells us, attempt to account for the variety of stuff by identifying a more basic stuff. One might, for example, identify mud as a combination of the earth and water. One might, for example, claim that there are four types of basic stuff: air, earth, fire, and water. In this way, a philosopher could explain the enormous variety of stuff by means of an account of more basic stuff. These philosophers attempted to find the most basic stuff. If this process ends in multiple basic material stuffs, the theory is a form of material pluralism. If the process ends in one basic stuff, which underlies all the variety of stuff, the theory is a form of material monism. We see both material pluralist and material monist theories among the early Greek philosophers. The theories claim that the basic stuff, whether singular or plural, functions as a persistent substratum. The substratum is "changing in its attributes," but the underlying substratum persists through change. In this way, the basic stuff neither comes to be nor perishes; instead it is always

---

[3] Aristotle, *Metaphysics* 983b6–13, A12, I. Aristotle's works are available online: http://classics.mit.edu/Browse/browse-Aristotle.html.

preserved. Modern science, it is worth noting, continues this search for the basic stuff(s). To date, we continue this ancient search, though we have not yet found it or them.

Aristotle develops an account of four causes: material, efficient, formal, and final. By talking about the substance water as a material principle, Aristotle places it in his theory as a material cause. We will get to Aristotle's account of the four causes in Section 5.2.3. At this point, it is important to avoid anachronism, as tempting as it might be, to frame Thales' account in Aristotle's subsequent theory. Aristotle hones in on Thales' particular theory, by noting that some early Greek philosophers are pluralists and some are monists in their accounts of the basic stuff. He identifies Thales as a monist.[4] Thales, Aristotle tells us, says that the only basic stuff is water and that earth floats on water. We can say with confidence that Thales holds these claims, but we are left to conjecture concerning Thales' reasons for holding them.

Multiple sources tell us that Thales offers a materialist account of natural phenomena. He offered an explanation for the flooding of the Nile. Thales claimed that the flooding of the Nile was caused by the Etesian winds and explained earthquakes by claiming that the earth floats on water. As a ship bobs in the waves, the earth quakes in the bobbing. This also explains, he thinks, that water is dispersed throughout the rivers of the earth. These reports credit Thales with an innovation worthy of repute. A physical explanation of the flooding revolutionizes the explanatory model. It ignores the mythological model of explanation, which cited Poseidon as the cause of flooding. Thales offers a physical explanation, which cites natural phenomena as the cause. Other sources report that Thales explanatory model expands from water to the whole of the world and the heavens. First, there is water. The condensation and compaction of water forms the earth. From water and the condensation of the earth come wind, earthquakes, and the movement of the stars. Thales was the first to explain the heavens and the earth through an eternal element that underlies all changes. There are many things in need of explanation here. If we accept the first claim, water is the only thing. What changes the water and makes it condense? How can you condense water enough to get earth? Both of these concerns point to motion. The concerns condense into the question: What causes the changes in water? We need some explanation of motion in the account.

---

[4] Aristotle, *Metaphysics*, 983b19–21.

Thales imports motion elsewhere. He argues that the soul is a source of motion, in the way that magnets move objects. Aristotle argues that Thales infers the power of motion in the soul from the ability of a magnet to move iron. If we follow the model so far, water is condensed into earth. Now we are told that two forms of the earth (condensed water) can move each other (loadstone and iron). Put this together. The soul is the animating force. It is an attraction–repulsion relation between two objects. Both objects are forms of variously condensed water. If this is true, then the soul is everywhere, since water is everywhere, and the soul is just a form of water. As we saw, water is immortal, so it is God. Thales' position is expansive. He starts with one thing – water – and from it, he explains the earth, the wind, earthquakes, the flooding of the Nile, the motion of the stars, and the entire cycle of nature. It is difficult to confidently say much about Thales' beliefs and reasons for his beliefs. Testimonia does give us confidence in holding that he was reputed as holding certain beliefs and that he had some justification for holding the beliefs. If Thales offered a naturalistic account of natural phenomena, then he deserves to be credited as the first Greek philosopher. If Thales did not offer a natural account of physical phenomena, then he is not worthy of repute as the first Greek philosopher. Philosophers disagree about whether he was the first philosopher or not.

Aristotle offers a controversial interpretation of Thales' claims about water. According to Aristotle, Thales held that water is a source or governing principle. In Greek the term is *arche*. This is a central concept in Aristotle's philosophy. The term "arche" can have multiple meanings: (1) a base element from which other elements come, (2) a base element that makes up the world, and (3) the governing principle used to explain the world. We do not have any evidence that Thales actually employed the concept of *arche* in this way. While these concepts play a big part in Thales successors and in Aristotle's philosophy, Aristotle's application of the term "*arche*" and its various meanings to Thales is now believed to be anachronistic. Interpreters today are skeptical of Aristotle's interpretation, and they offer an alternative view of the meaning and function of water for Thales. We can recall that Homer and Hesiod placed Oceanos surrounding the earth and that Oceanos was the begetter of gods. Oceanos was said to be in motion and it generated the rivers and freshwater wells. We also saw that Oceanos functioned in a mythological and not philosophical explanatory model. When we see Thales' account in the historical context of Homer and Hesiod, we see that his account is reminiscent of the earlier mythological accounts. This is now taken to be the more likely meaning and function of "water" in Thales' claims. The early Greek philosophers hailed Thales as their founder. Aristophanes has a character jokingly say, "The man is a Thales!"[5] The joke only works if Thales is believed to be philosophically wise.

1.1.2 Anaximander

Our best sources tell us that Anaximander was the son of Praxiades of Miletus. Anaximander was 64 years old during the second year of the fifty-eighth Olympiad (547/6 BCE). This would make Anaximander about 15 years younger than Thales. Anaximander was an associate and student of Thales. Though the early Greek authors did not tend to title their works, a common practice was to give them a title after the fact. *On Nature* was the most popular title of works by these early Greek authors, and Anaximander was the first to write such a work.

Anaximander was also the first Greek cartographer to write a schematic map on a wall. The map had Europe and Asia in equal size with the ocean flowing around it. Anaximander was also reputed to be the first person to bring the gnomon to Greece. He placed one in Sparta. This gnomon marked solstices and equinoxes and the hours of the day. Anaximander offers a cosmogony, a history of the origins of the *Kosmos*. This testimonia comes to us at some remove. Simplicius reports that Theophrastus reports that Anaximander's view on the origin of the *Kosmos* names the source of all things as *apeiron*. It is not an element, such as air, earth, fire, and water. The term "*apeiron*" comprises two parts. The "*a*" is an alpha-privative, and it means "not." The term "*peiron*" is derived from a root term used to form the verb "*perao*," meaning "to travers or to pass through," or "*peras*," meaning an end, limit, or boundary. When we combine the parts, we see that *apeiron* means "boundless or unlimited," or "cannot be traversed or passed through." The *apeiron* is eternal, always moving, and it surrounds the *Kosmos*.

At first glance, we might interpret the translation of *apeiron* as having only spatial reference. It is conceived as being so vast that it is infinite. There is a difference between what is boundless and what is infinite. If there is nothing beyond the boundless, then we cannot go beyond it. Even there we should be cautious to interpret the term as "infinite," except in certain of Aristotle's uses and other later authors. Spatially we can say that there is nothing outside of or beyond *apeiron*. While the term can have a spatial

---

[5] Aristophanes, *Birds*, 1.1009. Aristophanes' plays are available here: http://classics. mit.edu/Browse/browse-Aristophanes.html.

reference, it can also have a conceptual reference. The *apeiron* is generative of all the elements in the *Kosmos*, and some of these elements have opposite features: hot and cold, and dry and wet. There is a cycle that begins with the *apeiron* and the process of separating. The separation generates all things, the *Kosmos*. Over time the elements combine to reform *apeiron*. Some interpreters mention a natural regulation to the length of the cycles. The cycles are repeated endlessly. This shows that the *apeiron* is boundless also in its capacity to generate elements because when the elements are compared to each other they have opposite features and *apeiron* generates all elements of the *Kosmos*.

Anaximander had a detailed account of the *Kosmos* in its current generation. Plutarch and Hippolytus give us the following information about Anaximander's account of the *Kosmos*. The heavenly bodies are fire separated from the sun, and they are in air.[6] There are tubes or holes for breath like spokes in a wheel, through which we see the stars, the moon, and the sun. The sun is 27 times larger than the earth. The moon is 18 times larger than the earth. The sun is the farthest from the earth, and the stars are the closest. The earth is suspended in air, equidistant from everything. It is round, concave, and cylindrical. The depth of the earth is one-third of its width. Anaximander describes a hocky-puck earth equidistant from the heavenly bodies with specific proportions in relation to the sun and moon, or the apertures of the elements in the spoked wheel. The spokes in the wheel give him access to explanations of heavenly phenomena. He explains solar and lunar eclipses through the breathing holes and the waxing and waning of the moon. He invokes the winds to explain numerous natural phenomena such as thunder, lightning, and hurricanes. His explanation is that when the clouds surround the wind, the clouds are less dense than the wind. There is then a violent interchange, which causes a tearing and produces various phenomena. The wind is the prominent and consistent factor in Anaximander's explanation of natural phenomena.

Anaximander describes the stages in this current earth cycle in very general terms. The *apeiron* separates into the elements; then after a cycle governed by cosmic justice, these elements combine to be *apeiron* again. Also, he tells us that the earth is in the process of drying out. It is going from wetter to dryer, as the moisture dries from the heat of the sun. The vapor from the drying water produces winds. The process of the world drying up

---

[6] See Hippolytus Refutation 1.6.3–7 as found in Daniel W. Graham's *The Texts of Early Greek Philosophy* (Cambridge: Cambridge University Press, 2012), vol. 1, 57.

helps him explain the origins of human beings. Human offspring are not able to care for themselves when young. It is a wonder that the first humans survived. To explain the survival of humans, he claims that they come from nonhuman animals. He suggests that humans originally came from fish or smaller animals. The humans matured to puberty in these aquatic animals, whatever they were, and then burst forth from the aquatic animals.

Anaximander offers a revolutionary account of the *Kosmos*. He uses his model of the *Kosmos* to explain heavenly phenomena, such as eclipses and the phases of the moon. He charts the seasons and equinoxes by means of the gnomon. He offers a thoroughgoing physical account, where the gods of the mythic age have no place. The gods have become superfluous. Rather than explaining lightning and thunder by means of Zeus, we get an explanation in terms of wind, rarity and density, and friction. Rather than explaining the behavior of water through Poseidon, he invokes wind and pressure. His account employs phenomena that we can demonstrate at a smaller scale and then amplify the implications of the phenomena to apply to large-scale Kosmic phenomena. His explanation of the place of the earth in the *Kosmos* is especially interesting. Aristotle tells us that Anaximander places the earth in the middle of the *Kosmos*. The earth is held in stasis, held in by contrary forces. In this way, the earth and the heavens are placed by necessity. Interpreters notice that this explanation employs what Leibniz will subsequently call the Principle of Sufficient Reason.[7] Aristotle describes Anaximander as having what is now called sufficient reason to place the earth anywhere except at the center, since he has no reason to place it higher, lower, left, or right. Unless there is some sufficient reason to place the earth elsewhere, there can be no explanatory justification for placing it elsewhere.

Anaximander's account is revolutionary not just in his consistent use of physical elements interacting with physical elements to generate phenomena, but in his conceptual and explanatory form of justification. Unlike Thales, we know that Anaximander committed his thoughts to writing. His work, *On Nature*, was groundbreaking and seminal. Many subsequent authors wrote books titled *On Nature* or had their works known by this commonly used title. He wrote in prose and not poetry, which marks a clear stylistic break from the poets Homer and Hesiod. The papyrus informs subsequent interpreters in a way that gives us insight into his thoughts in a way that we lack concerning Thales. The particulars of Anaximander's account

---

[7] See Richard D. McKirahan's *Philosophy Before Socrates* (Indianapolis: Hackett Publishing Company, 1994), 40.

show ingenuity and creativity in their explanations of natural phenomena. Even more remarkable are his theoretical commitments underlying his explanations. He clearly sees the problem of accounting for the elements, earth, air, fire, and water in terms of each other or in terms of any one of these elements. His invocation of *apeiron* as an underlying substance is theoretically brilliant. True, he does need, but does not provide, an explanation of how *apeiron* can generate elements with opposite features. He does, however, see that to account for the opposite features of the common elements, he needs a genesis from a different sort of stuff. He does not tell us what *apeiron* is, but he does make it function in his explanations in a novel way. Finally, his invocation of what would later be called the Principle of Sufficient Reason shows that he is concerned as much with the structure of his explanations as he is with their content. In light of this, there are reasons to hold that Anaximander is the first Greek philosopher.

1.1.3 Anaximenes

Anaximenes' biography is obscure and there is not much that we can say with certainty. It might be true that Anaximenes of Miletus was the son of Eurystratus and that he died in the sixty-third Olympiad (528/5 BCE). Plato never mentions him by name and Aristotle is the first to name him. We can say with more confidence that he was from Miletus, that he was a student of Anaximander, and that he was the last in our record of the Milesian philosophical school of thought.

Anaximenes holds that air (*aer*) is the *arche* of the *Kosmos*. He posits air as the first element and the source of the other elements. The term "*aer*" is used by his predecessors. Among them, we should focus on Anaximander's use of the term, which leads contemporary translators to render the term *aer* as "dark mist." This is distinguished from the higher regions in the skies that are called ether or more precisely *aither*. Anaximenes is referring to *aer* or air, insofar as it has no perceptible qualities. In some form, it is the stuff that we take for granted. Until it becomes tainted, we take it as given. Suppose that one fish asked another fish, "How's the water?"[8] Until the water is tainted and somehow off, the fish takes the water for granted. *Aer* functions in a similar way; it is imperceptible and as yet unknown. Anaximenes calls *aer* boundless and this echoes a concept from

---

[8] You might know this term by its modern use. "Ether" is a gas used as an anesthetic or solvent (aka laughing gas).

Anaximander. For Anaximander, *apeiron* has the capacity to separate and become all things. Anaximenes argues that the indeterminate *apeiron* is determinate. He determines the indeterminate in *aer*. The element *aer* is that sort of stuff, that stuff that you do not notice until it is not there, or until it becomes different or unfit. He refers to the substratum of nature singular and *apeiron*. He specifies *apeiron* to be *aer*, which can rarify or condense. In rarified form *aer* becomes fire. When condensed it becomes water, earth, and rock. Anaximenes holds that motion is an eternal force in the *Kosmos*. Everything that exists comes from *aer* and motion.

It is difficult to conceive that air is the basic element and that it is generative of the others. Yet, this is what Anaximenes attempts to show. Anaximenes offers the following to explain how the diversity of the world comes to be from *aer*. Air changes as its density and rarity change. We think of density and rarity as quantitative concepts that apply to how much of a given substance occupies a certain volume. Let us say that we have a container with a volume of 1 and we have x amount of an element in that container. If we can have more of an element in the same volume, then we have a denser element. Interpreters are quick to point out that these are sophisticated ways of thinking about rarity and density, and that we cannot have confidence in thinking that this is the concept Anaximenes employs. The rarest form of air is fire; as the fire becomes denser, it becomes wind, denser and it becomes cloud, denser and it becomes water, denser and it becomes the earth, and even denser it becomes stones. This gives us a list of seven elements that we can place from most rare to most dense: fire, air, wind, cloud, water, earth, and stones. All other things come from the seven elements. We should not think that we can explain air in terms of fire or stone. Air is not a denser form of fire and air is not a less dense form of stone. We can explain fire and stone in terms of air and not vice versa. If we could explain any of the elements by means of any other element, then no element is *arche* more than any other.

Anaximenes has more to say about air. He takes hot and cold as accidental and not essential features of matter. The following sentences show why he thinks the features are accidental. He explains hot and cold in terms of rarity and density. As justification for the connection, he offers an experiment that each of us can do at home. He claims that when you exhale with open lips the air is hot, and when you exhale with pursed lips the air is cold. This empirical evidence is meant to justify his claim that air can be both hot and cold. Anaximenes has air function in a way that is different from the other elements. Air alone, plus motion, rarity, and density, explains hot and cold. Air alone functions to explain the accidental features of the other elements. No other element functions in this way. We can now better understand how air functions as *arche*.

1.1.4 Xenophanes

Xenophanes of Colophon was a philosopher and minstrel. He tells us that he was born in Colophon in Ionia about 570 BCE. Xenophanes was part of the philosophical movement in Miletus. In about 546 BCE, he left Ionia and traveled widely. He spent most of his time in Sicily and southern Italy, where there were Greek colonies. He lived to be over 90 years old and died around 478 BCE.

Xenophanes does not offer a cosmogony, an account of the genesis of the *Kosmos,* and the diversity of genesis within the *Kosmos.* He does, however, discuss the *Kosmos,* the heavens, and the principal elements. So, he continues the discussion of principal stuff that is familiar among the Milesian philosophers. In addition, he is traditionally credited, going back to Plato and Aristotle, as the founder of the Eleatic school of thought in southern Italy. He was reputed to have been an associate and teacher of Parmenides, the most famous of the Eleatic philosophers. Recently, interpreters have become skeptical of the claim that Xenophanes was the teacher of Parmenides. Nevertheless, we can see that Parmenides reiterates some of Xenophanes' ideas and so we can say that his ideas had some influence on Parmenides. Xenophanes was a pivotal figure, forming a bridge between the end of the philosophical movement in Miletus and the beginning of the philosophical movement in Elea.

Xenophanes does not accept the traditional mythological Greek gods as real; instead he explains them away by substituting natural phenomena. He does not think that a rainbow is the goddess Iris, but he explains it as cloud and light. Xenophanes tells us in a fragment that certain elements are primary, but we get conflicting evidence on this point. One fragment says that he posited the earth as the only *arche*. Other, more numerous sources tell us that he takes the earth and water to be *arche*. The evidence does not allow us to determine whether there is one or two principal elements for Xenophanes. Possibly the earth dissolves into water, but more likely the earth and water are in a cyclical relationship with each other. He does tell us a bit more about the earth. The earth stretches from our feet downward without end. So, there is more to the earth than what we see. The air extends above us to the heavens. We can say with confidence that he does not take air as a principal element. He tells us that water, the ocean, makes wind. It also makes clouds and rain. He tells us that the sun warms the earth and we can suppose it warms the water too. He describes a process where water generates clouds through what we would now call evaporation. The clouds carry water through the sky. The rainwater falls back to the earth supplying the water for rivers. We now call this process the water cycle.

Xenophanes holds not only that water cycles from sea to cloud to rivers to sea, but testimonia tells us that he thinks the world goes through a process from wet to dry and back to wet again. He offers empirical evidence for the cyclical process. He argues that sea shells are found in the mountains. Impressions of seaweed, coral, and sea animals are found scattered about. These remnants are far from and above the sea. He infers that water and earth, wet and dry, undergo cyclical periods of dominance. Humankind will come to an end when the earth dissipates into the water. Xenophanes makes a remarkable claim about fossils and he takes that physical evidence into account when supplying his explanation of the phenomena. This is an important feature of science, namely that the explanation for physical phenomena must be grounded in physical evidence. His account shows that he continues with the themes of the Milesian philosophers. Though he does not give us a cosmogony, he does give us novel twists in his account of the *Kosmos*.

He is a focal figure of early Greek philosophy because of his comments on epistemology, ethics, and theology. We start with his epistemological skepticism. He argues that we do not *know* the plain truth about the gods or coming to be and perishing. All that we think we know actually is *opinion*. This is a puzzling passage since it seems to refute itself. If the plain truth cannot be known, then Xenophanes cannot tell us the plain truth. This response to the passage is too easy and it misses the point. Xenophanes is contrasting the plain truth or knowledge with opinion. We offer opinions; although these opinions can be true, they do not constitute knowledge. So, it can be the case that what Xenophanes is saying is true, but we just cannot claim that it is known. Though he offers a healthy skepticism through his division of knowledge and opinion, he does not offer a nihilistic skepticism. He argues that there are better and worse opinions. By investigating, using reason and observation, we can come to better opinions. Many people claim that the gods have revealed all things to them. He rejects this. It is not the gods that give justification to opinions, but instead humans must seek out true opinions for themselves. Through a process of seeking the truth, we can suppose, as Xenophanes sees it, that humans can gain better and better opinions. So, there is some hope of gaining true beliefs. He urges us to believe his claims as if they were true. Still, though we can have true opinions and we can be justified in believing the opinion as if it were known, we cannot have knowledge.

Xenophanes is committed to natural explanations of the *Kosmos* and he is skeptical of claims of knowledge. So, it is not surprising that he is relentless in his attack on the traditional Greek beliefs about the gods. One line of critique focuses on epistemological concerns about our knowledge of the gods. Humans think that gods are born, wear clothes, speak, and have bodies like humans. Gods end up being very much like humans. He offers more specific indications of humans anthropomorphizing gods. In Africa, the gods are black and snub-nosed. In Thrace, they have blue eyes and red hair. That is remarkable indeed. Xenophanes is incredulous about the widespread opinion that gods look just like the humans that worship them. The method that humans employ when envisioning the gods has other unwanted implications. If humans do this, what would other animals do? Xenophanes opines that if cows had hands, they would draw the gods in their own image. Cows worship cow-morphic gods. Horses worship what we can call *hippomorphic* gods. He concludes that the other animals would follow in the same manner. This species-centered *morpho* of the gods generates incredible results. So, no sooner should we believe that the gods look like us than we should believe that the gods look like horses, lions, or any other such things. Xenophanes is not done with his critique of traditional beliefs about the gods. There are not only epistemological reasons to reject the traditional beliefs about the gods; there are ethical concerns too. Homer and Hesiod attribute many morally vicious and disgraceful acts by the gods. Adultery and deception are just the start of the list. Xenophanes has ethical commitments that apply not only to human beings but also to the gods. There is one standard for both and this standard cannot credibly be inferred from the traditional Greek theological beliefs. We do not know much about Xenophanes' ethical theory, but it is safe to say that it forbids theft, adultery, and some forms of deception. When faced with a choice between his reasoned opinions on ethics and the behavior of the gods as depicted in Homer and Hesiod, Xenophanes sides with his reasoned opinions.

Despite his rejection of traditional Greek theology and his refusal to have the gods function in his physical account of the *Kosmos*, Xenophanes has beliefs about one God. He holds that there is one God and that God is unlike man in body and thought. God sees and hears everything, according to Xenophanes. To be consistent, Xenophanes needs to hold that God sees, thinks, and hears in a way very different from humans. While he does not tell us anything about how God sees or hears, he does tell us something about God's thinking. God thinks and moves all things; he causes earthquakes or anything else, simply by his mind. God is not a superhuman. God's thought is not that of a superhuman. God is not an anthropomorphic extreme. God's thought is not different in degree, but it is different in kind from human thought. Xenophanes also insists that God does not move. God does not move or change location. God is not fixed in some particular location and bounded in one place. This is not why Xenophanes claims that God does not change location. God does not change location because God is everywhere always.

1.2 Elea

1.2.1 Parmenides

Parmenides was from the city of Elea, which was a Greek colony in southern Italy (aka Magna Graecia). Plato gives us the best information on the dates of his life.[9] He was born c. 515 BCE and died in about 450 BCE. Inspired and influenced by Xenophanes, Parmenides is credited as the founder and most influential member of the Eleatics, a pre-Socratic school of philosophy.

Parmenides' most influential contribution comes in a lengthy fragment of text, 154 lines long. The text is written in poetic verse, in dactylic hexameter to be more specific. The pattern is based on long and short syllables, where the length of the syllable is determined by the length of the vowel. A short vowel takes about half as long to pronounce as a long vowel. A dactyl is a long syllable followed by two short syllables. A "hexameter" is six metron. Take the pattern long-short-short and repeat it five times. The sixth metron is two long syllables, a spondee. This is the same rhythmic (metric) verse that we see in Homer's and Hesiod's poems. It is also the rhythmic verse that Xenophanes sometimes uses and that Empedocles uses in all his works.

Parmenides' poem has three main sections: (1) the Proem or prologue, (2) the Way of Truth, and (3) the Way of Mortal Opinion. The Proem begins in grand poetic style with three mares carrying Parmenides. The chariot makes its way, with an axle that screeches like a pipe. The daughters of the Sun guide him. They lead him out of the night to the Gates of Night and Day. Justice is the key to unlock the gates. Justice requires strategic words and persuasion. The daughters of the Sun guide Parmenides beyond the gates of day and night. This is not the end of the Proem, but it is a good

---

[9] *Parmenides* 127.a7–c5.

place to sort things out. The first lines describe a trip led by mares to a deity. The deity is the goddess that we meet at the end of the passage. It is a common device in ancient Greek poetry to invoke the muses or some other deity at the beginning of a poem. The hope is that the deity will inspire the poet in crafting the poem. It also functions to put the poet in a position of privileged access to information, since the deity can tell the poet things that we cannot know. Parmenides has invoked this common poetic device, but he makes novel use of it.

The Proem continues, and Parmenides argues that there are only three ways of thinking or inquiry. These are paths into which one can inquire. One path inquires into what-is. This path holds that what-is is and that it must be. This path is *knowable* and it is the way of *truth*. The second path inquires into what-is-not. It holds that what-is-not is not and what-is-not must not be. This is an *unknowable* path. The third path inquires into both what-is and what-is-not. It holds that what-is and what-is-not are the same and not the same. This is the backward-turning path of mortal *opinion*. There is no truth in this path. Parmenides identifies three paths: the true, the unknowable, and the false.

As we saw, Parmenides claims that what-is *is*. There are at least three possible interpretations of "is." The term comes from the verb to be (*enai*). It is the third-person, singular, present, indicative, active form, translated into English as he, she, or it, is. There are three main uses of the verb "to be": (1) the *veridical* use, meaning "is true;" (2) the *existential* use meaning "exists;" and (3) the *predicative* use that attaches a predicate y to the subject x, in the form x is y. The veridical use takes a proposition as its object. One person could say, "this chariot is junk." Another person could respond by saying "it is." "It is" means that the proposition "the chariot is junk" is true. The existential use claims that an object exists. After putting the final pieces of the chariot together Milo exclaims, "There it is!" Milo means that the chariot exists. The predicative use attaches a predicate to a subject, "the chariot is wood." Here the predicate "wood" is applied to the subject "chariot." It is not clear how these three possible interpretations apply to Parmenides' claims. Interpreters disagree about which of the three interpretations apply to which of Parmenides' claims. Possibly, Parmenides applies only one of the three interpretations to all of his claims. It seems more likely that he employs more than one meaning of "is" in his claims.

Parmenides tells us that the second path holds that "what-is-not is not and what-is-not must not be." He says that this path is unknowable and unsayable. We can dismiss the second path as unknowable, but this is a curious dismissal. How can we know that something is unknowable? Can one think about a circle-square? You might suggest a "squircle" is the object of your thought, but that is neither a circle nor a square. There is no object to conceive of that is a circle-square. This is a possible interpretation. Can we utter anything about a circle-square? We can name it, but we are naming nothing. We can make the sounds of the utterance but the utterance has no meaning. We cannot think about or talk about nothing. So, Parmenides rejects the second path.

The third path holds that what-is and what-is-not are both the same and not the same. This is the opinion of mortals. Parmenides tells us that the breast leads mortal. The body leads the mind for mortals. They use their senses to try to find the truth, but they are deaf, blind, and confused by the senses. Since humans hold that what-is and what-is-not are both the same and not the same, humans find contradictions and oppositions in all things. Objects of the senses were not here in the past and then they are here in the present. When the objects of sense are here, they are both here and not there. So "not then" and "not there" are supposed to be objects of thought, inquiry, understanding, knowledge, and truth. The backward-turning mortals chase being and not being as if they are the same, since they are both supposed to be objects of thought. Yet humans also think that being and not being are different, since the one is and the other is not. This path is led by an unseeing eye. We can see why Parmenides calls mortals "two-headed" and "backward-turning." The senses often give us deceptive or false information and reason often disagrees. A straight stick in water looks bent, but it is not. A mirage in the desert looks like water, but it is not. Also, relational terms are challenging, since a person can be taller than x and shorter than y. Is the person tall? Yes and no. We are to avoid our habitual use of the senses to gain truth. If the path of what-is is conjoined with the path of what-is-not, then a contradiction results. What-is is and what-is-not is. We might suppose that the path is both knowable and unknowable, both true and false. Instead, Parmenides says there is no truth in this path of mortal opinion.

Parmenides rejects the unknowable path of what-is-not and the false path of what-is and what-is-not. Parmenides turns to the only path remaining, what-is is and it must be. He applies a series of predicates to what-is; ungenerated, imperishable, a whole of one kind, unperturbed, and complete. He offers a series of arguments in support of the predicates. To show that what-is is not generated and imperishable, Parmenides engages in rebuttals that he might face. A contrarian might claim that what-is came into existence at some time. Parmenides replies with a question, from what did it come? Since what is not cannot be spoken of or conceived, we cannot have what is not as the originator of what is. This is our first statement of the *Parmenidean Constraint*: Nothing comes from nothing, or something cannot come from nothing. Since the constraint is true, there must be something that has always been. If a contrarian claims that what-is came about at some time, then Parmenides invokes what we now call the *Principle of Sufficient Reason*. There is no reason for what is to have come to be at some earlier time, some later time, or any time. There is no reason for it to come to be at any particular time. Since there is no reason for it to come to be at any particular time or all the time, what is must be imperishable. So, he holds that what-is is timeless. We need to be careful here, since the term "timeless" has more than one meaning. "Timeless" can mean outside of time or through all time. We can determine which meaning Parmenides references, since he does not think that time applies to what-is. Consider the timeless truths of mathematics and geometry, a Euclidean triangle has 180° as the sum of its interior angles and the proposition $1 + 1 = 2$ did not come to be or come to be true at some time. The proposition exists, or is true, without any reference to time. So, Parmenides holds that time is not a predicate of what-is.

Parmenides argues that what-is is a whole of one kind. He tells us that what-is is alike throughout, continuous, holds together as one, and is not divisible. So, we cannot say that it is more here than there. Parmenides applies predicates to what-is to show that it does not admit of internal distinctions of any sort. Here we encounter an analogous ambiguity as we noticed with the term "timeless." Rather than saying that what-is is everywhere, we should say place does not apply to it. Parmenides tells us that what-is is unperturbed and motionless. We already saw that place or location does not apply to what-is; it follows that there can be no motion. After all, motion is movement through space. We might be inclined to understand "motionless" as meaning "being in one location." Instead, I suggest that we think of it as we did with time and place. Thereby, we understand Parmenides to mean that motion does not apply to what-is. Parmenides tells us that what-is is complete and lacks nothing. What-is cannot become more complete or gain some predicate that it needs. These predicates indicate the timeless and unchanging nature of what-is.

1.2.2 *Zeno*

Zeno was from Elea, born about 490–485 BCE, and flourished in the mid-fifth-century BCE. He was an associate and advocate of Parmenides. We have one fragment from Zeno. It focuses on plurality, the dichotomy between one and many. The first part of the fragment states that "If there are many things, it is necessary that they are just as many as they are, and neither more nor less than that."[10] The fragment continues by holding that there are only so many of the things that are. It concludes that the-things-that-are are limited. So far we have half of the dichotomy. The second part argues that if there are two things, then there are other things between the two things. Then again, it continues, there are others between them and so on for an infinite regress. He concludes that things are unlimited. One branch of the argument aims to show that pluralists must hold that things are limited and the other shows they must hold that things are unlimited.

Zeno challenges pluralists by holding that they must be able to tell how many things there are. This is a reasonable challenge to the pluralist. It is as if to quip, "You say there are many things, how many are there?" Should the pluralist respond with, "a lot," we would be unsatisfied. It is tempting to consider a context for Zeno's claim and take up some sort of thing. Possibly he is thinking of numerical things, or maybe it is physical things he references. Limiting his challenge to one context or another is a mistake. Zeno is making a claim about any sort of thing, the pluralist must say how many there are. Zeno's claim might be true of some sorts of things, but his challenge requires that the claim be true of all things and all sorts of things. An exception to Zeno's claim must show that there is more than one thing, but there are not an infinite number of them. So, if there is one context that shows Zeno's claim is not true, then his claim is simply false. There are reasonable responses available to the pluralist. They could claim that there are an infinite number of things. This might seem overkill, since Zeno only called for an account of how ever many things that there are – even if there are only two things – and now the pluralist has responded by going to infinity.

Alternatively, he takes up from Parmenides and examines the move from one thing to many things. Focus on the move from one thing to two things. His teacher distinguished thing instead of nothing and instead of many things. The many things were a mixture of things and nothings; this was nonsense. But if they are as many as they are, then they are neither more nor less than that. So, if they are as many as they are, they will be limited. "If there are many things, the-things-that-are are unlimited; for there are always others between the-things-that-are, and again others between those. And thus

---

[10] See G.S. Kirk, J.E. Raven, and M. Schofield, *The Presocratic Philosophers*, 2nd ed. (Cambridge: Cambridge University Press, 1999), 266.

the-things-that-are are unlimited."[11] It is difficult to understand why Zeno holds that when we accept that there is more than one thing, we must accept that there are an unlimited number of things. Consider the most basic division into thing A and thing B. If there are two things, then they must differ. They differ because A has at least one feature, a quantity or quality, that B lacks. Consider quantity, for instance the number one and the number two. They differ in many ways, since one is half of two, and two is twice one. Zeno argues that the division of one into two establishes an infinite regress resulting in an unlimited number of things. Suppose that there are many things, start with two. The two things must differ from each other.

Zeno had four arguments about motion.[12] The first argument is known as "The Dichotomy," and Aristotle calls the second "Achilles." The dichotomy argues that if there is motion, then to move from any point to any other point one must cover half of the distance. Then again one must cover half the next half distance, and so on. The half distances are infinite and one cannot get through what is infinite. So, there is no motion. We can see that the argument is called the dichotomy because it splits the distance, again and again, into two parts. The Achilles argument makes the same point but in a slightly different way. Suppose that Achilles races a tortoise, but the tortoise gets a head start. To catch the tortoise, Achilles must get to the point from which the tortoise started the race. From that point, he must get to the point where the tortoise was when Achilles got to the point where the tortoise started the race. This process goes on infinitely. Achilles never catches the tortoise. So again, there is no motion. Zeno employs the infinite divisibility of space to show that there is no terminating minimus for half the distance. There is always a half of a half of a half and so on ad infinitum.

The Arrow argument holds that time is composed of a series of instants called "now." At each moment of now, the arrow occupies a space that is just as much as the arrow or that is equal to the arrow. At each moment "now" the arrow is motionless. So, the arrow is both moving and not moving. This is false, so there is no motion. Zeno urges us to consider our idea of motion and time. If motion is like a movie running at a certain number of frames per second, then the composition of "now" moments will generate a paradox. If we think that motion is not a series of "now" moments, then we

---

[11] See G.S. Kirk, J.E. Raven, and M. Schofield, *The Presocratic Philosophers*, 2nd ed. (Cambridge: Cambridge University Press, 1999), 266.

[12] Aristotle, *Physics*, 6.9239b9–11.

need to offer an account of it. Aristotle rejects this argument by rejecting the idea that time is composed of "now" moments.

We have two more arguments. In the paradox of place, Zeno asks us to consider the place of place. Here Zeno asks us to consider the existence of what we call "place." We do say that each and every thing is in a place. Place is something, so place must be in a place. If place is in a place, then that place is a place too, and so on. This is an infinite regress. Ancient sources reject this argument, by rejecting the assumption that everything that exists has a place. Such things as numbers do not have a place. Thus, we avoid the infinite regress. Alternatively, we might accept that all physical things have a place, but their place is just where they are. So, although place has a place, it is the same place in each case.

The final argument that we will consider is called The Millet Seed. Zeno argues that when you drop a single millet seed or some subpart of the seed, it does not make a sound. When you drop a bushel, it does make a sound. So, millet seeds make a sound and do not make a sound. This argument points to the limitations of the senses, but it also indicates the limitations of any form of measure. Suppose you get an amplifier so that you can hear the millet seed hit the ground, you might think that the problem is solved. Not so fast, there will still be some sub-portion that does not make a sound. We can amplify the import of Zeno's argument. Suppose we consider the argument as directed not toward sound, but toward weight. Take the millet seed or some sub-portion of the seed that does not register as weighing anything. Then take a bushel of seed on the scale. The bushel will have weight. You might think that you just need a better scale, but at some point the scale will not register weight and then as more seeds are added, it will measure weight.

It is tempting to think that it is easy to answer Zeno's arguments. There are ancient sources that offer accounts of certain arguments and then point to fallacies in Zeno's position. In some cases, the critiques are correct. Also, armed with our contemporary understanding of math, physics, and logic, it might seem easy to solve Zeno's arguments. Of course, Achilles will overtake the tortoise. Of course, the arrow will hit the mark. We do Zeno's arguments a disservice by interpreting them in this way. Zeno is claiming that our understanding, coupled with our perceptions, leads to illusions of time, space, motion, and place. We have the impression of motion and time, but we lack an account. So, motion and time, he argues, are illusions. We can see that they are illusory, by considering the account we can offer for the illusions. The account we offer generates paradoxes and contradictions. If there really is such a thing as motion and time, Zeno is arguing that we cannot offer a coherent account of them.

1.2.3 Empedocles

Empedocles lived from about 495 BCE to 435 BCE. This makes him younger than Parmenides and a contemporary of Zeno and Melissus. He lived in Acragas, a Greek city in the south of Sicily. He was wealthy and involved in politics. Some people knew him as a religious leader, a physician, and even a magician. His dress was extravagant, with bronze shoes, a purple robe, and a gold crown. Some cities hailed him as a god.

He wrote numerous works, two of which were *On Nature* and *Purifications*. We should remember that often works were not titled by the author but by others. We have a large collection of his works in numerous fragments and testimonia. He composed tragedies, historical texts, religious poems, medical texts, and philosophical writings. Empedocles has connections with Pythagorean philosophy. His philosophical writing form is heroic dactylic hexameter. In keeping with the form, his style employs figurative and symbolic references. *On Nature* focuses on cosmogony and physical science. *Purifications* focuses on religious principles.

Empedocles is a pluralist, since he holds that what-is is more than one thing. He holds that there are four basic elements, or more specifically roots (*rizda*). This term refers to the roots of a living thing. He does not call them four "elements"; instead he calls them "roots" and imbues them with life. He refers to them in poetic style, naming Zeus (fire), Hera (air), Aidoneus or Hades (earth), and Nestis (water). The four roots in his physics are irreducible and indestructible. His cosmology places the four roots into an eternal cyclical process governed by the principles of "love" and "strife." Here again we see poetic language in his use of terms: "love" refers to attraction, mixing, and combining the roots and "strife" refers to the separation of the roots so that each is just what it is isolated from the others. Empedocles says that the genesis of mortals is double. He tells a story with two parts: one of increasing love and the other of increasing strife. In this way, the roots eternally become one, then many, and then one again. At stage one, there is love that is dominant, as the roots mix and combine. At stage two, there is maximal love, as the roots are mixed together. At stage three, the roots then separate. At stage four, there is maximal strife and all the roots are separated. Then comes love again and the process continues. This process of love and strife is governed by necessity. Empedocles accepts the ontological status of time, since he applies time references to the process. He refers to past, present, and future.

At every stage in the mixing of the roots, the Kosmos is a sphere. The sphere is a plenum; there is no void. The roots are in motion by exchanging places. The combining and separating roots mix in the form of a vortex. He draws an analogy between the vortex motion that occurs from the circular motion of liquids and air. Employing this argument by analogy is a useful strategy in science and more broadly. He argues that just as the larger and heavier things move to the middle of the vortex in water and air so too do such roots move to the middle of the Kosmos. The heaviest root is the earth and it is at rest at the center of the Kosmos. Surrounding the earth are concentric rings of water, then air, and finally fire. Empedocles offers an explanation for the phenomena of the heavens that we observe. By relying on observations that we can make in water and air, Empedocles argues that we can account for phenomena that we cannot currently observe.

According to Empedocles, we are in the stage of increasing strife, in maximal strife, or in decreasing strife. One thing is for sure, we are not in maximal love. If we were in maximal love, then there would be one living thing. The more strife, the more variety, separation, and dissimilarity physical things, and living things, have with each other. We live in a world of strife and many things. Eventually, all the roots will become one again. Empedocles enlivens the interaction between love and strife, by interweaving a zoogony. At stage one, when love comes to dominate, the roots attract. Empedocles invites us to consider all sorts of combinations. Today we are accustomed to distinguishing mixtures from compounds. You can mix oil and water, but they remain oil and water. Compounds involve a chemical reaction and the initial components cannot be separated. Bread dough is a compound of flour, yeast, and water. Though you can remove the water from the dough, you cannot separate the yeast from the flour. Empedocles is not thinking of mixtures and compounds in our contemporary terms. He invites us to think about all sorts of combinations. Empedocles describes a series of generations. In the first stage of generation, all the parts of plants and animals were split apart. In the second generation, the parts come together in the most imaginary ways. In the third generation come plants and animals. In the fourth generation comes reproduction among the plants and animals, such as we know them today. Empedocles invites us to employ our imaginations in this process. As love dominates the Kosmos there comes to be a bunch of parts of plants and animals. Then they combine to form animals. During this stage, we can imagine two humans joined back-to-back or ox-headed humans. We can imagine centaurs, gorgons, and all other manners of creatures. This is the age of mythical beasts. They did not reproduce in our time. In the final stage, the love is so dominant that the living things attract each other so strongly that they reproduce. Today we are in the zoological age.

Empedocles offers a novel and detailed account of perception. He argues that objects emit a stream of particles or effluences. The various effluences streaming from an object travel from the object to the perceiver. The particles in the stream are of various sizes. Some are the right size to flow into the eye, others to the nose, and so on. In this way, he explains how the eye perceives visual information, as opposed to other information such as scent. The visual information is the correct size to penetrate the eye, but not the right size to penetrate the nose. We see with the eyes and perceive scent with the nose, because the particles in the effluences are the correct size to penetrate that certain organ of perception. His account of perception is remarkable, since it is the first account of perception and is entirely grounded in his physicalist commitments.

We have focused, so far, on Empedocles' account of nature but he also had important religious commitments. We can see these two features of his philosophy in the two titles of his works. *On Nature* clearly focuses on the material world. *Purifications*, in contrast, focuses on religious matters. A purification in ancient Greece was meant to remove moral pollution from the person and the community. There were various purifications and the necessary steps to follow to remove the pollution were various. Empedocles holds that there are beings called *daimones*. They are composed of the earth, air, fire, and water. They live a very long time and are reincarnated many times. The *daimones* became morally polluted because they killed. This feature of his religious views explains why he prohibits killing and why he prohibits eating meat. Interpreters disagree about whether the two texts are consistent. Recent scholarship is mixed but tends to favor interpreting the texts as consistent. For our purposes, we should note the material nature of the *daimones* and recognize Empedocles' consistent dedication to a materialist account of the cosmos.

2

IONIA AND THRACE

2.1 Ionia

2.1.1 Pythagoras

Pythagoras was not only a philosopher but also a politician, a religious leader, and the founder of a distinctive way of life. He was born near Turkey on the island of Samos (c. 570 BCE). He left Samos when he was about 40 years old and emigrated to Croton in southern Italy. He died in Italy (c. 490 BCE). Though we have numerous stories and claims about Pythagoras, it is challenging to verify any of them. We do not have any writings from him. Despite the challenges in determining the accuracy of the biographical reports, we can say some things with confidence about his religious sect and about his philosophical commitments. Over the 200-year history of Pythagoreanism two branches diverged in their focus. One group was the *akousmatikoi* and the other was the *mathematikoi*. The term "*akousmatikoi*" comes from the Greek term "*akousma*," which means the "things heard." This branch of Pythagoreanism consists of certain sayings, cryptic and symbolic, that guided their lives. There were three main types of *akousma*: what a thing is, what is something to the greatest extent, and what behavior must or must not occur. The *mathematikoi* followed the mathematical and geometrical teachings of Pythagoras. The term *mathematikoi* derives from the Greek term "*mathema*" meaning that which is learned, knowledge, science, and mathematics. They were the first to distinguish the odd and even, prime, and square numbers. They also had categories of numbers that we no longer use. This branch of Pythagoreanism marks a revolutionary turn in early Greek thought, by turning from a focus

This Is Ancient Philosophy: An Introduction, First Edition. Kirk Fitzpatrick.
© 2024 John Wiley & Sons, Inc. Published 2024 by John Wiley & Sons, Inc.

on the material world to a focus on numbers, geometry, and mathematics. The teachings of the *mathematikoi* had a profound influence on Greek thought, and their ideas continue to be of interest to this day.

The two branches of Pythagoreans held common beliefs. They believed in the immortality of each soul. They make a radical move, since it gets rid of the difference between humans and gods. The one essential difference between humans and gods was that gods are immortal and humans are not. There was a common shorthand reference to gods, by calling them the immortals (*athanatoi*). Likewise, the shorthand reference to humans was mortals (*thnetoi*). They held that all living things have souls. Some Pythagoreans made a close connection between the soul and air. In fact, the pronunciation of the Greek term for soul (*psuche*) requires that one aspirate, breath out, when saying the term. They thought of the soul as a proper fitting together or *harmonia*, of parts that are represented by certain mathematical relations. Human souls were not necessarily in human bodies. The Pythagoreans believed in what might be called the radical transmigration of souls. Accordingly, when a body dies, the soul leaves the body and enters a new body. The soul does not necessarily enter another human body. It might enter the body of some other animal. There is a story about Pythagoras, where he tells someone to stop hurting a dog because he can tell from the dog's whimpers that the soul of his deceased friend is now in that dog. Thus, we can describe their account of the transmigration of souls as a radical transmigration. Since human souls can embody other living things, the Pythagoreans had a strict prohibition against killing. This covered not just the killing of human beings but extended to all animals and all other living things. We have some reports that an evolved soul might cease to be embodied again.

The Pythagoreans used their account of numbers to offer an account of the physical world. The concepts of odd and even are connected, somehow, with the concepts of the limited and unlimited, respectively. The One is both odd and even and the One generates, somehow, numbers. Numbers, in turn, constitute the universe. This is abstract, and without the needed context or explanation, it does not offer much help in our understanding of the Pythagorean belief that the *Kosmos*, the world, and the physical objects in it are numbers. The claim that the universe is number or that physical things are numbers is ambiguous. In ancient Greek, as in English, the claim is open to multiple interpretations.[1] The claim that "*x* is *y*" can mean that the two things are identical. This interpretation of the Pythagorean claim

---

[1] The Greek term "*homoios*" means both the same and similar.

renders it untenable. Alternatively, the claim can mean that x is composed of y. The claim that this flour is wheat makes a composition claim. This interpretation of the Pythagorean claim is untenable, as it claims that the compounding elements of flour are numbers.

Aristotle indicates a third alternative. He argues that the Pythagoreans hold that the universe is number, in part, because the features of numbers are in music, the *Kosmos*, and all other things. In this interpretation, x and y have attributes in common. We need to investigate the examples that Aristotle offers to understand the Pythagorean claim. We will start with the claim that the attributes of numbers are the attributes of the musical scale. Pythagoras was the first Greek to express the musical scale in mathematical terms. The tetractys was a 10-member triangle. It has one point at the top, then moving down it has two, three, and four. They sum to 10:

The tetractys

Figure				*Ratio*	*Geometry*
▲					Point
				1 : 2	
▲	▲				Line
				2 : 3	
▲	▲	▲			Plane
				3 : 4	
▲	▲	▲	▲		Solid

He offers ratios that allow one to derive the musical scale. The ratio 1 : 2 is the ratio of the octave. The ratio 2 : 3 is the ratio of the perfect fifth. The ratio 3 : 4 is the perfect fourth. The figure is even more instructive than it seems at first glance. The relation between 2 : 3 and 3 : 4 is 9 : 8, which is the whole step. The whole step is used to set the other notes in the scale. There you have it, the major scale. More importantly, we have a mathematical account of it. You can hear it with your ears and understand it with your mind. Pythagoras heard and understood this possibly for the first time in Greece.

The tetractys was also important for the Pythagorean understanding of geometry. Moving from the top of the figure to the bottom, the first row represents a point. The second row has two dots, which represent the two points that make a line. Three points are needed to make a plane figure. Four points are needed to make a solid, or a three-dimensional figure. This gives us an indication of the relations between numbers and physical things. We saw that numbers, through certain ratios, are associated with the musical scale. Through the tetractys, we can see that numbers are associated with geometric objects. Turning to three-dimensional objects, which require at least four points, the Pythagoreans begin with the tetrahedron. This is a pyramid, with four vertices and four triangular faces. Next comes the cube, with eight vertices and six square faces. The octahedron has six vertices and eight triangular faces. The dodecahedron has 20 vertices and 12 pentagonal faces. Finally, the icosahedron has 12 vertices and 20 triangular faces. These five three-dimensional geometric objects are called the five regular solids. We can see that the Pythagoreans extended their mathematical account to cover three-dimensional objects that require more than four points. The Pythagoreans held that there were four basic physical elements; earth, air, fire, and water. They correlate each element with four of the five mathematical solids or regular solids. Fire is associated with the pyramid, earth with the cube, air with the octahedron, and water with the icosahedron. This correlation has fire associated with four vertices, earth with six, air with eight, and water with 12. The dodecahedron is not associated with any of the four elements, but it is associated with the sphere.

The geometrical account of solids, correlated with the elements, functions as an account of the *Kosmos*. The number 10, which we saw represented in the tetractys, functions in the Pythagorean account of the *Kosmos*. Accordingly, there are 10 planets but the earth is not at the center. They place fire at the center of the *Kosmos*. The fiery center is orbited by a series of spheres: Counterearth, Earth, Moon, Sun, Mercury, Venus, Mars, Jupiter, and the fixed stars. There are two noteworthy features of the Pythagorean account of the *Kosmos*. They do not accept the geocentric model of the *Kosmos*. First, the earth is not at the center of the *Kosmos*. Second, the earth is not just round like a plate; the earth is a sphere. One final feature of their account of the *Kosmos* fits together, and harmonizes the account of music with the *Kosmos*. The Pythagoreans hold that the spheres in the *Kosmos* make sounds as they orbit the fiery center. They are spaced relative to each other and to the fiery center in proportions that produce the harmony of the major musical scale. This account of the *Kosmos* is called the music of the spheres, the harmony of the spheres, or the sirens' song. The Pythagoreans hold that we cannot hear this music because it is always present. So, we do not notice it.

Pythagoras offers a theory of opposites. Though other philosophers mention and employ opposites in their accounts, the Pythagoreans attempt to delimit their number and types. Aristotle tells us that the Pythagoreans hold that there are 10 pairs of opposites. Aristotle attributes this account of the Pythagoreans to Alcmaeon of Croton, but also suspects that it is Alcmaeon's addition. We can arrange them in columns:

Thesis	Antithesis
Limit	Unlimited
Odd	Even
One	Plurality
Right	Left
Male	Female
Standing	Moving
Straight	Bent
Light	Dark
Good	Evil
Square	Oblong

This list is worth examining, since it organizes opposite qualities according to numerous categories. We could take any one in the pairs of opposites and organize the others around it. First, let us identify the categories. I separated the opposites and looked at the two groups separately. On the one side, we have limit, odd, one, right, male, standing, straight, light, good, and square. On the other side, we have unlimited, even, plurality, left, female, moving, bent, dark, evil, and oblong. It seems to me that the male has better attributes than the female. It is especially notable when the female is associated with the dark and evil. The Greek language designates three genders: male, female, and neuter. Many contemporary languages do so as well. In general, the masculine is associated with action and the female is associated with being acted upon. So, we expect that the term for farmland is feminine, and the term for plow is masculine. What is odd about the list is that the male is standing and the female is moving. More conceptually, and for the Pythagoreans more centrally, the male is associated with the odd and the female with the even. Given that the male is associated with the limited and not the unlimited, it is odd to see the male associated with the odd and not the even. Furthermore, the male is associated with the square and not the oblong, but it is also associated with the odd. Intuitively, the square goes with the even and the oblong with the odd.

The Pythagoreans identified and categorized opposites. They are the most general of qualities, the limited and the unlimited. Not surprisingly, there are qualities of numbers starting with the one and the two. Then, there is the odd and the even, and even the even/odd. There are geometric qualities, such as straight and bent and square and oblong. There are sensory qualities, such as light and dark. There are sex identifications, such as male and female. Finally, there are moral or normative qualities, such as good and evil. We are missing at least one important opposite from this series of Pythagorean opposites. Given that the list mentions sensory phenomena, it should mention the musical opposites of concordant and discordant. Though they are mathematical at root in their explanations, the musical feature of Pythagoreanism implies that the terms for musical opposite should be included.

The Pythagoreans introduce many novel features in early Greek philosophy. They argue that the soul is immortal. They ground their account in mathematics and geometry, instead of the physical world. They offer a correlation between math and music, which gives us an account of the harmony in the major musical scale. The harmonious ratios found in music are also found in the soul, in the material world, and in the whole of the *Kosmos*. The mathematical features of Pythagoreanism are augmented by the religious features. By observing the religious principles, commands, and prohibitions a person can bring his soul into harmony with the whole of what-is.

2.1.2 Anaxagoras

Anaxagoras was born (c. 500 BCE) in Clazomenae, a major city in Ionia. Clazomenae was part of the Persian Empire and he served in the Persian army. He was a contemporary of Zeno and Empedocles. He was the first early Greek philosopher to live in Athens, residing there for about 30 years. He was an associate of Pericles, but had little interest in politics. He wrote in prose and produced just one work, *Physica*. Though he was older than Empedocles, he published his work after Empedocles. Eventually, he was charged and convicted of impiety, the first in a line of philosophers to be convicted of impiety in Athens. After his conviction, he returned to Iona and subsequently died in Ionia in the city of Lampsacus, c. 428 BCE.

Anaxagoras is a *pluralist*. He holds that there are many, maybe countless many, basic substances. These basic substances are irreducible. There are two main types of substance, things have a portion of everything and mind, which is infinite (*apeiron*) and self-ruled (*autokrates*). No thing is isolated by itself. This passage places the unmixed substance, mind, in contrast to mixed substances, all other things. Though mind and other substances have a feature in common, they are both basic substances, and the features of mind differ from the features of the other things. Mind is alone by itself, meaning that it is not mixed with other things. Mind rules itself, all other objects, and all souls. Mind set the *Kosmos* in motion, structured its progression through time, and arranged the stars, sun, and moon. Mind is the purest and finest substance. In addition to mind, Anaxagoras posits other substances and certain governing principles of the *Kosmos*. All other substances are mixed by having a portion of everything in them. The kinds of things that he posits are various. We have familiar elements such as earth, air, aether, and water. He posits clouds and stones. Surprisingly, he posits hair, flesh, and bone. He also posits qualities such as sweet and bitter, wet and dry, hot and cold, bright and dark, black and white, and dense and rare. Notice that some of the mixed substances contain opposites, two things of the same kind that are as different as possible. Functionally these are governing principles and not substances of the same sort as earth, air, or water. Finally, though this does not complete his potentially endless list of substances, he posits what he calls seeds (*sperma*). Each seed is a mixture of all things.

Anaxagoras adopts the Parmenidean constraint, nothing comes from nothing. By accepting that what-is does not come to be or perish, he posits what-is as timeless. Since he accepts the reality of processes through time in the *Kosmos*, he holds that what-is is through all time. At the start of the *Kosmos*, all things were one. If you were to cut it into smaller parts, you would always get the same thing. Aristotle called this substance *homoeomeries*, since it is the same, or similar, throughout its parts. The term denotes having the same parts. The term comes from *homo*, same, and *meros* meaning part. This term requires that all the parts be the same, in that they all have a portion of everything in them. Anaxagoras does not hold that there is a smallest division of what-is; there is an infinite division. He holds that it is one and the same thing through all the divisions.

The start of the *Kosmos* had everything together, all mixed up in equal portions with opposites imbued equally in each part. Recall that for Anaxagoras there is no smallest part, since what-is is an infinitely divisible plurality. At that time all things were one, such that an imagined observer would see one undifferentiated thing. There is nowhere to look in this original state, since all vantage points are the same. It is not that there is nothing to see; it is that one would see everything everywhere. Then mind set things in motion according to its governance. Mind, for Anaxagoras, is both a substance and a governing principle. It is the finest and purest substance, but it also governs and directs the *Kosmos*. The circular motion causes a vortex, and it causes like things to gather with like things. Anaxagoras does not give a sufficient reason for the motion or for it occurring when it did. Regardless, he has mind cause a vortex motion. The air and aether were the first to separate. We can imagine that through time lumps of flesh and chunks of bone formed. There were probably hearts, arms, and hands whirling around. The things, according to Anaxagoras formed all sorts of odd compounds, possibly including the formation of mythological compound creatures. The earth sits fixed in the vortex, held up by air. As things separate off in the vortex, there is more and more of the arrangement we see today.

Anaxagoras does not think that we get flesh by some combination of earth, air, fire, and water. Even though he mentions earth and the other elements, these things are no more basic than the other substances that he mentions. For Anaxagoras, earth is not more basic than flesh. The separation of basic elements into lumps and chunks is puzzling. It helps to think of this distinction. Anaxagoras holds that each part of what-is has a qualitative feature, no matter how small a part; it *has a part* of everything in it. He does not hold that each part *has an equal part* of everything in it. As we saw, or rather could imagine not seeing, in the beginning what-is was mixed equally. Then mind caused motion, which caused separation and congregation into lumps and chunks. It continues to be true that each part has a part of everything, but it is no longer true that each part has an equal part of everything in it. In this way, we get lumps and chunks of basic stuff as some basic element composes the largest portion in that lump or chunk. To identify some lump as flesh is to identify flesh as having the largest portion of basic elements in the lump. There is no coming to be and perishing; there is just the changing proportions of basic elements.

Anaxagoras made some notable observations concerning phenomena. He explained the light of the moon as a reflection of the sunlight and rainbows as reflections of clouds when enlightened by the sun. Despite these observations, he rejects the senses as authoritative for knowledge. Anaxagoras offers a justification for his rejection of the senses. When we have a mixture of white and black pigments and then add the smallest amount of one color or the other to the mixture, we cannot see the difference. Yet, we understand that there is a difference. What we see is an appearance of what we cannot see. What we cannot see is what-is. Anaxagoras has argued that mind is the guide to understanding what-is and, by implication, that our minds are our guides to understanding reality.

Anaxagoras' texts challenge interpreters to develop a coherent account of his philosophy given the testimonia and fragments that we have. It is difficult to coherently interpret the texts that we have, and we know that not all of the texts are equally worthy of credibility. We can add to this that the texts we have seem to imply a novel and very detailed account that incorporates all things in everything and opposites in all things. There is so much unsaid for us, given the texts we have and so much unsaid, possibly, for Anaxagoras. We must employ the principles of charity and fidelity to interpret the texts.

2.1.3 Heraclitus

Heraclitus was from the city of Ephesus in the region of Ionia. He lived to be about 60 years old (c. 535–475 BCE). Though Ephesus was a Greek city and Heraclitus was Greek, the city was part of the Persian Empire. He was from a ruling family that had rights to the kingship, which was largely ceremonial. Heraclitus is said to have abdicated the kingship and handed it over to his brother. We have seen other philosophers from Ionia, but by the time Heraclitus flourished both Pythagoras and Xenophanes had left the region. So, Heraclitus was probably an isolated presocratic philosopher. He wrote at least one book, possibly titled *On Nature*, which was deposited in the temple of Artemis at Ephesus. He claimed to have learned philosophy autodidactically, through self-teaching.

Heraclitus does not have a high opinion of other philosophers and earned a reputation for being a misanthrope. His scorn for other philosophers is legendary. His vitriol is directed toward Homer and Hesiod, but he is especially hostile toward Pythagoras. He even criticizes Xenophanes, despite their both having a dislike for mythological explanations. His attitude toward Thales is notably less caustic than toward other philosophers, and he does not assail the Milesian philosophers. He offers high praise for Bias of Priene, one of the seven sages. His general contempt for other philosophers may be part of a larger contempt for the majority of human beings. He was not a supporter of the Athenian democracy or of democracy in general. He clearly holds that almost all the philosophers before him were grossly mistaken.

We have over 100 fragments from his book and a lot of testimonia about his philosophy. We even have lengthy fragments that stood as the first lines in his book. Yet, we do not know how the book was organized. This has led to speculation about the composition of the text, with some interpreters thinking that it was simply a list of sayings in no particular order and others thinking that the sayings were organized by topic. Contemporary interpreters not only organize the fragments by topic but also acknowledge fragments that fit into more than one category. It is helpful to keep this in mind when one reads the fragments organized by topic. There is a tendency to read the fragment as just related to the topic it is placed under, without remembering that placing that fragment under that topic may well be an anachronism. Still, the topic headings are useful in our study of Heraclitus, as they highlight certain recurrent themes in his thought.

Heraclitus has a writing style that is compact, elegant, and full of word-play. His passages are often short and cryptic. The common themes in the passages encourage us to find connections among them, though their style demands careful attention to each passage on its own. Despite the amount of material that we have from Heraclitus, interpreters offer a dizzying variety of characterizations of his philosophy. According to Plato, Heraclitus' main idea is that everything is in flux. According to Aristotle, Heraclitus was squarely in the Ionian tradition. He thinks Heraclitus was a monist, choosing fire as his basic element. The Stoics find Heraclitus' view to foreshadow their own views. The texts seem to function a bit like a Rorschach test, by generating interpretations that tell us more about the interpreter than they do about Heraclitus' philosophy. We cannot simply dismiss the various interpretations of his philosophy, since the same interpreters also give us the fragments and related testimonia. We cannot take their telling of the fragments as authoritative while dismissing their commentary. Also, many of the interpreters had more texts and more commentary about the texts than we do today. We must judiciously use the resources that we have, by carefully evaluating their credibility in light of all the evidence that we have.

The *logos* is the central concept in Heraclitus' philosophy. When Sextus Empiricus tells us of the beginning passages from Heraclitus' book, the fragment's first words are *logos*. In the passage, Heraclitus claims that everything happens on account of the *logos*. Heraclitus tells us not to listen to him but to the *logos*. According to the *logos*, everything is one. The term "*logos*" in Ancient Greek is difficult to translate. The term can refer to words that express any inward thought. It can refer also to a speech, saying, maxim, or proverb. Then again, it can refer to a thought, an account, or a reason in support of an opinion. It is the etymological root of the noun "logic." It is often translated as "word." The noun *logos* is cognate with the verb *legein*, meaning to say or to speak. Heraclitus is well aware of this term's range, and he exploits it in his writing. For instance, he can move from talking about the logos to talking about what people say, and even to what people say about the logos. In Greek, one word can move from meaning what-is, to the account of what-is, to saying or thinking something about what-is. As you have seen, I render the term "*logos.*" To make matters more challenging, Heraclitus uses the term in idiosyncratic ways. Even native speakers of ancient Greek would puzzle at some of his uses of the term.

The *logos* functions to account for the wholeness or oneness of the *Kosmos*. According to the *logos*, "things together are wholes and not wholes . . . one thing comes from many things and many things come from one thing."[2] Given the different meanings of *logos*, we can interpret this in many ways. At least we must accept that the one, unity, and the many, plurality, are both true of the *Kosmos*. Despite the apparent temporal implications of the terms "comes from," we should not think that Heraclitus limits this claim to change over time. He accepts that the opposites can follow each other temporally, but he also accepts the bolder claim that they can happen synchronously.

Heraclitus argues that change over time comes in an eternal cycle governed by the *logos*. Hot things become cold. This change has a persistent subject that takes on opposite features at different times. A different kind of change over time comes in the alternation between day and night. Sometimes cutting the body or causing it pain is good, when it cures a disease. Sometimes, causing pain or cutting the body is bad, when it is caused by a disease. Heraclitus thinks the *Kosmos* has always existed and always will exist. The gods did not create it. The *Kosmos* is a non-generated constant of what-is. *Logos* directs the *Kosmos*. Fire is the coin of the realm in the *Kosmos*. It is like gold, silver, or currency in that you can exchange it for anything. Heraclitus thinks that fire is quenched by turning into water, which in turn changes into earth. In a similar fashion, the soul turns into water, which in turn changes into earth. Water from the sea turns into fire and earth by means of a waterspout engulfed in lightening. There is a proportion among the elements. Two units of sea transform into one unit of fire and one unit of earth. These elements remain in a constant proportion through the changes. Matter is thus neither created nor destroyed. In this way, Heraclitus insists on the conservation of matter throughout the transformation of elements. Fire is the primary element because of its ability to transform elements into other elements.

Heraclitus also holds that opposites can exist in an object at one time. In this way, what-is is a unity and a plurality at one time. The opposition is

---

[2] Daniel W. Graham offers the Greek of text B10 in *The Text of Early Greek Philosophy* (Cambridge: Cambridge University Press, 2012) 158 (DK B10).

composed of things at variance from each other, but together they form a harmony (*harmonia*). Heraclitus gives the bow as an example of a unity that is composed of opposites at the same time. In one respect of the bow, the limbs push apart. In a different respect, the string pulls the limbs together. Without the counteracting forces, there is no bow. The bow is a unity from opposing forces. The bow is meant to exemplify the *Kosmos*. Heraclitus offers many examples of opposites at the same time but with some distinction between the opposites. The beginning and end of a circle are the same. The road to the top of a hill and down from the top are the same and not the same. In a different case but at one time, seawater is good for ocean fish but bad for human beings.

One notorious example of opposites is especially challenging to interpret. Plato tells us that according to Heraclitus "you cannot step into the same river twice."[3] Plato and Aristotle take this to show that Heraclitus holds that everything is in flux. Accordingly, change is a cosmic constant for all things. One challenging feature of Plato's is that there is no persistent subject. If you cannot step twice into the same river, then there is no same river that persists through time. If this is an accurate attribution, then Heraclitus does not think that things stay the same by changing. In other words, he does not think that a unity is formed by yoking opposites. Applied to the *Kosmos*, this interpretation implies that there is no persistent *Kosmos*. The analogy between the bow and the *Kosmos* implies that there is a whole or a unity that is composed of opposites. Though Plato's paraphrase is often cited as a Heraclitean dictum, we can see there are good reasons to question its legitimacy. There is an alternative river passage that is attributed to Heraclitus, "Upon those that step into the same rivers different waters flow . . . They scatter and . . . gather . . . come together and flow away . . . approach and depart."[4] This passage assumes that there is a "same" river. It has the person step into the same river, but the river is composed of different waters. The water is constantly changing. It exhibits opposites: scatter and gather, coming together and flowing away, approaching and departing. This passage has a unity that is composed of opposites. The river is a unity that exhibits opposite qualities in ceaseless flux. The *logos* offers an account of the river, but *logos* also means "word." We do use the same name through time with reference to a river, but we understand that the river is constantly

---

[3] My translation of Plato's, *Cratylus* 402a.

[4] Kirk, Raven, and Schofield, *The Presocratic Philosophers*, 2nd ed. (Cambridge: Cambridge University Press, 1999) 195 (DK B12).

changing. The same word names an ever-changing thing. With this interpretation, we can see that the river passage is consistent with Heraclitus' other passages about unity and opposites.

The previous paragraphs attempt to treat Heraclitus' account of opposition into opposites that occur at different times or at one time, but there are subtleties in the examples that need mention. Some of the opposites are different qualities in the object, such as hot and cold. Other opposites are qualities that the object has in relation to other objects, such as seawater being healthy for fish but not for humans. Some opposites do not seem to have a persistent subject, such as fire transforming into other elements. There is no way to capture his account of opposites as being of one type or even of two types (e.g., asynchronous and synchronous). This is one of the many challenges that Heraclitus presents to interpreters.

Heraclitus offers moral principles as well. A wise person follows the *logos*, but most people do not follow the *logos*. So, they are not wise. He thinks that drunk people act like ignorant children and that true happiness is not found in bodily pleasures. He thinks that insolence (*hubris*) is a vice and he warns that violent passions damage the soul. By knowing the *logos* and following it a person can attain virtue and happiness. Heraclitus has not just offered moral claims; he has grounded his moral theory in a larger theory of the *Kosmos*. In this way, he has initiated a rational principle as justification for his ethical claims. This account makes the question of how we should live open to rational inquiry. It also places virtue within the grasp of every person.

2.2 Thrace

2.2.1 Leucippus and Democritus

Though some interpreters claim that Leucippus is a fictitious figure, it is more likely that he was a philosopher and that he produced some texts. We do not know where Leucippus was born, since we have conflicting reports of three possible birthplaces. He is credited with writing at least one work, *The Great World System*, and possibly another titled *On Mind*. It is likely that he proposed his theories sometime about 440–430 BCE. We do not have any fragments of texts from Leucippus. Possibly some of the fragments and testimonia that we do have are from or about Leucippus, even though they are attributed to his student Democritus. We can be more confident in our claims about Democritus. He was born in the city of Abdera in Thrace, which was an Ionian colony (c. 460 BCE). Abdera also produced Protagoras the sophist. Democritus was about 10 years younger than Socrates. He traveled so much that he was reputed to be one of the most widely traveled of the early Greeks. He ventured to Egypt, India, and elsewhere. He lived a long life, possibly to the age of 90, 104, or even 109 years. Probably, he lived to be about 90–100 years, which puts his death at about 370 BCE.

Leucippus was most probably the originator of Atomism. Though it is difficult, if not impossible, to separate the contributions of Leucippus from those of Democritus, it is most likely that Leucippus proposed the initial tenants of Atomism, and Democritus fleshed out the theory. Democritus was among the most prolific authors of Greek philosophy. He was definitely the most prolific of the early Greek philosophers, authoring over 70 titles. Thrasylus (aka, Thrasyllus) organized a subset of Democritus' texts into 13 tetralogies (sets of four texts), with 52 works in his collection.[5] The works covered a wide range of subjects, organized under four main topics. He wrote at least 8 texts on ethics, 16 works on physics, 12 works on mathematics, and 8 works on music. Recall that the subject of music covered a broader category than music, since the study of music was also a study of language and literature. He wrote on other subjects as well, including medicine, military strategy, and farming. The collection of his works included some spurious works as well. We have a large collection of fragments from Democritus, but almost all the fragments that we have come from his works on ethics. On the other subjects, we must rely on testimonia.

The first tenet is revolutionary and foundational; there are two sorts of basic stuff: atoms and void. The English term "atom" is derived from the Greek term "*atomos*." The term is a combination of an alpha privative (*a*) meaning not and *tomos* meaning cuttable or divisible. So, "*atomos*" means uncuttable or indivisible. Atoms are what-is. They are also called "being," "full," "solid," and "compact."[6] "Void" is a translation of multiple Greek terms. The term "*kenos*" means "empty," and the term "*ouden*" means "nothing." So, the Greek terms are translated as the English term "void." The void is what-is-not. The atomists had a crafty linguistic way to denote the contrast. They took the term "*ouden*," and cut off "*ou*" (not) to leave "*den*" or (hing). This then gives the contrast between "hing" (aka thing) and

---

[5] Thrasylus also organized Plato's works into tetralogies. Greek tragedies were usually arranged in tetralogies as well.

[6] Ancient atomic theory is importantly different from modern atomic theory. The objects of modern theory are cuttable; they come apart.

nothing, what-is and what-is-not.[7] Atoms and void do not come to be; they are eternal. The atomists maintain a version of the law of sufficient reason: There is no more reason for something to be than not. They must hold that there is sufficient reason for there to be both atoms and void. Atoms account for material stuff and the void makes room for the movement of the atoms.

The void is what-is-not. It is half of the whole, which contains atoms and void in equal proportions. The void has a place but it is not a thing or "hing." The void is the space between the atoms. It has a place in the whole, as do the *atoms*, but, it is nothing. The atomists might seem to violate the Parmenidean constraint, which held that nothing comes from nothing. The constraint was also interpreted as something that cannot come from nothing. The atomists did not get something from nothing, since they hold that the atoms are eternal. They do violate the constraint that nothing can come from nothing, because they give nothing equal place in the whole. They deny that the whole is one. The whole is two, atoms and void. There is also eternal motion in the universe.

The second tenet is that everything occurs by necessity. The atomists were the first Greeks to distinguish the universe (*pan*) from the *Kosmos*. The universe is the whole, everything, or all existence. The *Kosmos* is an ordered system, a regulated system, or a well-ordered or well-regulated system. Though there is one universe, the atomists claim that there are an unlimited (*apeiron*) or infinite number of *kosmoi*, the plural of *Kosmos*. By holding that there are *kosmoi*, the atomists hold what we would call a multiverse theory. The multiverse theory holds that our universe is not the only one. There are potentially infinitely many other universes. The atomists establish a similar theory, by claiming that within the whole there are *kosmoi*. In the atomists' view, the whole is atoms and void.

The *atoms* have three primary qualities: (1) shape, (2) arrangement, and (3) position. "Shape" refers to geometric organization, which is also translated as "structure." The atomists refer to *ruthmos*; in English, it translates to "rhythm." Shape and structure are rhythm in geometric structure and rhythmic composition. These patterns are metric and geometric. Interpreters use the alphabet to explain the three features. They say that A (*alpha*) and B (*beta*) are different in shape, AB and BA differ in arrangement, and AΩ (*alpha omega*) differ in position. There are 26 letters

---

[7] The atomists were not the first to make this clever etymological move, cutting "*ou*" and using "*den*" as "*hing*" or "thing." See, McKirahan, *Philosophy Before Socrates* (Indianapolis: Hackett, 1994) 307, fn., 9.

in the English alphabet; we have both upper- and lowercase letter shapes. So, we have 52 geometric shapes. This way of thinking about the atoms seems limited by the alphabets employed. The atoms have an infinite number of shapes and rhythms. This is one way to exemplify the relations, but there are others. The *ruthmoi* are geometric shapes, with edges, outcropping, concaves, hooks, and an infinite variety of shapes or structures. The letters in the alphabet have parts, certain strokes in common with other letters. We must not think of the strokes as actually separable parts, though they are conceptually separable. We must think of the letter as one thing that does not have separable parts. There are 24 letters in the ancient Greek alphabet, and there are only uppercase (majuscule) letters. Yet there are an unlimited, or infinite, number of atoms and an infinite number of types. So, we can think of the letters as an example, as long as we do not think of them as having parts or being limited in number.

The atoms not only have different shapes but also have different sizes. Nothing prevents there being an atom the size of the *Kosmos*. The different sizes of atoms indicate that they have different amounts of matter and different weights. Larger atoms weigh more. The second feature of atoms is their arrangement. This feature refers to the way that atoms combine to form compounds. Two atoms in different arrangements form different compounds, such as AB and BA. The third feature of atoms is position. This feature shows that the same atom can form different compounds, by being in different positions relative to the other atoms in the compound. The same atom in different positions can form compounds that demonstrate different features.

Kosmoi (plural of *Kosmos*) form through the features of the atoms and collisions among the atoms. A *Kosmos* is formed when some atoms in the universe come together and they form one vortex. They collide and bounce around in different ways. The atomists do not offer an account for the cause of motion. It seems that they are content with assuming a first collision between, or among, the atoms. Once we have one collision, the collisions would increase through the entire universe. The atomists hold that like atoms stick with like atoms. As the vortex rotates, the smaller atoms move to the outside of the vortex and depart back into the universe. The remaining atoms in the vortex form a spherical shape. Within the spherical shape, the earth forms when the atoms combine in the center of the vortex. The combination and separation of the atoms in the *Kosmos* are what we call coming into being and passing away. In reality, there is no coming to be or passing away, though compounds give the appearance of such phenomena. Each *Kosmos* forms in a similar way, but the features of atoms combine in different arrangements and positions. As a result, the various *kosmoi* demonstrate different features. Some *kosmoi* have living things and some do not, some have people and some do not.

The atomists claim that the earth formed before the stars. The earth rests on air. The atomists account for the colder regions in the north and the warmer regions in the south by claiming that the earth is tilted to the south. The abundance of vegetation in the warmer regions makes the southern part of the earth heavier than the northern part. The moon is the closest star to the earth, followed by the sun, and then stars. Alternatively, they tell us that the sun is the farthest from the earth. Possibly the different claims about the sun mark a disagreement between Leucippus and Democritus. The planets are at various distances from the earth.

The soul is material, just as is everything else except void. The soul accounts for life, sensation, and thought. The soul comes from moisture, and it imparts life. It is composed of spherical atoms in a certain arrangement and position spread throughout the body. At death, the soul separates from the body and spreads out of the body over time. Sensations occur by contact among atoms. Touch is the primary sense, in that the explanation of touch by physical contact is the model for the explanations of the other senses. Taste occurs through physical contact. The physical objects emit effluences through the air that impact the bodily organs. This explanatory model is used to explain sight, smell, and hearing. The explanatory model is extended to account for thought. There are effluences of atoms that impact the soul to cause thought. In addition to sensing and thinking about sensations, not all that we think about is grounded in sensations. The thoughts that are not grounded in sensory experience are caused by the effluences of other sorts of atoms. They are caused by atoms that are not related to sensation-causing atoms. The atomists are consistent in maintaining their materialist convictions, but when their convictions are applied so broadly, they strain credulity.

The connection between atoms and sensation might seem straightforward. It might seem that there are sweet atoms, sour atoms, white atoms, and red atoms. It might seem that there must be a correspondence between the features of the atom that cause a certain sensation and the sensation. This is not the account that the atomists offer. Instead, they argue that it is by convention (*nomos*) that some things taste sweet or bitter, hot or cold, or that they appear to have a certain color. The same atoms could taste different to a different animal. The atoms do not necessitate the particular sensation that we experience. There is a correspondence between the atom and our experience of the atom. It might be the case that sharp atoms correspond to bitter tastes, but there is no necessity for that atom to cause that sensation in an animal. The atoms do not have any necessary sensory qualities. There is a familiar distinction between nature (*phusis*) and custom (*nomos*) in early Greek thought.[8] Things that exist by *phusis* are objective features of the *Kosmos*; they do not change through time or location. Things that exist by *nomos* are different in different places and times. The atomists explained how it is that something might taste a certain way at one time for a person and a different way at a different time. For example, when a person is healthy a certain food might taste one way, but when sick it tastes another way. Even in good health, the senses change over time and place. Atoms are by nature, sensations are by custom. The distinction between atoms and the sensation of atoms, between nature and custom, gives the atomists good reason to distrust the senses. They condemn the senses and take judgments that are based on the senses as illegitimate. *Nomos* does not provide good epistemological justification for knowledge.

The third tenet of atomism is that the good life is "well-tempered" (*euthumos*). The Greek term combines the prefix *eu* meaning "well" and *thumos* meaning "temper." *Thumos* is rich in meaning, and it can also be translated as anger, courage, desire, mind, soul, and spirit. When we add the prefix and employ it as a verb (*euthumeo*) we get being well with anger, courage, and the rest. The atomists hold that a good person is a well-tempered person. A well-tempered person avoids excess and deficiency in desire and consumption. This person should avoid envy, covetousness, jealousy, and malice. The person is moderate, temperate, well-disposed toward anger, and content. There is a balance and equilibrium to this person that is analogous to the balance exhibited by the earth in the *Kosmos*, though there is no tilt in the well-tempered person. The discussion of ethics is a notable contribution from the atomists. They do not just make claims about the good life. They offer reasons to adopt certain ethical positions. Just as there is balance in the universe, atoms, and void, earth and air, there is also a balanced way of life concerning desires, the soul, and temper.

The atomists hold that the universe is what-is and what-is-not, being and not being. They defy Parmenides by positing what-is-not. They do not defy the Parmenidean constraint, since there is no coming to be of what-is. They hold that atoms are non-generate and eternal. They attempt to block Zeno's claims that the pluralists must accept the infinite divisibility of what-is, by

---

[8] The term "*phusis*" can be translated as either "nature" or "physics." This book uses both translations.

arguing that atoms are not divisible. Instead, the atoms are unlimited (*apeiron*) or infinite. They do not specify any limited collection of natural elements, such as earth, air, fire, and water, from which all things are composed. The geometric shape of the atoms and other factors account for the strong bonds in granite and the weak bonds in papyrus. The distinction between the features of the atom and the features of the experience of the atom aims to show that sensory knowledge is not a legitimate epistemological justification for knowledge of the universe and reality. There must be more to reality than the senses alone can reveal. Finally, they ground their ethical theory in their cosmology, providing the possibility for the individual to be in harmony with the *Kosmos*.

3

THE PHILOSOPHIC TURN

Western philosophy did not start in what we would think of as Greece, but it was initiated by the Greeks in a region that was Greek. This Hellenic, or Pan-Hellenic, region stretched from what we now think of as Italy, through Greece, and through the western coast of modern-day Turkey. These communities were united by their ties to the Greek language and to the worldview of Homer and Hesiod. The first Greek colonies were founded as the Dorians moved from Greece to the western coast of Turkey in about 1050 BCE. The Greek colonies were not governed by any central organization. Some of them in Ionia were within the Persian Empire. They were either an independent *polis* or under some alliance. An alliance means that the ally is subordinate to another *polis* or alliances of *poleis*. When you look at the map, you can see that they are all connected by the Mediterranean Sea. This fact is obvious in the epic poems of the *Iliad* and the *Odyssey*. The catalog of ships in the *Iliad* speaks to the seafaring tradition of the Greeks. With the *Odyssey*, the journey involved wandering in the sea. The Dorians move from the north of Greece through Greece. They tend to keep separate by founding their own settlements in Greece. Sparta was reportedly a Dorian settlement. The culture spread through Greece. It comes with poetry and religion. At the same time, it spreads to both the east and the west. It spreads through the north of the Aegean Sea, through the polis of Abdera, and the region of Thrace. To a much lesser degree, it spreads through southern Italy and into the southernmost Sicily. The Greeks expanded to the southernmost parts of Italy and the southern parts of Turkey. The Greeks expanded to set up colonies and establish trade routes among them. Maritime travel across the Aegean Sea was essential to the trade routes.

This Is Ancient Philosophy: An Introduction, First Edition. Kirk Fitzpatrick.
© 2024 John Wiley & Sons, Inc. Published 2024 by John Wiley & Sons, Inc.

We turn to the philosophical progression through time and ask these philosophers one question. What is the matter? Thales (*fl.*, c. early sixth century) is credited by Aristotle and others as the founder of philosophy. We have two main interpretations of Thales' philosophy, the Aristotelean and more recent interpretations. The more recent interpretations argue that Thales did not employ water as a basic element in a philosophical account, but instead employed it in an account that was more mythological than philosophical. Despite the different interpretations of Thales' views, there is no doubt that he was recognized as the founder of philosophy and that his legacy led to the revolution that was Greek philosophy. Furthermore, his legacy gives us a distinctive style of philosophy that focuses on reducing the enormous variety of phenomena that we experience to an elegant account of the *arche*. From these elements, the Milesians sought an account of all natural phenomena and the entire *Kosmos*. Water is the matter, since it is the *arche* of the *Kosmos*.

Anaximander (*fl.*, c. 570 BCE) does not identify any element as the *arche*. Instead, he identifies the *apeiron,* or the unlimited, as the basic element. The *apeiron* is unlimited in space and in time. It is also unlimited in its qualities or features. All other materials, for instance water, are limited. The limited materials have definite properties that circumscribe the possible features that the material can embody or exhibit. *Apeiron* functions as both the basic material of all things and a principle governing the material. If Anaximander had selected a familiar element, such as earth, air, fire, or water, he would then have needed to offer an account of the other elements coming from the one and the one coming from the others. That is a difficult challenge to meet. By positing the *apeiron*, Anaximander avoids the need to derive the other familiar elements from any one familiar element. From where do the familiar elements come? They come from an element at one remove from the familiar elements. We cannot directly experience *apeiron*, since it does not have any definite features. The limited familiar elements display opposite features when considered in relation to each other: some elements are hot and some cold, some are wet and some dry. If Anaximander had taken any one of the familiar elements as *arche*, he would have needed to account for other familiar elements that have features opposite to the *arche*. How might Thales account for fire, if he names water as *arche*? A difficult if not impossible challenge. The matter is *apeiron*, since it is *arche* of the *Kosmos*.

Anaximenes takes up the challenge (*fl.* 550 BCE). He inherits the ground-breaking approach of water as the basic element from Thales and the brilliant move to *apeiron* by Anaximander, but adopts neither water nor *apeiron* as *arche* of the *Kosmos*. His account takes air as *arche* of the *Kosmos*. We saw that there are challenges with taking water as *arche*, and there are challenges with taking *apeiron* as *arche*. It is hard to see how water can be fire, and it is hard to see how we can have any material evidence for *apeiron*. Anaximenes uses air to account for opposites, such as dense and rare. From there he can account for hot and cold. With these two pairs of opposites, he offered an account of the *Kosmos*. Anaximenes forsook the advantages of *apeiron* in Anaximander's system and brought his account back to the sensible world. He invites us to run an experiment. Purse your lips and blow, then open your lips and blow. What is the difference? He claims that the pursed lips make the air colder and the open lips hotter. Rarity and density offer an account of hot and cold that can be verified at home, so he says. This is a powerful redirection from the abstraction that Anaximander posited through *apeiron*. Air and wind combine in different circumstances with different results in sensation. In some contexts, compressing the wind makes it feel cooler while in others it makes it feel hotter. So, we can offer counterexamples to his claim. At this point in time, raising the counterexamples misses the historical point. The return to material elements that Anaximenes instigated makes the *arche* observable, testable, and verifiable (or not). This is a return to the founding ideals of the Milesian association, if Aristotle is correct. The matter is air, since it is *arche* of the *Kosmos*.

Xenophanes was born in Ionia but moved to Elea (*fl.*, c. 540 BCE). He is credited as the founder of the Eleatic movement. Xenophanes is the only minstrel among the early Greek philosophers. There is no doubt that all the Greeks who could sing sang. They just did not do it to their own works. Xenophanes probably sang his own works, since they were written in poetic verse and music often accompanied bards. It must have been shocking to hear him sing, since his performance was like a performance of the *Iliad* or *Odyssey*. Yet, he denies the gods of Homer and Hesiod. He offers explanations for natural phenomena without referencing the gods. Instead, he offers earth and water, or just the earth, as the primary material elements. He was the first to identify what we now call the water cycle. Xenophanes is the only philosopher to claim, on some reports, that earth is the primary element. Whether it was one basic element or two, he offers a materialist account of the *Kosmos*. This he holds in common with his Milesian predecessors.

Xenophanes is epistemologically skeptical about our knowledge of the gods. We can guess that his parents wanted him to be a theist and held that there are gods. He is not a theist. Homer and Hesiod are polytheists, they believe in many gods. His parents probably hoped for this theistic commitment in particular. No such luck. Then again, monotheists believe there is one and only one God. Xenophanes went in a radically different direction. It is easy to think that Xenophanes is an atheist or an agnostic. It is not that simple. The primary feature of a god, of whatever sort in the ancient world, is immortality. Xenophanes holds that there are immortal natural elements in the *Kosmos*. The non-generated timeless *Kosmos* has the features of a god, but it is not personified or anthropomorphized. The atheists believe that there is no god. They believe that they have an argument in support of their view. The agnostics believe that there is not sufficient evidence to believe in God or gods. They claim not to know if there is a God or gods. Xenophanes' claim that people from different places each have gods that look like them warns us about deifying ourselves. The gods in Africa look like Africans and the gods in Greece look like Greeks. Once he points it out, it is not hard to spot the pattern. He speculates that cattle and lions would draw gods in their own image too. Xenophanes forces us to ask if we have any good reason to believe in whatever gods or God is being honored in some particular epoch. There is no doubt that Xenophanes broke with tradition in denying the gods of Homer and Hesiod, but he put immortal things in place of them: earth and water, the world, and the *Kosmos*. Xenophanes is a Homeric god-slayer. The problem is that Homer, Hesiod, and everyone else talk about fictitious gods.

Pythagoras comes next chronologically (*fl.* 540 BCE). Though he was born off the Ionian coast on the island of Samos, he flourished in Croton in Magna Graecia. He offers a theoretical branch of his philosophy and a practical branch. He comes from Samos, an island off the east coast of Ionia near the island of Chios. He emigrates from Ionia to Elea at about 40 years of age. In southern Italy, he founds a philosophy that has a theoretical and a practical branch. Though the two branches are unified in a single philosophical system and a corresponding way of life, the branches eventually split. The *mathematikoi* follow the theoretical and mathematical teachings and the *akusmatakoi* follow the precepts governing behavior. There is an expansiveness to Pythagorean philosophy that challenges supposed divisions between philosophy and religion. The Pythagoreans offer novel theorems in geometry, such as the Pythagorean theorem and they are the first to give the ratios of the musical scale.

The Pythagoreans did not follow the Milesians in creating a materialist cosmology that identifies some element, such as water or air, as a basic substance. The Pythagoreans go in a different and more abstract direction. Among their most challenging and novel claims was that the world is number. An uncharitable interpretation takes the claim as an identity claim, for instance, this bread is a number, and a number is this bread. We find a more charitable interpretation when we consider their account of the musical scale. The musical scale can be expressed through numerical ratios. The mathematics gives an account of the musical scale or it rationalizes the scale. Mathematics and ratios are also employed to account for the soul, the world, and the whole of the *Kosmos*. The goal is not only to account for the *Kosmos*, but also to give an account that allows each person to harmonize with the heavens. The matter is number, since it is *arche* of the *Kosmos*.

Heraclitus is the next to flourish (*fl.*, c. 500 BCE). He lived in Ephesus in Ionia and produced his philosophy isolated from the other philosophers of his era. Heraclitus' account of the *Kosmos* has both conceptual and material aspects. Conceptually he argues that the *logos*, or the account of what-is is one. Yet, the *logos* is an account of opposites. The bow exists, for example, only by the counteracting forces of pushing and pulling. The bow is a harmony, *harmonia*, in the way that the parts fit and function together. The *logos* is also the word. We call a river, for example, by the same name over time, but different waters always flow from one moment to the next, and the river changes course over time. One word for something that is constantly changing. Heraclitus runs the difference between one and two, one and many. They are not ever meant in the same way and this keeps him from contradiction. He always invokes some difference in time, relation, respect, or some other feature. Heraclitus does not offer contradictions; he offers dichotomies and paradoxes. A contradiction is the claim that x is both y and not y. A dichotomy is the claim that x is y in one way and not y in some other way. The ways of distinction are many: time, relation, respect, and other features.

Heraclitus also offered a materialist account of the *Kosmos*. The elements did not come into being; they have always been. So he does not create something from nothing. He puts fire as the basic element that transforms into the other elements and back into fire. There is a proportionality to the changes and there is a conservation of matter through the process of change. The process of change is eternal and it is governed by the *logos*. We can see that there are both theoretical and material features of his account. The *logos* is both one and many, and the material account places one element as central among many. The matter is that fire is the primary element in the *Kosmos* and the *logos* unifies opposites.

Parmenides was from Elea on the west coast of southern Italy (*fl.*, c. 480 BCE). He writes in poetic verse, a style that harkens back to the works of Homer and Hesiod. Despite the similarity in style, his content is radically different. When he wonders about what-is, he wonders about what exists, what we can think about, what we can inquire into, and what we can know. The first path holds that it is. The second holds that it is not. The third holds that it is and is not. These are the three paths he discusses. The second path is rejected because what-is-not is not an object of thought, existence, or truth. The third path can now be rejected, since it assumes what-is-not. What-is remains as the only object of being, thought, and knowledge. It is non-generated, timeless, and unchanging. It turns out that there is not a lot to say about what-is. The truth is pretty simple. It also turns out that most of what we think, say, and believe we know cannot possibly be true. The third path is the way of human opinion and it is all mixed up. It mixes now and then (not-now), true and false, being and not being. Parmenides leaves us the Parmenidean Constraint, nothing comes from nothing or something cannot come from nothing. The matter is that people mix what-is and what-is-not. What-is-not is not, and nothing comes from it. Get your head straight and see that what-is is all that is.

Zeno (*fl.*, c. 460 BCE) offers vivid reasons to accept Parmenides' position. Suppose you do not take his position. Zeno argues that the path of two-headed mortals will inevitably end in impossibilities, absurdities, paradoxes, or contradictions. Zeno's Dichotomy and Achilles puzzles each in their own way argued that if motion exists, then an object would need to cover an infinity of mid-points to get anywhere. You cannot cover infinite space in some finite time, so there is no motion. It is tempting to think that we can refute these arguments with ease, by means of contemporary mathematics. The audience can refute the arguments in fact. They could invite Zeno to stand in front of the target, while he offers the arrow puzzle. Yet, this response misses the point. For Zeno, our understanding of the phenomena is the problem. Any measurements that we take are only so precise. Though one millet seed weighs nothing, a pile does have weight. We cannot get something from nothing. There is always a space between the calculations and the truth, between the measurements and the fact. The infection in our conceptions, calculations, and measurements is that they are infected with what-is-not or not-being. Zeno is a puzzle-master for his time. His use of the *reductio ad absurdum* argument form is a notable contribution to the history of logic. If you believe x then you must believe y, but y is absurd, paradoxical, or a contradiction. This form of argument still applies to mathematics, physics, biology, and all the sciences. The argument form applies not only within each STEM discipline and among the disciplines, but also in all other disciplines. The matter is that pluralists think they can account for time and change. They cannot, since their accounts always end in absurdity, paradox, or contradiction.

Anaxagoras was born in Clazomenae, a large city-state in Ionia (*fl.*, c. 460 BCE). He produces his work as a contemporary of Zeno. He works within the Parmenidean Constraint: the basic elements are non-generated and timeless. There are two basic types of elements: the unmixed and the mixed. Mind is unmixed with any other basic element. All other basic elements are mixed; they have a portion of everything other than mind in them. The mixed elements were called homoeomeries, by Aristotle, meaning that the substance is the same in all parts. Every substance other than Mind contains opposites. This element, or elements, is strange. Anaxagoras does not just have the standard elements such as earth, air, fire, and water. Anaxagoras includes seeds (*sperma*), flesh, bone, teeth, and other body parts as basic elements. We have encountered many monists. Anaximander is a monist; for example, the *apeiron* is the one basic element. Parmenides is a monist; all true concepts are of one thing. Anaxagoras breaks with his predecessors and contemporaries by adopting pluralism. He accepts basic monist principles, such as the Parmenidean Constraint, but he does not think that what-is is one. There are two basic elements, the unmixed and the mixed. The unmixed element, Mind, governs and directs the *Kosmos*. The matter is that there are two sorts of things, unmixed and mixed. Mind is unmixed and it is the *arche*. The mixed substances and seeds have a portion of every limited thing in them, every part of them.

Melissus was from Samos, a city near Miletus in Ionia (*fl.*, c. 450 BCE). He was Parmenides' student and remained a defender of his work. Accordingly, he adopts many, but not all, of Parmenides' convictions. For instance, he accepts that what-is is one thing, that it is non-generated and unchanging. He argues that it is unlimited (*apeiron*). If what-is were two things, he argues, then each of the two things would be limited by the other. It is likely that Melissus means unlimited (*apeiron*) in space and time. He rejects the existence of the void, arguing that to accept it would be to accept what-is-not or not-being. Parmenides held that what-is is timeless, meaning that it is outside of time. Melissus argues that what-is is timeless, meaning that it exists through each moment of time. This divergence by Melissus would motivate many of the arguments he offers. Since what-is is in time and space, he needs to show that one thing through all time and throughout all space. It also opens lines of criticism. If what-is is spatial and temporal, why in the world does it seem that there is so much change and diversity through time and space? We do not have fragments that will allow us to construct a reply for Melissus. Possibly he did not have a reply; more likely is that he did for better or worse. The matter is that what-is is the *apeiron* and it is through all time. It is not outside of time or space, but throughout all time and space.

Empedocles lived in Acragas, south of Elea on the southern Italian coast (*fl.*, c. 450 BCE). He was a contemporary of Zeno and Melissus, but his views differed widely from the two monists. Empedocles was a pluralist. His philosophical connection is to Pythagoras and his religious connection is to the Orphic mystery cults. He wrote in the old style of Homer, a heroic dactylic hexameter. Writing in poetic meter lends itself to figurative language and symbolic reference, even at the expense of descriptive precision. This is true of Empedocles' writings. When we decipher the imagery, we see that Empedocles holds that there are four basic things: earth, air, fire, and water. Rather than calling them "elements," he calls them "roots" (*rizda*). This reference breathes life into the roots. The roots are non-generated in a Kosmic cycle of motion governed by the principles of love and strife. "Love" and "strife" are images of attraction and separation, coming together and going apart. The *Kosmos* is a sphere with a vortex forming as the roots exhibit maximal love at some times and maximal strife at others. His argument in support of the vortex is an argument by analogy from the observable phenomena of liquid in circular motion. Here, he holds that the small-scale observable phenomena explain the larger-scale, non-observable phenomena. Another remarkable feature of his philosophy is his explanation of perception. He argues that there are particles or effluences that are emitted from objects to other objects. Each perceptual organ accepts particles of a particular size, and so we smell with our noses, hear with our ears, and taste with our tongues. This means that perception is by material contact and explained entirely in physical terms. Empedocles' religious views governed the soul, which was taken to be composed of the roots. He prohibited killing of any kind and he prohibited eating meat. The goal was to keep the soul pure and avoid moral pollution. The matter is that what-is is more than one. The *Kosmos* is earth, air, fire, and water; these are the eternal living roots. They are in an eternal process of attraction, love, and separation and strife.

Leucippus (*fl.*, c. 440 BCE) founded the theory of atomism, but we have no fragments from him. Though some texts are attributed to him, it is difficult to distinguish them from passages attributed to his student, Democritus (460–370 BCE). He was born in the city of Abdera in Thrace, at just about the northernmost part of the Aegean Sea. Democritus developed the theory of atomism to the version that both ancient and modern critiques evaluate. Democritus was probably the most well-traveled and a prolific writer of the early Greek philosophers. He traveled throughout the Greek world, to Egypt, India, and elsewhere. There is no doubt that his travels informed his writings and his philosophical point of view. The atomists come late in the time-line, since Democritus was a contemporary of Socrates.

The atomists argue that there are two basic things, atoms and void. The atoms are what-is and the void is what-is-not. Clearly, they reject the Parmenidean views in some way, but it is not clear that they violate the Parmenidean Constraint. They do not violate it by claiming that atoms, something, came from nothing, void. They claim that atoms and void are non-generated timeless things. They do not claim that nothing, void, came from nothing, void, since void always is. They do violate Parmenides' views by holding that nothing is. Though nothing is not a thing, it is somewhere and functions in the whole (*pan*) by providing space for movement among the atoms. By distinguishing *pan* from the *Kosmos*, they made room for multiple ordered universes or *Kosmoi*. Each *Kosmos* is a vortex in the multiverse.

The atomists offer a materialist account of the *Kosmos*, even though they accept the void. What-is are *atoms*. The soul is composed of atoms, as are all other physical things. The different shapes and sizes of the atoms help to explain the variety of things that we encounter in the world. It is the shapes and sizes of *atoms* that account for stronger and weaker bonds in the physical world. The atoms also explain sensation, but the different atoms that arouse sensation have no necessary correspondence to any certain sensation that they arouse. We experience sweetness because of us in relation to the atoms. We cause the taste of sweetness. The atom that causes this in us may well cause a different sensation in a different animal. On its own it has no taste, smell, appearance, feel, or sound. Democritus severs the sensations we experience from the atoms in the *Kosmos*. He severs our sensory knowledge of the world from the qualities of the *Kosmos* in itself. Despite the indifference of the *Kosmos* in relation to our ability to experience the *Kosmos*, Democritus has a plan for the good life. He wrote much on ethics and his goal was a well-tempered life. We should live moderately with respect to food and drink. We should be mindful of our temperament of anger and competition. We should temper our desires for honor and victory. The atomists offer a compelling, detailed, and long-lived account of the *Kosmos*. The matter is that what-is is atoms and void.

The first philosophers were isolated from other philosophers simply by their rarity. There were not many of them. Philosophers are still rare to this day. Still, the Greek colonies were well connected by sea. Trade and travel were common. When we consider the philosophers through time, we can see that more and more, they informed and influenced each other. The spark occurred first in the materialists Milesians, Thales, Anaximander, and Anaximenes, then to Xenophanes the minstrel philosopher, who was born in Ionia and settled in Elea. Then comes Pythagoras, who was born on the island of Samos in Ionia and moved to Croton in southern Italy, and the

Pythagoreans. Heraclitus composed his works in relative isolation. Parmenides then founded the Eleatic movement in southern Italy, which included Zeno and Melissus. Empedocles lived farther south in Italy than Elea and Croton. He lived in Acragas on the east coast, opposite Syracuse on the west coast. Leucippus and Democritus bring atomism from Thrace, about a mid-point in the landmass from Athens to Miletus. The early Greek philosophers came from the eastern Greek colonies and moved to the western Greek colonies. Greece, as we know it, was a hub of transportation and commerce, of ideas and philosophical texts. The early Greek philosophers were from the outskirts of the Greek-speaking world.

We have a chronology of philosophers, from certain regions, offering their distinctive philosophical ideas:

Flourishing chronology BCE	Philosopher	City/region of flourishing	Philosophy
Early sixth century	Thales	Miletus/Ionia	Water is *arche*
570	Anaximander	Miletus/Ionia	*Apeiron* is *arche*
550	Anaximenes	Miletus/Ionia	Air is *arche*
540	Xenophanes	Miletus/Ionia	Skepticism
540	Pythagoras	Croton/Magna Graecia	*Kosmos* is number
500	Heraclitus	Ephesus/Ionia	*Logos* unites opposites
480	Parmenides	Elea/Magna Graecia	Nothing comes from nothing
460	Zeno	Elea/Magna Graecia	Pluralism entails paradox
460	Anaxagoras	Clazomenae/Ionia	Unmixed mind and mixed seeds
450	Melissus	Samos/Ionia	*Apeiron* through all time
450	Empedocles	Acragas/Magna Graecia	The four roots are *arche*
440	Leucippus and Democritus	Abdera/Thrace	Atoms and void[1]

---

[1] This chart benefited from Peter Adamson's *Classical Philosophy, A History of Philosophy Without Gaps* (New York: Oxford University Press, 2014), xix–xx.

When we ask these philosophers what is the matter, they each have something to say. The Milesians were the spark that ignited the philosophical inquiry. They focus on the basic elements as *arche*. They also abstract from earth, air, fire, and water to *apeiron*, rejected the Homeric gods, and unified the opposites through the *logos*. They attempted to do so, which is more than had ever been done before. There is an alternative movement in Magna Graecia. They tend to abstract from physical matter and place the *arche* of the *Kosmos* in numbers and reasoning, where numbers are the *Kosmos* and nothing comes from nothing. Let us add the absurdities, paradoxes, and contradictions of pluralism. Melissus stands out in Magna Graecia, by endorsing the Ionian materialist commitments and placing the four elements as the "roots" of his system. Then, there were the Thracians from Abdera who claimed that there are only atoms and void.

To understand the philosophical turn, we need to consider the history of the region that gave birth to Western philosophy. Miletus is in the southern part of Turkey. The region was called Anatolia and Asia Minor. It is at the border of Europe and Asia. During the thirteenth century (1300–1201 BCE), the Carians spread to and settled in the area. Other Greeks followed into the region near the end of the century. In about 1000 BCE, Greek colonies spread west and east. To the west, the Greek colonies spread through southern Italy in the eighth century BCE, in a region that was later called Magna Graecia. To the east of the Greek homeland, colonies spread throughout the Aegean Sea. The Greek colonies spread to the Aegean islands and along the shore of Aegean. On the eastern shore of the Aegean, the Greek Ionians settled in Miletus. Greek philosophy began in Miletus in the early sixth century.

During the Mycenean period (c. 1450–1100 BCE) in the late Bronze Age, Mycenae expanded to Miletus. The city was a thriving and powerful Greek colony. It was a military power and a well-connected hub of trade. During the Mycenean period, the city was partially destroyed by fire. At the end of the Bronze Age, foreigners attacked Miletus again and destroyed it by fire. Miletus went through cycles of flourishing and decline, periods of building, and periods of destruction. During the Greek Dark Ages Miletus formed close attachments to Athens, a relationship that would subsequently serve the city well during the Greek and Persian wars. During the sixth century (600–501 BCE), Cyrus the Great extended the reach of the Persian Empire to include Miletus. Miletus was a powerful maritime and land trade hub. It was the most powerful city among the eastern Greek colonies. Thales came about this time, with Anaximenes continuing the examination into basic elements (*fl.* 550 BCE). Xenophanes was born in Ionia but moved to

Magna Graecia. Pythagoras was born in Ionia, but moved to southern Italy too. Heraclitus flourished about 500 BCE in the southern region of Ionia in the city-state of Ephesus.

At the beginning of the fifth century, at about 499 BCE, Aristagoras led the Milesians in a revolt against the Persian Empire. Darius the Great led the suppression and the Persian victory over the Milesian rebellion. The Persians were brutal in their retribution for the rebellion. They killed all the men, enslaved the women and children, and they castrated all the boys. The Persians tried to preclude any Milesian progeny. The second Persian invasion of Greece spread to Boeotia in southern Greece. In 479 BCE, the Greeks faced Xerxes there and an alliance of the Greeks from different Greek city-states defeated Xerxes on land in the battle of Plataea. The Greek battle at Plataea was part of a larger plan; the same day the Greeks launched a naval battle. They won the battle of Mycale in the Aegean. The land and naval battles proved decisive for the Greeks against the Persians. As the Persian Empire contracted, the Greeks expanded back into the colonies of Ionia and the city-state of Miletus. During this time (c. 479 BCE), the city was repopulated primarily by Greeks from the Ionian region. No longer under the influence of the Persian Empire, Miletus expanded its trade network to spread across the Aegean Sea. Miletus functioned as a central hub of commerce, trade, transportation, and services. This trade network spread throughout the Aegean, to southern Italy, Egypt, the Black Sea, and India. In 460 BCE, Anaxagoras produced his work in Ionia; Melissus did the same about 10 years later (fl. 450 BCE). The city must have been vibrant with foreign merchants, trade from far-off cities, and exposure to diverse cultural ideas.

There were other factors that set a context for the birth of Western philosophy. Though the Greek world accepted Homer's epic poems and worshiped the Olympian gods, Homer and Hesiod's works were not sacrosanct. The Homeric worldview was not taken as dogma. The Greeks had wide room for interpretation of the texts, for reinterpretation of them, and for creative license. For these reasons, Homer's texts did not function as the Bible of the ancient Greek world. The governance of Miletus compartmentalized city functions. It kept religious practices, military affairs, bureaucratic city of the functions, trade, and legal affairs largely separate from each other. Legal affairs were settled by arguments in court, employing a standard of reasonableness and persuasion to determine outcomes. The invention of coinage in Lydia set broad regional commensurate standards of value and a more abstract conception of value. The scales that commensurate value in trade correspond to the scales of justice that commensurate competing claims. Just as coinage sets a neutral standard of value in trade, rational argument sets a neutral standard in legal disputes. Literacy was not restricted to a small ruling class in the Greek world. It was widespread, as was access to ideas, information, and speculation. These factors combined with the influx of Egyptian and Oriental ideas as parts of the milieu that allowed for the birth of Western philosophy. These features of Miletus, or some subset of them, were probably necessary features for the birth of philosophy, but they are not sufficient since they also existed elsewhere. What distinguishes Miletus from elsewhere is the audacity, originality, and genius of the men that initiated the philosophical and scientific turn.

The move from mythological explanations to philosophical arguments is difficult, at best, to determine in the abstract. Fortunately, we have some historical fragments and testimonia. The textual records will allow us to get an initial definition, one by example. The earliest philosophers tried to explain what-is in terms of the material world and provide material explanations for physical phenomena. They use observable phenomena to make inferences about unobservable cosmic phenomena. They explain a wide variety of phenomena by means of a few materials. They stress the importance of reason in our understanding of the *Kosmos*. Some place the *logos* at the center of their account and use it to unify opposites. Others offer theories of mathematics and apply them to account for music, the planets, and the *Kosmos*. Some argue that there is just one thing; others argue that there are many things. Some argue that what-is-not is not and others argue that it is. Some argue that there is no void and others argue that there is. The Parmenidean Constraint is still applicable. One can argue that the Atomists' claim is among the most important claims that science has ever had. It is applicable still. So we could say that early Greek philosophy is simply what these exemplars did. Yet, this definition by example is inadequate.

There are some things that we can say with confidence about the early Greek philosophers. They subjected Homer and Hesiod not just to speculation but also to interrogation. Since the epic poets' mythology was a traditional belief, challenging it at a basic level or rejecting it is a revolutionary act. It is not the case that everyone walked around dogmatically believing the poems of Homer and Hesiod. The Greeks have a lively tradition of playing off of those poems and changing things to make a good story. Yet their reworking of the poets' views occurs within limits. There are gods and there are certain gods. The gods are the account of all natural phenomena and the *Kosmos*. The mythological view is justified by how long it has been believed, by how many people believe it, and by the social/political structures that celebrate and enforce the view. We know now that the justification for the mythological view commits certain informal fallacies; namely, the appeal to tradition, the appeal to the many, and an implied appeal to force. The philosophers offer an alternative. They refuse to accept the content of the mythological view, because they refuse to accept the justification for the mythological view. Xenophanes, Parmenides, and Empedocles wrote in the same poetic verse as the poets. Despite the common style of composition with the poets and allusions to the Olympian gods, these philosophers emphatically do not accept the poets' explanations. All three philosophers rejected the traditional gods. Xenophanes directly berates the poets' views about the gods and points to their anthropomorphism of gods. Parmenides thought there is just one thing, hardly leaving room for the Greek pantheon. Empedocles holds that there are four roots and gives them the names of the Olympian gods. Their references to the gods are actually references to earth, air, fire, and water. Even the most sympathetic philosophers in style among the early Greeks reject the poets' theology/mythology, and they reject the justifications for it.

The early Greek philosophers did not just reject the traditional mythological standards of justification; they did adopt a new standard of justification. They rejected the appeal to tradition and appeal to authority. The early Greeks accepted a *Kosmos*, an ordered universe. Hesiod accepted a *Kosmos* as well. What makes the philosophers different is their standard of justification. They take reason as the guide to offering an account of the *Kosmos*. With the appeal to reason comes an appeal to rational justification for their claims. Some authors, such as Parmenides, appeal to rational constraints that limit not only what-is but, more importantly for our purpose here, how we can reason about what-is. Zeno makes use of an argument form that we now call a *reductio ad absurdum*. This form guides his reasoning. We see arguments by analogy and arguments from generalization. We see multiple authors invoke what we now call the law of sufficient reason. Though some of the early Greeks offer more claims than reasons, it is reasonable to interpret the claims as conclusions of arguments. We are missing the reasons that were offered for the conclusions; they are lost from the historical record. We do not know that there were always reasons offered in support, and it is likely that, in some cases, there were no reasons offered. Still, we see a consistent, thoroughgoing, use of rational justification that runs among the Greek philosophers. Despite radical differences among the philosophers, they each implicitly appeal to reason and rational argument as the standard of justification. The early Greeks matched wits to find the truth.

When you match wits with people in power, traditional belief systems, or authority figures in the city, you will often pay a price. The elders in town do not take kindly to being questioned, challenged, and taken as an equal. They have tradition, popular opinion, and political power at their disposal. Some sources report that the Pythagoreans had their meeting house burned, with the adherents trapped inside and immolated. Anaxagoras was convicted of impiety and he had to flee Athens. The social costs were also true for the later Greeks that we will discuss in this book. Protagoras was banished from cities. Socrates was convicted of impiety and executed. Aristotle was convicted of spreading Persian ideas and he ran away from Athens to save his life. Look at the history of the West. It features numerous and prolonged persecution of philosophers. Look around the world today. In much of the world, philosophy is a dangerous endeavor. In some countries, it is either formally illegal or practically illegal. To this day, some countries confiscate the works of Plato and Aristotle at the border, banning the possession, dissemination, and discussion of such texts. The philosopher is always a minority and in danger of arousing the anger of traditional seats of power. The early Greek philosophers were not just embodiments of genius and revolution but also brave and audacious.

Part II

THE GOLDEN AGE

4

PLATO

4.1 Biography and Texts

Plato was born into an aristocratic family in Athens (427 BCE).[1] "Plato" means "broad," and it was his nickname given for his broad physical stature. His birth name was Aristocles, a family name from his grandfather. Plato's father was Ariston. He traced his lineage back to Codrus, who was the last king of Athens. His mother was Perictione. Her family claimed to have had a relationship with Solon, the great Athenian lawgiver, one of the seven sages, and the man who revised Draco's draconian laws. Plato had a sister, Potone, and two older brothers, Glaucon and Adeimantus. Plato lived to be 80 or 81 years old. He died in 347 BCE.

Plato received a typical Greek aristocratic education, beginning with gymnastics, music, and poetry. He was about 20 when he started associating with Socrates. In some reports, he is said to have been about 18, while in others, he is in his early twenties. It is likely that Plato met Socrates when he was even younger, since his mother's cousin Critias was associated with Socrates. Plato was also in his early twenties when Athens fell to Sparta. Following this defeat, Athens was ruled by the Thirty Tyrants. Plato was associated with and related to some of these Tyrants. In the wake of Socrates trial and death (399 BCE), Plato left Athens and traveled extensively. He was in his late twenties at the time. Possibly, he went to Megara to visit with

---

[1] Some report his birthplace as Athens and others report it as Aegina. See W.K.C. Guthrie's *A History of Greek Philosophy*, vol. IV (Cambridge: Cambridge University Press, 2000), 10.

Euclides, who was also an associate of Socrates, was present at Socrates death, and was the founder of the Megarian school. We know that he went to the Greek colonies in southern Italy and there he met with philosophers, mathematicians, scientists, and tyrants. He also met with the Syracusan tyrant Dionysius I, reputed to be among the worst of tyrants. He subsequently returned to meet with the son of Dionysius I, the tyrant Dionysius II. The *Letters* offer an account of Plato's visits with the Tyrants. Plato also visited a Greek colony in Egypt, Naucratis. In his travels he was twice taken and either sold into slavery or held for ransom. We cannot be sure of the precise chronology and order of places that Plato visited.

When Plato returned to Athens, probably after his first trip to southern Italy, he founded his school. The Academy was founded sometime in the early 380s, probably about 387 BCE. The Academy got its name from its location, a sacred grove of olive trees associated with the Greek hero Academus. Today we call education "academics" in honor of Plato's Academy. The Academy was unusual, since it allowed women to study there. Plato's Academy had competition in Athens. Isocrates founded a school in about 392 BCE. Isocrates' school in Athens was very popular and very expensive. Although he is called a "philosopher," he specialized in rhetoric and the management of aristocratic wealth. Isocrates was a skilled orator and he often argued cases in court. The aristocratic students at the Academy had a more theoretical education than did Isocrates' students. We can be sure that the dialectical method functioned somehow and that there were lectures on texts or readings of texts. We cannot be very precise about the curriculum at the Academy. We should not assume that the aristocratic Athenians submitted to the brutal education outlined in the *Republic*. We do know that a person could spend decades studying at the Academy.

Plato's texts were collected by Thrasyllus in the first century CE; the edition remains the canon to this day. The collection had 35 dialogues and 9 platonic letters arranged into 9 tetralogies. Grouping the texts into tetralogies, sets of four works, was reminiscent of the same practice in Greek tragedies. The *Oresteia* that we encounter today has only three works. There was a satyr play added to a trilogy of plays, to make a tetralogy. The satyr play connected the three tragedies to a worship of the god Dionysus. Historically, the fourth part of the tragedies is lost to us.[2] Though the tragedies had four parts, the first three parts were the body of the play. We do

---

[2] We are missing the satyr play, a fourth part of a tetralogy that connected the other three parts with the worship of Dionysus.

know that the fourth part was a celebration. Practically, there are three parts to a Greek tragedy. The first three parts tell the story. Thrasyllus organizes Plato's work to make full use of the four parts:

Tetralogies	Texts 1	2	3	4
1	Euthyphro	Apology	Crito	Phaedo
2	Cratylus	Theaetetus	Sophist	Statesman
3	Parmenides	Philebus	Symposium	Phaedrus
4	Alcibiades*	Alcibiades II‡	Hipparchus‡	Rival Lovers‡
5	Theages‡	Charmides	Laches	Lysis
6	Euthydemus	Protagoras	Gorgias	Meno
7	Hippias Major*	Hippias Minor	Ion	Menexenus
8	Clitophon*	Republic	Timaeus	Critias
9	Minos‡	Laws	Epinomis‡	Letters*‡[3]

Some of these tetralogies are conceptually coherent, such as tetralogies one and six. Tetralogy one covers the trial and death of Socrates. The first three entries in tetralogy six cover certain sophists, and the fourth entry, *Meno*, discusses a common question for sophists. Can virtue be taught? Despite the historical import of the tetralogy and the conceptual coherence of some groupings, many of these tetralogies are not so conceptually coherent. Also, the groupings mix texts that are Plato's with texts that might not be his and texts that probably are not his. This gives us good reason to think that if Plato did arrange his dialogues in tetralogies, he did not arrange his dialogues into each of these nine tetralogies. Thrasyllus believed some of the texts to be spurious, so he placed them at the end of his collection. In the Hamilton-Cairns edition of the complete works of Plato, we have none of the spuria and only 29 texts in total. In Cooper's more recent edition of the complete works of Plato, we get both authentic and spurious texts. Though we will focus on Plato's authentic texts, all the texts are valuable historical documents and worthy of our study.

---

[3] The "*" means that there is no consensus about whether Plato wrote the text or not. The "‡" means that there is consensus that Plato did not write the text. The "*‡" means that different letters among the texts have different evaluations as to whether Plato wrote them or not.

4.2 The Socratic Dialogues

Socrates was born in 470 BCE. His father Sophroniscus worked with stone, and his mother, Phaenarete, was a midwife. Socrates served in the military, suffering hardships without complaint. He was described as having an odd habit of wandering off and standing still for hours. He claimed to have a daimon that spoke to him, telling him what not to do. We do not know what he did for a living. He tended to be unkept, wore old clothes, and bathed infrequently. He was notoriously unattractive, with a pug nose and a big belly. He avoided politics and the law courts. He was not at all the ideal Athenian man. He was moderate in his consumption of food, sex, and drink. He married Xanthippe and they had three sons. After being convicted of impiety and corrupting the youth, he was sentenced to death. He was ordered to drink hemlock, which he did, and he died at the age of 70 in 399 BCE.

Socrates wrote nothing that survived. He is described as composing hymns in his last days. He does not seem to be a writer of philosophy at all. No source tells us that he authored a book or disseminated texts. It is clear that he spent his time talking to people in the marketplace (*agora*). The *agora* is on the north side of the Acropolis in Athens. In addition to markets, temples, and gymnasiums, it has law courts. Aristocratic Athenians would go to the *agora* to argue their cases and lawfully settle disputes. Socrates is referenced by numerous contemporaneous authors. Plato places him at the center of almost all his dialogues; Xenophon writes the *Memorabilia of Socrates* and an *Apology of Socrates*; and Aristophanes pillories him in popular plays. We might hope to disentangle Socrates from the depictions of him. We cannot. Xenophon is a valuable historical and biographical source, but not so philosophically astute. Socrates claims do not find full expression in his analysis. Aristophanes makes little or no attempt to take Socrates seriously. His texts are valuable for their historical portrayal of Socrates and his repute, but not so much for their philosophical import. We might hope to have an objective view in Plato. No such luck.

The so-called Socratic Problem is that we cannot separate Socrates the man from the portrayals we get of him from contemporaneous authors. We have Socrates as a character in Xenophon, Aristophanes, Aeschines of Sphettus, Antisthenes, and many others. Socrates the historical figure, the man, is not the same as Socrates the character at the end of any writer's pen. We look to Plato because he gives us the best analysis of what Socrates said, thought, and believed philosophically. Still, Plato is not an objective historian, if there is such a thing. He is a writer and thinker who has his own purposes in using Socrates' as a character. It is difficult, if not impossible, to separate Socrates from Plato's account of Socrates. Nonetheless, interpreters have attempted to do so. Since we get stories of Socrates from many sources and he never writes anything philosophical, we are left with various accounts. Some interpreters divide the dialogues conceptually and some divide them chronologically. Some interpreters divide Plato's texts into three periods: early, middle, and late. Other interpreters divide his works into two. Some subsets of the early dialogues are Plato's so-called Socratic Dialogues. The Socratic dialogues are generally accepted to represent Socrates' views and not Plato's. In these dialogues, Plato gives life to the man, Socrates. Though they are not verbatim transcriptions of Socrates' claims, the Socratic dialogues are taken to represent his views. Here is a list of Socratic dialogues:

The Socratic Dialogues		
Apology	Charmides	Crito
Euthydemus	Euthyphro	Gorgias
Hippias Minor	Ion	Laches
Lysis	Protagoras	

This list is not without controversy. The *Protagoras* and *Gorgias* are excluded by some because of their complexity and length. The *Phaedo* is not included because of its metaphysical focus and the distinctly Platonic theory of forms. The Socratic dialogues are the early dialogues, and they are understood to represent Socrates' views. The Platonic dialogues, in contrast, are understood to represent Plato's maturing views.

Socrates knows nothing of the soul, let alone the tripartite soul. He knows nothing of the heavens or the earth and nothing of the basic elements. Socrates conversed with people for free in the surroundings of the law courts. He did not inquire about the basic elements. He wanted to know what it is to live well. This requires courage, temperance, knowledge, and wisdom. The Socratic method of refutation, or the *elenchus*, is his famous method of questioning. The method follows a form. Socrates asks, what is *x*? where *x* is a virtue or he asks, can *x* be taught? Consider the question, what is *x*? The interlocular, who is often a sophist, is at the ready with definitions. So, the interlocular offers a definition of *x*. Socrates then tests the definition to see if it is too narrow, too broad, or in conflict with something else we believe. The sophists' attempts inevitably fail. Then Socrates invites them to revise the definition and try again. Some sophists withdraw from the discussion during or after the first round, while others revise and resubmit a definition. Consider a tidy example of *elenchus* from Book I of *Republic*. This dialogue is not a Socratic dialogue, but there is debate about whether Book I of *Republic* was originally a stand-alone Socratic dialogue. Regardless, it is a masterful demonstration of the *elenchus*, and it ends in an *aporia*:

The Socratic Method		
Stages and Character	*Questions and Answers*	*Example from Republic, Bk. I, Socrates and Cephalus*
Stage one Socrates	What is *x*?	What is justice?
Stage two Interlocular	*x* is *y*	Justice is keeping your promises and paying your debts.
Stage three Socrates	*y* is too broad, too narrow, or in contradiction to something we also believe	If you promised to return the weapon at some time, then it is not just to return the weapon to the person in a fit of madness at the agreed time.
Stage four Socrates	Invitation to revise *y*	Invitation to Cephalus to revise his definition of justice.
Stage five Interlocular	Start over at stage two, or abandon the inquiry	Cephalus abandons the inquiry. His sons take up the challenge and start anew at stage two.

A distinctive feature of the Socratic dialogues is that they do not come to a definition of the key term. They end in *aporia*. So, they are called the aporetic dialogues.

There are four dialogues in the trial and death of Socrates: *Euthyphro*, *Apology*, *Crito*, and *Phaedo*. The first three dialogues are Socratic and the fourth is Platonic. The Socratic dialogues focus on two features: Socrates' trial and his interactions with the sophists. Plato tells us about Socrates' walk to trial, his defense, his decision to remain in Athens, and his execution. In the walk to trial, Socrates encounters Euthyphro, a publicly outspoken orator on piety. Socrates mentions that this is good luck for him, practically a godsend, that he would run into Euthyphro. Socrates asks for a definition of piety and employs the *elenchus*. Piety is the proper observance of the gods or God. Euthyphro shows no hesitation, or humility, in his initial stage two definition. He says that piety is doing what he is doing, prosecuting his father for murder. This is an example, and he offers other examples of piety. Socrates tests the definition, by pointing out that he did not ask for examples of piety. He asked Euthyphro to tell us what piety is. Things continue, and Euthyphro modifies his failing definitions. Socrates poses a dilemma. He notes that Euthyphro holds (x) piety is (y) what is loved by all the gods, or if there is only one God by the God.[4] Socrates then asks about two options: (1) Is something pious because the gods love it? (2) Do the gods love piety because it is pious?[5] Are these pious observances good in themselves or are they good because the gods think them good?

The Euthyphro Dilemma		
Premise 1	If something is pious because all the gods love it, then there are no bounds to what the gods can deem pious.	The challenge is that all the gods might think that something bad is good.
Premise 2	If the gods love piety because it is pious, then the gods are irrelevant.	The challenge is that we and the gods love piety for the same reason.
Premise 3	Either something is pious because all the gods love it or the gods love piety because it is pious	P1. If A, then B P2. If C, then D P3. Either A or C Conclusion. Either B or D
Conclusion	Either there are no bounds to what the gods can think good or the gods are irrelevant.	The challenge is that there is no boundary on what the gods think good, or there is no reason to worship the gods.

The challenge can be expressed in more natural language. Socrates wonders about two options, given Euthyphro's definition of piety. First, is something (piety) good because all the gods love it, or do all the gods love the good thing (piety), because that thing (piety) is good? In the first case, Socrates raises what has come to be known as the problem of abhorrent commands. If something is good simply because the gods love it, then it is possible that all the gods could love something that is not good. Suppose all the gods love murdering innocent children in a certain town. Does that make murdering children in that town good? It is not credible to think that just anything that

---

[4] *Euthyphro,* 10d.
[5] *Euthyphro,* 11a.

all the gods love is good, simply by being loved by all the gods. In the second fork of the dilemma, Socrates raises the question of the need to worship the gods. If the gods love piety because it is pious, then we can love piety for the same reasons. We too can love piety because it is piety. In which case, the gods become irrelevant and superfluous. There is no reason to worship the gods. This dilemma remains a challenge to divine command theories of ethics, which hold that moral goodness is doing what God (or all the gods) commands and abstaining from the things that God (or all the gods) forbid. Socrates leaves his meeting with Euthyphro disappointed, since Socrates is on the way to defend himself against the charge of impiety.

In *Apology*, Socrates gives his defense.[6] The term "*apologia*" means "defense" in ancient Greek. The English term "apology" is the transliteration of the Greek word into English meaning "defense." In this case, the term refers to a legal defense. Before turning to Socrates' defense, we should note a couple of features of his defense that are not easily seen in the English translation. First, Socrates begins by reminding the jury of 501 members that he is not accustomed to making speeches in court. He invokes *xenia*, a standard of behavior that governs host and guest. This standard goes back before Homer. The term "*xenia*" is an abstract noun, meaning "the rights of a guest," or "hospitality." *Xenia* comes from "*xenos*" meaning guest-friend, foreigner, or stranger. Socrates is not a foreigner in Athens. Though he left Athens to fight in wars, he is known for being an Athenian homebody. Second, he distinguishes two groups of accusers: the first accusers and the second accusers. The first accusers are from the generation before the second accusers. They are the parents of the second accusers that comprise the jury. Socrates says that the first accusers are more "*deinos*" than the second accusers. The term "*deinos*" is ambiguous. In one sense, it means terrible, dire, and fearful. Alternatively, it means mighty, clever, and marvelous. Socrates' use of the term plays on the ambiguity, by inviting the jury to interpret the term as meaning terrible. Thus, the jury understands Socrates to mean that the first accusers are more terrible than they are (the second accusers). At the same time, we can interpret Socrates as saying that the first accusers are mightier and cleverer than the second accusers. These are just a few examples of the brilliant wordplay in Plato's dialogues. *Apology* begins after Meletus makes his accusations. The dialogue starts with Socrates' response.

---

[6] Xenophanes gives us a dialogue on Socrates defense, also titled *Apology*. It is available here: http://www.perseus.tufts.edu/hopper/text?doc=Perseus:text:1999.01.0212.

We can discern certain charges. Meletus claims that Socrates is guilty of wrongdoing on five counts. The first charge is that Socrates studies things in the sky and below the earth.[7] According to this charge, Socrates believes that the sun is made of stone and the moon is made of the earth.[8] Meletus' reference is rich, since doxographers tell us that Anaxagoras was the first to philosophize in Athens and the first philosopher to be prosecuted there. Anaxagoras does not limit his account to physical matter; he posits mind too. Meletus focuses on his materialist commitments. Accordingly, Anaxagoras account is atheistic. This charge accuses Socrates of following in the path of the first philosophers. Plato tells us elsewhere that Socrates read Anaxagoras' works with a focus on his account of the "mind."[9] Socrates was dissatisfied with his account of mind as a cause because he thought that it did not function meaningfully in his account. So, Socrates was familiar with Anaxagoras' philosophy, but he was not an adherent of it. Socrates argues that anyone in Athens can purchase a copy of Anaxagoras' works. It is unreasonable to think that Socrates is spreading Anaxagoras' ideas through town, when they are already widely available and well known. Socrates believes that the sun and moon are gods. So, the charge that Socrates is a materialist and atheist is false. In addition, the charge that he is spreading such ideas to the youth is also false. From what we know of Socrates' focus on ethics and his lack of interest in metaphysics, the charge is clearly misguided. It does indicate that there were common and long-held accusations against philosophers.

The second charge is that Socrates makes the weaker argument into the stronger argument.[10] Accordingly, he also makes the stronger argument into the weaker argument. This charge accuses Socrates of being a sophist. It claims that Socrates uses sophistic reasoning to make good reasoning look like bad reasoning, to make true claims look false, and to undermine commonly held beliefs. Socrates' defense of this charge is twofold. The sophists charge money for their instruction, but Socrates does not. By arguing that he does not charge a fee, Socrates also tries to avoid the charge that he is responsible for what people do after associating with him. The second feature of Socrates' defense against this charge is that he does not have the wisdom that the sophists claim to have. They claim to have wisdom

---

[7] Plato's *Apology*, 19b.
[8] *Apology*, 26d.
[9] *Phaedo* 97c.
[10] *Apology*, 19b.

concerning excellence, human and social excellence, to be precise.[11] Socrates explains that he does not have such wisdom, though he does have wisdom of a different sort. He recounts a trip he made to the oracle at Delphi and the subsequent events that made him so unpopular with powerful men in Athens. Socrates visited the oracle and she told that there was no one wiser than him in Athens. He thought that this claim was obviously false.

So, he tested the oracle at Delphi. He went back to the people in Athens who were thought to be wise and who thought themselves wise: the politicians, the generals, the poets, and the artisans. He questioned them and found that they were wise in their respective areas of knowledge. The politicians were wise about politics, the generals about warfare, and so on. Yet the politicians also thought they were wise about warfare, poetry, and the arts. In like fashion, the generals thought themselves wise about politics, poetry, and the arts. In each case, these people were not wise, when speaking about any area of knowledge outside of their own. They thought they were wise about everything, but they were not. Unlike the people who were thought to be wise and thought themselves wise, Socrates knew that he did not know anything about politics, generalship, poetry, or art. That is when he understood that the oracle was right. Wisdom does not require specialized knowledge about politics, warfare, or human excellence. Wisdom requires that a person know the difference between what he knows and what he does not know. Not one of the local wise guys knew the difference between what they knew and did not know. They thought that they knew many things that they did not know. In contrast, Socrates did know the difference between what he knows and does not know. He knows that he does not know anything about such things. Even if he is wise, he does not have the sort of wisdom that Meletus accuses him of having. The process of questioning powerful people in Athens involved public conversations where the powerful people ended up revealing their gross ignorance to everyone present. This was embarrassing for them. It made them angry and resentful toward Socrates. The three men involved in drafting the indictment against Socrates were angry on behalf of certain groups that Socrates questioned. Meletus was angry on behalf of the poets, Anytus for the craftsmen and politicians, and Lycon on behalf of the orators. Socrates claims that these men and others have slandered him for a generation. These three men are representatives of the so-called first accusers.

---

[11] *Apology*, 20b.

Turning to the third charge, it accuses Socrates of not believing in the gods of the city and believing in strange new divine beings.[12] Socrates points out that he participates in all the public religious observances and he makes sacrifices. He had already talked about visiting the oracle of Delphi, who is devoted to Apollo. It is true that Socrates believes in a strange divine being. He tells us that there is a divine being who speaks to him. This divine being is a daimon. This being is not necessarily a god. Traditionally in Greek literature, a daimon is an intermediary between humans and gods. Socrates claims that a daimon is either a god or the offspring of a god, and Meletus agrees.[13] When Socrates presses Meletus on the incoherence of his charge, Meletus states that he is charging Socrates with not believing in gods at all.[14] He subsequently claims that Socrates does believe in divine things.[15] The full charge is incredible to Socrates, since it is so ill-conceived. If divine beings are gods or the offspring of gods, one cannot believe in divine beings and not believe in gods (*theoi*). Meletus is caught between two prongs of his attack. Socrates and the other philosophers are atheists. Socrates believes in a novel daimon that speaks to him. Trying to have it both ways dooms Meletus' position to incoherence.

Meletus charges Socrates with corrupting the youth by teaching the things mentioned in the other charges to the youth of Athens.[16] The final charge functions as an addendum to the other charges. By studying things in the heavens and below the earth, by making the stronger argument appear to be the weaker argument, by not believing in the gods of the city, by believing in strange new gods, and by teaching these things to others, Socrates is guilty of corrupting the youth. Socrates asks if Meletus thinks he corrupts the youth willingly or unwillingly. If he thinks that Socrates is unwillingly corrupting the youth, then the proper response is to take Socrates aside and counsel him. Show him that what he is doing corrupts the youth. Meletus has never done so. Meletus responds that he thinks that Socrates is willingly corrupting the youth. Socrates responds that no one willingly causes harm to his associates. By corrupting his associates Socrates is going to be harmed by their corrupt ideas and behavior. By harming his associates, Socrates is harming himself. Yet, Socrates holds that no one

---

[12] *Apology*, 24c.

[13] *Apology*, 27d.

[14] *Apology*, 26c.

[15] *Apology*, 27d.

[16] *Apology*, 19b and 24c.

willingly harms himself. Socrates counters Meletus' charge with a dilemma. If he is unwillingly corrupting the youth, then take him aside and do not bring him into court. If he is willingly corrupting the youth, then he is voluntarily harming himself. Yet, Meletus brought Socrates into court, and Socrates cannot be voluntarily harming himself. Either way, Meletus' charge cannot be accurate.

After Socrates' speech, the jury of 501 citizens voted to find him guilty. At that point, the two sides offer their requested punishment. The jury must accept one punishment or the other; they cannot craft an alternative punishment. Meletus calls for Socrates to be put to death. Socrates first suggests that he should receive free meals for life, just as the Olympic victors receive. His friends then provide him with some money, and he offers to pay that money as a penalty. With just these two options, the jury sentences Socrates to death.

Plato also writes a dialogue that takes place after the verdict. The *Crito* portrays a conversation, probably fictitious, between Crito and Socrates. Plato uses the dialogue to explain why Socrates did not flee Athens after the guilty verdict. The majority, *hoi polloi*, of Athenians would have been perplexed by Socrates' insistence to stay in Athens before the trial and after the verdict. Socrates did not think he was guilty of the charges. Why would Socrates remain in Athens to suffer the death sentence? Crito makes the point well by saying that this entire affair is a triple fiasco. First, Socrates did not need to go to trial, since he could have left Athens. Then there was Socrates' conduct in the trial, where he antagonized the jury and did not offer an effective defense. Finally, there is his insistence on remaining in Athens after the trial to suffer the unjust verdict. Crito is concerned that people will blame him for not rescuing Socrates. Crito offers Socrates the chance to escape. He has bribed the guard, he has a disguise (53d) for Socrates to wear, he has money to help with travel, and he has safe places for Socrates to stay throughout his escape. It is all arranged and ready to go.

Socrates responds by directing Crito to not worry about what the majority of people think. Instead, he urges Crito to examine both sides of the debate. Crito presents reasons for leaving. Socrates offers the other side. He begins by arguing that one must never do wrong or one must never do injustice (*adikos*).[17] He then uses this proposition to infer that one must never return a wrong for a wrong, or an injustice for an injustice.[18] He warns

---

[17] *Apology*, 49b.
[18] *Crito*, 49b.

Crito not to accept this proposition without due consideration, since the majority of people think that it is right to return a wrong for a wrong. Most people think that it is just to return injustice for injustice. He says that these two sides have always and will always look at the other side with contempt. He has an elegant argument:

Premise 1	Returning wrong (injustice) for wrong (injustice) is doing a wrong (injustice)
Premise 2	Never do wrong (injustice)
Conclusion	Never return a wrong (injustice) for a wrong (injustice)

Socrates has a valid argument, though the other side in the debate will think that the first premise is false and interpret the argument as unsound. Socrates then moves to establish another basic principle: One must honor all just agreements.[19] He does not claim that one must honor all agreements, only just agreements. The subsequent discussion shows that he is concerned with excluding unjust agreements, such as those that are made under duress, coercion, misrepresentation, and fraud. We can think of the *Crito* as having two main parts. The first part concludes at 50a, and the second part runs through to the end of the dialogue. The first part concludes with these three principles: never do wrong, never return a wrong for a wrong, and honor all just agreements.

In the second part of the dialogue Socrates speaks on behalf of the "Laws." The personified "Laws" (*nomoi*) represent the existence of law and order in the city. Before they founded the city there was nature (*phusis*) and they carved out a space for the Laws (*nomoi*). By leaving, Socrates is contemplating undermining the Laws and doing all he can to destroy them. If no one follows the laws, then there are no laws. The Laws argue that leaving the city would be harming the city and wronging the city. Wronging the city is committing an injustice. A city cannot exist, if people do not follow the laws governing the city. They argue that leaving is returning a wrong for a wrong. Here they argue that Socrates was not wronged by the city. All the rules governing trials in the city were followed in his court case. If Socrates was wronged by anyone, he was wronged by the jury. If Socrates leaves, he is returning a wrong for a wrong in a misguided way. He is wronging the Laws, but they did not wrong Socrates. His fellow citizens wronged Socrates. Even if Socrates was wronging the ones who wronged him, he would still be

---

[19] *Crito*, 49e.

doing a wrong for a wrong. Yet this is farcical, since Socrates would be returning a wrong for a wrong but doing the wrong against one who did not wrong him in the first place. The third principle compels Socrates to honor all just agreements. The Laws argue that they have a just agreement with Socrates. They let him see how the city is governed and they did not force him to stay in Athens. When Socrates was a young man, he approached the city and formally requested to be a citizen. Furthermore, the city allowed Socrates to plead his case; and all the rules for trials were followed. Socrates has a just agreement with the city. The Laws conclude that leaving would be unjust on three counts: it is doing wrong, returning a wrong for a wrong, and dishonoring a just agreement.[20] Crito does not have a counterargument. So, staying in Athens and suffering the execution is just and leaving is unjust.

The *Phaedo* is the final dialogue in the tetralogy of Socrates' trial and death, but it is not a Socratic dialogue. In the dialogue, the character Socrates espouses the theory of forms, which is part of Plato's philosophy. According to the narrator of the first part of the dialogue, Echecrates, Plato was not present because he was ill.[21] There are features of the dialogue that likely represent Socrates the man. Socrates was in good spirits in the dialogue. He made friends with the guards, spent time singing and composing poetry, and was eager to get on with the execution. In contrast, the people present were distraught, despairing, and crying. Early in the dialogue, Socrates remarks on the shackle around his ankle. It causes pain. When the shackle is removed he will experience pleasure. Though you cannot have pleasure and pain at the same time, he argues that pleasure and pain are two sides of the same coin. You cannot get one without subsequently getting the other. When you get pleasure, you will suffer pain in its absence. When you suffer pain, you will get pleasure in its absence. Yet, the good life is not one spent in the pursuit of pleasures or avoiding pain. For most of his life, Socrates has experienced neither pleasure nor pain with respect to his leg. This state of being, this unperturbed state, is the good life. This state is neither pleasure nor pain. The dialogue concludes with Socrates eagerly accepting the hemlock. He asks if he can pour a libation from it, but is told that there is just only enough of the poison to complete the execution. He drinks the poison, walks around a bit, and then lays down to let the poison work. His last words, as depicted in the dialogue were, "Crito, we

---

[20] *Crito*, 54b–c.

[21] *Phaedo*, 59b.

must sacrifice a cock to Asclepius."[22] This is ironic, since Asclepius is a god of health. Socrates claims that death is the cure for his sickness. Crito asks if there is anything else that Socrates wants, but there is no answer. The dialogue closes with Phaedo saying that Socrates was the "best," "wisest," and "most upright" of all men he has known.[23]

4.3 The Sophists

The term "sophist" comes from the Greek term "*sophos*," which means wise or clever. Specifically in this context meaning clever with arguments or speeches. Initially, the term was complimentary, being applied to Pythagoras, Solon, and the seven sages. By the time of Plato, however, it had become a term of derision. The group of people that we now call sophists are not part of a unified movement. They do not hold to any common philosophical, political, social, or ethical beliefs. Despite the variety of views that they express, they do have certain features in common. (1) They are teachers focusing on rhetoric and moral excellence (*arete*). The skill of rhetoric and oratory was especially useful in the Athenian democracy, where the freedom of speech and the participatory democratic service opportunities required argument and persuasion. The skill was also useful in other city-states, where the ability to persuade a tyrant or oligarchy could prove to be beneficial. All but one of them claims to teach excellence. Gorgias does not claim to know what excellence is or to teach it. (2) The sophists focused on practical affairs and not on abstract theoretical concerns. They were interested in success in the city, securing desired results, and in enhancing a person's standing, power, and wealth. They were not interested in developing abstract metaphysical theories or materialist philosophical accounts. They tended to be empirical and practical in their concerns. (3) The sophists traveled widely among the various Greek cities. They took their craft on the road to offer demonstrations and recruit new students. (4) They charged a fee for their instruction. Some of them charged large fees and thereby became very wealthy. Historically, the sophists predate Socrates and continue to thrive contemporaneously with him. (5) Each sophist disparages the others. There are a number of sophists out there selling their instruction. Each sophist needs to show that his product is better than the others on the

---

[22] *Phaedo*, 118a.
[23] *Phaedo*, 118a.

market. This leads them to argue that the ideas of the other sophists are inferior to their own. More practically, each sophist needs to show that he is better at debate than his competitors. The sophists see rhetoric as a tool used in fighting. They describe their debates as combat. The best embodiments of this adversarial stance are Euthydemus and Dionysodorus. These two compete in the *pancratia*, a brutal series of combat sports. They are eager to beat you up verbally, but they would probably prefer to beat you up physically.

We do not have many fragments from these figures. One notable exception is Gorgias, from whom we have a set of fragments arguing that nothing exists. Most of what we know of the sophists comes from Plato's dialogues. Many of Plato's dialogues feature sophists as primary interloculars or secondary attendees. Many of the dialogues focusing on a particular sophist are named after them, such as *Protagoras, Gorgias, Euthydemus*, and *Hippias Minor*. Other sophists function in dialogues that do not bear their name, such as Thrasymachus in *Republic*, Dionysodorus in *Euthydemus*, and Prodicus and Hippias in *Protagoras*. His dialogues serve to contrast the sophists against Socrates, highlighting the differences in their methods and opinions. This makes Plato's account of the sophists suspect, since he features them as antagonists to his mentor Socrates. Though some interpreters are willing to dismiss Plato's account of the sophists as biased and inaccurate, more recent interpretations balance Plato's account with other sources. These interpreters accept Plato's account in general, insofar as it is not contradicted by other evidence.

Protagoras of Abdera (c. 490–420 BCE) was probably the first sophist, and he was surely the most famous. He came from the same city as Democritus, the atomist, and some dubious sources say that Protagoras was his student. Plato's *Protagoras* focuses on the subjects that the dialogues namesake teaches. Protagoras claims to teach *arete*, and this calls up a more general question: Can virtue, excellence, or *arete* be taught? Protagoras must hold that virtue can be taught, since he makes great sums of money from teaching it. Socrates argues that wisdom holds the knowledge of all the virtues. Protagoras argues that different virtues require different knowledge. If Socrates is correct, then it is more likely that virtue can be taught. If Protagoras is correct, then it is more likely that virtue cannot be taught. The dialogue ends with a humorous admission that they have both got this "topsy-turvy and terribly confused."[24] Protagoras claims to teach *arete*. In

---

[24] *Protagoras*, 361d.

this way, Protagoras seems to teach people to be good. He has two types of patrons: (1) wealthy young men and (2) citizens who want to improve their status in the city. It is one thing to seem to be good and another to be good. It seems that Protagoras must hold that there is such a thing as good and bad, right and wrong. Protagoras' teaching produces good men. Yet, Protagoras is famous for claiming that "man is the measure of all things."[25] This is some form of relativism. It could mean that the general consensus of what-is is true or accurate. If human beings say that x is hot, then it is hot. This is a species of relativism. In this case, if you disagree with the general consensus, then you are wrong. It could be that if the consensus in some region or in some particular city-state says that x is good, then it is good. This is regional relativism. Protagoras, however, pushes the position. If you think that x is hot, then it is hot for you. If someone else thinks that x is cold, then x is cold for her. This concept delimits to the individual: This is Protagorean relativism. If each man is the measure of empirical phenomena and normative evaluations, then how can anyone go wrong? If we cannot go wrong, then no one needs Protagoras' instruction.

There is a difference between judgments about empirical phenomena and judgments about value. The empirical judgments allow us to engage a physical object and, at the same time, share that experience in groups. When we make judgments about right and wrong, good and bad, we do not have such an object. We do not know that the concept(s) we reference in the community are the same object(s) for each person. If I say that x is good and you say it is bad, then we do not know that x is the same object for both of us. For empirical objects, they are for each of us as they are experienced to be. Thus, the object is hot for me and cold for you. This is true of conceptual objects too. If x is good for me and bad for you, then so be it. Protagoras could make arguments on either side of a subject. He was skilled in the art of debate, contrasting two opposing arguments. Composing arguments on both sides, contrasting arguments (*dissoi logoi*), is the primary skill that Protagoras will teach you. For this art, Protagoras was accused of making the weaker argument the stronger. He can also teach you how to determine what is advantageous for you. We experience sensations that are hot or cold and we evaluate actions as good or bad. We struggle to employ these experiences and judgments to our advantage. This is what Protagoras teaches. He teaches the skills to determine what is advantageous to you. The outstanding problem for Protagoras is to state what the skill is. From there he could

---

[25] *Theaetetus*, 152a.

show that the skill is teachable. He cannot do either. Could the art of *arete* be good for me and bad for you? We cannot know until we determine the skill and its teachability. Protagoras cannot say that *arete* is good for everyone, since he is a relativist and he cannot say what *arete* is.

The interaction between Socrates and Protagoras is playful and demonstrates a mutual respect. Though they disagree and cannot resolve their disagreement, neither of them can propose a solution. We are left with two people trying to get to the truth and failing to do so. One way to understand this is that both of them agree that there is such a thing as truth. Socrates thinks it is objective, but Protagoras thinks it is subjective and relative. There is an obvious objection to Protagoras position. If truth is relative, then Protagoras' position is relative. If the claim that *arete* is teachable is relative, then it can be teachable for Protagoras and not for Socrates. Yet, Protagoras is not able to show that *arete* is teachable for him. Despite their disagreement about whether Protagoras can teach what he claims to teach, from Socrates' perspective Protagoras is on the right path concerning the big question about truth.

Gorgias lived in Leontini in Sicily (c. 483–376 BCE), but he was an Ionian. Leontini was a colony of Chalcidian Naxos in Ionia. He lived a long life; some estimates put his age as high as 105 or 109 years. Some reports tell us that he was a student of Empedocles. He wrote manuals for rhetoric and oratory. He also wrote a work titled *On What Is Not* or *On Nature*. This work argues in the Eleatic style of Parmenides and Zeno to the conclusion that nothing exists or that what-is-not is. The work is difficult to interpret, because it is not clear whether it is meant sincerely or as a parody of the Eleatic style. *On What Is Not* seeks to establish three main conclusions:

1. Nothing exists or what-is-not is.
2. If what-is is, then it is incomprehensible.
3. If what-is is and it is comprehensible, then it is not communicable.

Put simply, nothing exists. If something does exist, we cannot think of it. If we can think about it, we cannot communicate it to others. The Parmenidean style of this line of argument is clear. The question remains as to whether the arguments are made sincerely or in jest. It is more likely that it is a parody meant to show that the arguments used by the Eleatics are capable of demonstrating either the conclusion that what-is is or that what-is-not is. If this interpretation is correct, it is a demonstration of Gorgias' skill in the *dissoi logoi*, since when paired with Parmenides' arguments we get contrasting arguments. We can interpret Gorgias' arguments that nothing exists as making a serious point through parody. It is serious in its aim to show that the Eleatic form of argument can function to prove that nothing exists. It is a parody, since it aims to prove that nothing exists. In which case the argument does not exist. We do not need to see the two interpretive options as constituting an exclusive dichotomy. We do not need to saddle Gorgias with the view that nothing exists.

With this background information in hand, we turn to Plato's *Gorgias*. In this dialogue, Socrates attempts to determine what Gorgias teaches. He claims to teach oratory or rhetoric, the craft of persuasion through speeches.[26] This skill is the most valuable skill. It gives a person power in the city and leads to success in every venture. It is more valuable than the knowledge of medicine, since doctors cannot persuade patients but orators can.[27] Socrates tries to get a clear view of oratory, by distinguishing what sort of persuasion Gorgias teaches. He asks Gorgias if he thinks there is a difference between persuasion that comes with true convictions and persuasion that comes with false convictions. Persuasion that comes from false convictions does not involve knowledge but persuasion from true convictions does involve knowledge. Gorgias agrees that there is a difference.[28] So, one form of persuasion does not involve learning, true conviction, or knowledge. It is simply persuasion. The other form of persuasion does involve learning. Gorgias claims that he teaches the kind of persuasion that does not involve knowledge or learning.[29] This position allows him to claim that he does not know anything about the subjects he covers in oratory, such as medicine, shipbuilding, warfare, or statesmanship.

Recall that Protagoras claims to teach excellence, *arete*. Gorgias does not claim to teach excellence. This relieves him of any obligation to state what excellence is or whether it can be taught. Instead, Gorgias teaches oratory simply, which does not involve a knowledge of the particular subjects covered in the orations. Gorgias does not need to know what is true, what is just, and what is good to teach the kind of oratory he teaches. Now that Socrates knows this much about what Gorgias teaches, he can turn to determine if oratory is teachable. Gorgias needs to show that oratory is teachable, since he charges large sums of money for his teaching. If he cannot show that oratory is teachable, then he would be shown to be a snake-oil

---

[26] *Gorgias*, 452e.

[27] *Gorgias*, 456.

[28] *Gorgias*, 454e.

[29] *Gorgias*, 455a.

salesman, a huckster, and a charlatan. To determine whether oratory is teachable or not, Socrates distinguishes a craft from a knack.[30] A *craft* involves knowledge and technique (*techne*). Socrates argues that there is one craft for the soul and it is politics. There is one craft for the body but he cannot say what its name is. He does know that it has two parts: gymnastics and medicine. Legislation in politics is analogous to gymnastics, and justice in politics is analogous to medicine. Socrates' point is that the rules governing society, laws, are analogous to the rules governing physical fitness, gymnastics. Also, determining justice in court cases is analogous to determining medical treatments to achieve health. In each of these cases, a person must have knowledge. There is right and wrong in legislating. There is justice and injustice in court adjudications just as there is right and wrong in medical treatments.

In contrast, a knack (*empeiria*) cannot offer an account (*logos*) of the endeavor, and it cannot offer an account of the causes that produce the results.[31] A knack gives pleasure to others and flatters them. It is sometimes successful and sometimes not, but it cannot account for the causes of the difference between success and failure. For example, the same plate of food can give pleasure to some people and displeasure to others. The knack of cookery cannot offer an account of why the dish produced pleasure in one person and not in another. Socrates says that the knacks notice the crafts, but they don't know them. They guess and conjecture about them. The knacks put on the mask of the crafts; and they have the pretense of being crafts, but they do not act from knowledge. They impersonate the crafts. They aim to give people pleasure, rather than making people just or healthy. Socrates lists certain knacks, such as cookery, cosmetics and couture, sophistry, and oratory. Since each knack impersonates a particular craft, Socrates establishes correlations between each craft and a particular knack:[32]

Crafts	Knacks
Legislation in politics (soul)	Sophistry
Justice in politics (soul)	Oratory
Medicine (body)	Cookery
Gymnastics (body)	Couture and cosmetics

---

[30] *Gorgias*, 462.
[31] *Gorgias*, 465a.
[32] *Gorgias*, 465b–c.

Socrates argues that oratory impersonates justice, but it does not know what justice is. In addition, oratory cannot offer an account of itself. It cannot offer an account of the difference between successful persuasion and failure. The same plate of food can bring pleasure to some people and not others. The same speech can persuade one audience and not another. Oratory cannot account for the difference between success and failure. As it turns out, the orator simply has a knack for persuasion. Since oratory is a knack, Gorgias cannot offer an account of successful persuasion. So, he cannot teach people to successfully persuade others. This result is not good for Gorgias. It turns out that Gorgias is a charlatan. In the face of this unwanted result, Gorgias withdraws from the discussion.

4.4 Plato's Philosophy

4.4.1 Knowledge

Of Plato's texts, the *Theaetetus* alone devotes itself wholly to questions of knowledge. It is the earliest and the foundational text in epistemology. The initial exchange in the text comes between Euclides and Terpsion. Euclides reports that many years ago he attended a discussion with Socrates and Theaetetus, among others. Terpsion asks Euclides if he can recall the conversation. Euclides replies that he cannot recount it from memory, but he made notes about the conversation and he can have them read aloud.[33] This is a complex way for Plato to introduce a dialogue devoted to knowledge. We have a character who cannot remember the conversation in enough detail and who relies on notes he made after the conversation. Faulty memory begins the dialogue on knowledge.

Theaetetus considers three main definitions of knowledge. The first definition is that knowledge is perception. Perception alone can provide us with information gained through the senses. We can sense tactile qualities, colors, smells, and tastes. We can sense that some object is hard and some other object is soft. Yet, to know about these objects we need to employ certain concepts, such as like, unlike, same, and different. These concepts are not in the sensations themselves. Instead, they guide comparisons and relations by employing ideas about the objects of sensation. We also judge some objects to be beautiful or ugly. These are not sensations but judgments about objects sensed. To know that an object is hard, we need the concepts

---

[33] Ancient Greek was always read out loud.

of hardness and softness. To judge an object as beautiful, we need the concepts of beauty and ugliness. Sensation alone will not account for our knowledge of objects.[34]

The second definition is that knowledge is true judgment. We can see that this thesis follows from the failure of the first definition. There we saw that perception is not enough for knowledge. We also need a judgment that is true. True judgment is a step in the right direction. Socrates asks us to consider a jury in a court trial. They hear eyewitness testimony of things that a witness perceived. Suppose that the witness knows the truth about what happened in an assault or a robbery. He can be persuaded by the lawyer that the witness is telling the truth. Once the juror is persuaded, the juror comes to hold a true judgment. Yet, the juror was not there. So, he does not know. This counterexample shows that a person can hold a true judgment but not have knowledge.[35]

The third and final definition is that knowledge is true judgment with an account (*logos*). We can see how this follows from the failure of the second definition. As we saw, the juror lacked a proper justification, or account, for his true judgment. This allowed for the possibility of a juror to have true judgment but not knowledge. So, we turn to consider what is an account or a justification. If we can get clear on this concept, it is hoped, then we can add it to true judgment to get a definition of knowledge. Socrates asks us to consider a definition of an account. Suppose that we consider an account to be the naming of the elements of a thing. An account of mud, for instance, requires that we can name its elements as water and earth. Letters and syllables are the tools used in naming. Consider the name "Socrates" and focus on its first syllable. The syllable is "So." An account of the syllable names its elements, namely "S" and "o." Continuing, the account of "S" requires that we name its elements. Yet, "S" does not have any elements, and "o" does not have any elements. We can have an account of the syllable "So," but we cannot have an account of its basic elements, "S" and "o." Since we cannot have an account of them, we cannot know them. It is unacceptable to hold that we can know the syllable by naming its elements, but at the same time we cannot know each letter. In this view, we can know the name "Socrates" by having an account of the letters and their order, but we cannot know the letters themselves. How can you know both when you do not know either?

---

[34] *Theaetetus*, 186.
[35] *Theaetetus*, 201a–b.

Possibly we went wrong in treating the syllable as being composed of parts. It is true that the syllable is composed of letters, but it is also true that the syllable is one unit of the name. In this way, we can think of the syllable as some single thing that has its own nature different from the letters. We are not saying, on this hypothesis, that the whole is greater than the sum of its parts. We are saying that the whole is different from its parts.[36] If we consider the whole as one thing, then it does not have basic elements or parts. If an account requires us to name the basic elements of a thing and the syllable does not have basic elements, then we cannot have an account of it. If we cannot have an account of it, then we cannot know it. We face a dilemma either the syllable has parts or it does not have parts. If we consider a syllable to have parts, then we can account for the syllable but not the letters. If we consider the syllable not to have parts, then we cannot account for the syllable. Either way, we cannot show that we know the syllable.

Socrates urges us to try an alternative definition of an account. Suppose we define an account as being able to name some feature that distinguishes it from all other things.[37] In this way, we can tell what a thing is by its differentness from all other things. One has an account of Theaetetus, for example, when one can distinguish Theaetetus from all other people. We already had true judgment in our definition of knowledge. Socrates argues that holding a true judgment concerning Theaetetus would require the person making the judgment to distinguish Theaetetus from all other people. What are we adding to true judgment of the distinguishing difference when we add an account of the distinguishing difference? We must be adding something other than a judgment. It must be, according to Socrates, that we mean that the person must not simply make a judgment. Adding the account to the definition of knowledge requires the person to *know* the distinguishing difference and not simply *judge* the distinguishing difference. Now we have made a mess of things. Knowledge is true judgment and a knowledge of the distinguishing difference. It results that knowledge requires a person to already know.[38] Socrates broadens his rejection of this line of argument. When we think of various ways to define "account," Socrates argues, we see that they will add something to the judgment involved in true judgment. An account will require not judgment, but some knowledge about the judgment. The problem is not in the particular definition of account, but in its relation

---

[36] *Theaetetus*, 205b.

[37] *Theaetetus*, 208c.

[38] *Theaetetus*, 209d–210a.

to true judgment. Anything we add, Socrates argues, will produce the circular definition of knowledge.[39] *Theaetetus* ends in an *aporia*.

It is tempting to think that the failure to find a definition of knowledge in *Theaetetus* is due to limitations in the analysis of the Greek language. Possibly we need more to work with in the final attempt to define an account, more than judgment and knowledge. Maybe we need just one more attempt to define "account." These are worthy topics to explore, as are concerns about the other attempts to define knowledge as perception or true belief. As a result, we might think that we have made no progress in *Theaetetus*, because we did not get a definition of knowledge. Yet, we have made some progress. We are aware of the failings of some attempts to define knowledge. We can see that there are challenges in defining what an account is. These are valuable insights that we did not have at the start of the dialogue. What is Plato's definition of knowledge? He does not offer one. Though he does talk about knowledge in other dialogues, he does not define the term.[40] Nonetheless, *Theaetetus* makes a lasting contribution to epistemology. As we turn from knowing to knowing any certain proposition, let's call it p, the dialogue gives some important direction. To know p we can say that (1) p is true, (2) the person assents to p, and (3) the person is justified in assenting to p. We can see that this format requires that p be true, that it be judged to be true, and that the person have an account. Despite the modern terminology, the modern framework owes much to the *Theaetetus*. We struggle to this day to adequately characterize what is required for a proposition to be true and what it is to be justified in holding a belief. So, it is no surprise that Socrates discussion ends in an *aporia*.

4.4.2 The Forms

Before we turn to the forms themselves, we will examine the path that Plato charts from sensation to understanding. In *Republic*, Socrates tells us that there are certain sensations that call to the understanding or summon it.[41] Some sensations do not call up the understanding. Suppose you perceive three fingers: the middle, the ring, and the pinky. None of them is more or less a finger. It does not matter if they are long or short, fat or skinny, light or dark. Each of them is equally a finger. In this case and other such cases,

---

[39] *Theaetetus*, 210a.
[40] *Meno* 97c–98a and *Symposium* 202a come closest to a definition of knowledge.
[41] *Republic*, 523c.

there is no need for the understanding. Now consider the bigness and smallness of the fingers. The ring finger is bigger than the pinky, but smaller than the middle finger. It seems that the middle finger is big and small. Consider the sense of touch. This same sense perceives hardness and softness. When you touch an object, such as a bed, it resists the pressure somewhat and accepts the pressure somewhat. The bed is both soft and hard. This information is conveyed through the same sense, namely touch. Every sense is set over opposite qualities. Odors can be musky or putrid, sounds can be loud or soft, seen objects can be clear or obscure, and tastes can be sweet or bitter. Each of the senses perceives opposites at the same time and in the same object. These perceptions, Socrates tells us, awaken or summon the understanding, since they report that opposites are mixed together in one object. When you have the sensation of opposite qualities in one object, the understanding is summoned to determine whether it is the hard and the soft. The understanding determines that the hard is separate from the soft. For the understanding, hardness is one thing and softness is another. Yet for perception, the hard and the soft are mixed up together. These sensations are *summoners*, since they awaken the understanding. They call the understanding to inquire into each of the opposite qualities as separate ideas. This process leads the understanding to contemplate the concepts of bigness, smallness, hardness, softness, and the lot.

The difference between sensation and understanding is indicative of a larger distinction between the phenomenal world and the world of ideas. When you transcend sensations that report opposite qualities in one object and you contemplate the ideas themselves, you move from the phenomenal world to the world of ideas. In the world of ideas, bigness is distinct from smallness. This move to the understanding calls us to consider bigness itself. The concept of bigness is the capacity to exceed. This is the quality that all big things have in common. We can apply this same sort of concep-tualization to the other qualities, such as smallness, hardness, and softness. We can chart this by showing how the form transcends the particular instances. There is one form over many that participate in that one form. This confronts the relation between the form and the physical instances of that form. The understanding considers bigness in its own right, or bigness itself. It considers smallness itself, hardness itself, and softness itself. Plato calls the ideas of such things forms (*eide*). We can see what Plato is doing by observing his grammatical moves. Consider the subject and predicate in grammatical structure: the finger (subject) is big (predicate). Formally we can see structure, *x* (subject) is *y* (predicate). What Plato does is to place the predicate as a subject. Thus, we get bigness (subject) is the capacity to exceed (predicate). The form of bigness sets the standard for all of our perceptions. To say that an object has the quality of bigness is to say that the object has the capacity to exceed.

This account extends to mathematical and geometrical objects. Concerning numbers, two is even and three is odd. The number two has the quality of evenness and three has the quality of oddness. Plato refers to the quality of oddness and evenness as subjects unto themselves. Evenness is being divisible by two without a remainder. Moving to geometry, the circle itself is an enclosed figure equidistant from a center point. The triangle is a three-sided enclosed figure with interior angles that sum to 180°. Plato extends the concept of forms to include what many people would consider to be opinions that have no objective standard, such as beauty, justice, and courage. The cliché says that beauty is in the eye of the beholder, but that is not true according to Plato. There is a form, or idea, of beauty itself. This is the standard by which all beautiful things are beautiful. The same applies to justice itself. It is the standard by which all just things are called just. Though beauty itself is more difficult to define than bigness itself, the difference between the two is a difference in degree and not a difference in kind. The same goes for justice itself and courage itself. Plato argues that there is a conceptual standard for beauty, justice, and courage, however difficult it may be to understand the standard.

Most people think that the physical world is the real world. If they can touch it, smell it, see it, or taste it, they think that it is real. Most people are what Plato calls lovers of sights and sounds.[42] He contrasts the lovers of sights and sounds with the lovers of things in themselves or lovers of ideas. These references serve to distinguish the phenomenal world from the world of ideas. The phenomenal world is a world of becoming, coming to be, and passing away. Everything in the physical world is in flux; recall Heraclitus. Change is the constant in the phenomenal world. Everything in the realm of ideas is in the world of being. Objects in the realm of being do not come into being and they do not change. The circle itself has always been and will always be. It is non-generated and timeless; recall Parmenides. The circle itself has the only requisite feature of a god. It is immortal. Our ability to understand these timeless objects shows, Plato thinks, that we are kindred with or like the gods. Though we are embodied physical beings, we are able to contemplate timeless objects. So, there must be some aspect of us that is divine or like the divine. The circle itself is timeless, true, unchanging, and non-generated.

---

[42] *Republic*, 476b.

The circle itself references a *universal* term, since it applies to many physical particulars. This clock is circular, this coin is circular, and so on for the other circular objects. Yet, this clock and this coin are *particular* terms, since the terms apply to individual objects. No particular object is the circle itself. In fact, not one of these objects is a circle. Instead, these particular objects are circular. So too for triangular objects, square objects, and all other physical things. Objects in the world of becoming are imperfect appearances of perfect beings. The circle itself does not and cannot physically exist. If we were to be precise about these circular objects, we would see that they are not perfectly round. No matter how close a circular object might be to the circle itself, the circular object will always be imperfect. If you write the symbol "2" on a whiteboard, you have not put the concept of two itself on the board. There are many ways to reference the number two. Plato argues that there are timeless truths that we can apprehend in the forms. There are unchanging and non-generated truths that we can understand about bigness itself, the circle itself, and justice itself. In this way, the world of forms is the realm of truth. In the phenomenal world, there is no truth. For Plato, there simply is not anything true in this physical world. Plato expresses the relationship between the form and the particular object that has the qualities of the form by saying that the object participates in the form or has a share of the form. Though Plato makes extensive use of the concept of participation in his account of the relation between forms and physical objects, the concept of participation is not analyzed in any detail in *Republic*.

Plato offers a critique of his own theory, the theory of forms, in his dialogue with *Parmenides*. This dialogue is told by Cephalus, though not the same Cephalus as in *Republic*. This Cephalus tells of a meeting among Parmenides, Zeno, and a young Socrates. Parmenides and Zeno are concerned to show that there is one and not many. Socrates is concerned with showing that each form is one thing and that it has many participants in it. Parmenides offers at least six challenges to the theory of forms. We will examine three of the challenges. Parmenides challenges the theory of forms to account for the extent or range of the forms. Parmenides asks Socrates if mud has a form. He broadens the concern to wonder if undignified and worthless things have forms. Do injustice and cowardice have forms? Socrates is not sure about the extent of forms. He does not offer any principled reason to think that certain things have forms and other things do not. Socrates has no adequate answer to Parmenides' challenge about the extent of the forms. Parmenides asks about the relation between the parts and the whole. This criticism is often called the whole-parts dilemma. The physical objects are participants, they have a part, of the whole. Do the physical instances get their part from the whole of the form or a part of the form? If they get their part from the whole, then the whole is entirely present in the part. This cannot be. If part of the whole is in the participant object, then which part of the whole is it? As an umbrella covers a group of people, each part of the umbrella covers a different particular person. Parmenides concludes that if the whole has parts, then it is not a whole. There are two outcomes, either the whole is in every participant and it is not a whole or the whole has parts and is not a whole. Socrates fails either way, since he must hold that the whole is one and many.

Parmenides asks about the relation between the particular objects and the form. He argues that according to Socrates there are many physical instances of the form and there is one form. The physical things have a predicate, let us say big, and they call to mind an idea of bigness. The idea of bigness also has the predicate big. The form of bigness is the big itself. Since both the physical instances and the form participate in bigness, there must be a form in which they both participate. When we consider the particular instances and the form, we notice that both of them participate in a transcendent form. There must be a form for the particular/form relation, since they both have the predicate big. Yet now we have a form above the form. The form that is set over the particular and the form gives rise to another form, and another, and so on. This criticism is often called the third man argument, as it is applied not only to the form of bigness but also to the form of man. Parmenides shows that Socrates adopts a position that ends in an infinite regress. The young Socrates has no successful counter.

In *Parmenides*, Plato shows that he is aware of serious challenges to the theory of forms. To his credit, he does not hide his concerns about the credibility of the theory. He is concerned about the extent of the forms, about the relation between the parts and the whole, and about the forms in which particulars and forms participate. He offers other concerns as well. He is unclear about the relation between thoughts in a person's mind and the forms. The thought is a thought of the one form above the many particular participants of the form. Yet, this thought must be a form, since it is an idea of one form above many instances. It results that the form is a thought of a form. This raises the question of whether the thoughts are forms or are they separate from the forms? *Parmenides* does not exhaust the criticisms of Plato's theory of forms. Yet, it is an important place to start, since it offers the main concerns of the theory by its founder. This gives us insight into where Plato thinks more needs to be said and into the weaknesses of the theory from his perspective. We should not assume that these are the most difficult challenges that the theory of forms faces or that they delimit the possible lines of criticism. Plato invites the reader to critique his theory, to see either where it goes irreparably wrong or where it requires elucidation. In this way, we can participate in the theory of forms as both apologists and critics.

4.4.3 The Cave, Line, and Sun

We return to *Republic* and to its most famous images. The analogy between the sun and the good begins with the observation that the sun makes all visible things visible, but the sun is not an object of direct vision.[43] In the physical world, it is odd that the one thing that makes things visible, the sun, is not an object of vision. Plato argues that when we consider the world of ideas and of the forms, we see an analogous oddity. All forms participate in the good. In this way, the good is the form of all the forms. The good enlightens all the forms, and it allows the understanding to see, apprehend, the forms. Yet, the good is not a direct object of the understanding. The understanding cannot contemplate it directly. The good makes all intelligible things intelligible, but it is not an object of intellection. Just as the sun when viewed directly will destroy the person's eyesight, the good when directly contemplated will blow your mind. You are warned, do not think about goodness itself. Plato writes dialogues about many of the virtues and their forms, such as justice, courage, and temperance. He never writes a single dialogue about goodness or the form of the good. The analogy of the sun holds that just as the sun functions in the visible realm the good functions in the intelligible realm.

Plato next turns to the divided line.[44] He tells us to consider a line that is divided into two unequal sections. One section represents the visible world and the other represents the intelligible world. So, we have visible things that are not intelligible, and we have intelligible things that are not visible. He does not tell us which of the two main sections is larger than the other. Contemporary interpreters commonly hold that the section representing the intelligible world is larger than the section representing the visible world. These interpreters hold that there are more objects in the realm of understanding than there are in the realm of physical things. They can

---

[43] *Republic*, 507d.
[44] *Republic*, 509d.

argue that there are forms of things that no longer exist, that do not yet exist, or that will never physically exist. Alternatively, it may be that the section representing the visible world is larger than the section representing the intelligible realm. This interpretation holds that there are more physical things than intelligible things. Given what Plato tells us, we cannot know which interpretation is correct. In what follows, we adopt the contemporary interpretation. Plato makes two more divisions in the divided line. He tells us to divide each of the two sections into unequal sections that are of the same proportion as the first two-part division. Again, he does not tell us the ratio of the subsections. We now have two unequal subsections in the visible world and two unequal subsections in the intelligible world.

The smallest section of the visible realm is the smallest section of the line. This section represents conjecture (*eikasia*). The next section in the visible realm represents belief (*pistis*). Moving to the intelligible realm, the smaller section in this realm refers to thought (*dianoia*). The last section in the intelligible realm is the largest section in the line and it refers to understanding (*noesis*). In the visible realm, we can have conjecture about certain objects, which yields unreliable and untrustworthy information. Plato names different epistemological faculties ranging over the different parts of the line. These faculties correspond to different objects that these faculties perceive. We can have conjecture about shadows and reflections of physical objects. We can have beliefs about physical objects. In the intelligible realm, we can have thoughts about mathematical and geometric objects. Finally, we can have understanding about the forms. Plato is not arguing that we can have conjecture, belief, thought, and understanding about one and the same object. Instead, he is arguing that the faculties of conjecture, belief, thought, and understanding apply to different sorts or kinds of objects.

The final image of the three is the allegory of the cave.[45] Plato invites us to consider a group of people chained to a bench facing the rear wall in a cave. Their chains compel them to face the wall. The people can see shadows moving about and flittering on the wall. These people conjecture about the meaning of the objects and struggle in vain to say anything true about them. Suppose that we unchain one of these people and let him turn around. At first he can see nothing, because the light is so bright and his eyes are unaccustomed to it. After his eyes adjust, he can see that there are artifacts being transported across and in front of the fire. These are the objects that are making the flittering shadows on the wall. He no longer believes that the

---

[45] *Republic*, 514.

shadows are the real world and now believes that the physical objects are the real world. Suppose we take this person past the objects and the fire and take him up and out of the cave. The sun shines brightly and his eyesight is dazzled again. For a time, he cannot see anything. Then his eyes adjust and he looks into a lake. There he sees reflections of trees, animals, and other physical objects in the water. The water imperfectly reflects the objects. As his eyes adjust, he is able to look directly at the trees, animals, and other natural bodies. If he were to return to the cave and talk to the people chained to the bench about what he has seen, they would think he was crazy. Yet, he understands that what they take to be real is not real.

Now we can harmonize the three images. The sun ranges over the visible world and the good ranges over the intelligible world. Under the sun there is conjecture about the shadows and reflections of physical objects. There are beliefs about physical objects. Under the good, there are thoughts about mathematical and geometric objects. There is understanding of the forms. The parts of the cave allegory correspond to the parts of the divided line. The shadows on the cave wall correspond to the objects of conjecture. The artifacts in front of the fire correspond to the physical objects. The reflections outside of the cave correspond to mathematical and geometrical objects. The physical objects outside of the cave correspond to the forms:

The sun simile	The sun		The good	
The divided line	├────────┼──────────┼──────────┼──────────┤			
The two worlds	Physical world		Intelligible world	
Mental faculties	Conjecture	Belief	Thought	Understanding
Mental objects	Reflections	Physical objects	Mathematics and geometry	The forms
The cave simile	Wall shadows	Artifacts casting shadows	Reflections of physical objects	Physical objects

Interpreters often discuss the allegory of the cave on its own, though Plato does not present it this way. He offers it as a part of a larger tripartite image. He tells us to fit together the three images. We are to put the simile of the cave with the divided line and the analogy between the sun and the good. When we put all three images together, as Plato offers them, we get a grand image. Yet, the images are not the objects of Plato's account. The images are to be transcended through the faculties of thought and understanding. In Plato's works, readers should not focus on the image. Instead, transcend the image and employ the understanding.

4.4.4 The Soul

The term "soul" (*psuche*) is present in Homer's epic poems. There it refers to the breath that is life. In its primary meaning the term is descriptive. The term also refers to what a warrior risks on the battlefield, namely his life. The term applies to the disembodied shade or spirit that leaves the body at death and travels to Hades. In this way, the soul is distinct from the body. The term applies broadly to the life force in all living animals and by extension to all living things. When a person is alive, he has breath. When dead, he has no breath. Over time the term undergoes changes, becoming broader, subtler, and a technical term of art in some writers.

In *Apology*, Socrates tells us that he does not know what happens in the afterlife.[46] He does not know if death is the greatest of blessings or the greatest of evils. In *Phaedo*, Socrates argues that the soul is invisible, and it stands opposed to the visible body.[47] The soul is embodied during life and it uses the bodily senses to experience the world. The soul also investigates and understands ideas that are not tied to the physical senses.[48] The more tied to the body the soul is, the less understanding it has. The goal of philosophy is to free the soul from the body as much as possible when alive. The freer from the body the soul is the more understanding it will achieve. In *Phaedo*, the soul is more or less rational, depending on its connection with the body. We should notice, though, that the entanglement with the body engenders irrational bodily drives and desires. A soul that is tied most with the body sees opposites in the same object, is confused by ideas, and succumbs to ignorance.[49] The ignorance is indicative of irrational thoughts and desires. Though Plato does not distinguish a rational and an irrational part of the soul in *Phaedo*, we can see that the soul is capable of irrational and rational functions. A survey of Plato's texts shows a decided preference in his account of the human soul. The soul is bipartite, having a rational part and an irrational part. The soul existed before being embodied and it will exist after death. The soul is the principle of life. It is deathless, immortal, and indestructible.[50]

Plato offers a divergence from the bipartite account of the soul in both *Phaedrus* and *Republic*. In *Phaedrus*, we get the image of a charioteer

---

[46] *Apology*, 29a.
[47] *Phaedo*, 79b.
[48] *Phaedo*, 83.
[49] *Phaedo*, 82e.
[50] *Phaedo*, 106e.

driving two winged horses.[51] The charioteer represents the rational part of the soul. One winged horse represents the irrational appetitive part of the soul. It is unruly and ill-behaved. The other horse represents the spirited part of the soul. This horse is of good stock and it helps the charioteer steer the chariot. We should notice that this image is introduced with qualifications. Socrates tells us that an account of the actual structure of the soul requires a lengthy discourse. Though we humans cannot give a full account of the soul, we can describe what the soul is like. In *Republic*, we get a more detailed account of the structure of the soul. This account also comes with qualifications. Socrates tells us that his present method of argument will not generate a precise answer to the questions about the structure of the soul.[52] A precise account would require a different inquiry, both longer and deeper. Nonetheless, he says, the account that he will offer is good enough for the present circumstances. Having said this, Socrates turns to a difficult topic about the soul. We have different desires and pleasures in the soul. Through the soul we learn, we get angry, and we experience physical desires. Do we experience these things through the same part of the soul or through different parts? Socrates wonders if the soul has parts. If it does have parts, how many parts does the soul have?

To offer an account of the parts of the soul, Plato offers what we will call the principle of opposition (PO). The principle states that one thing cannot do or suffer opposites at the same time (*hama*), in the same relation (*pros*), and in the same respect (*kata*).[53] If we see the soul doing or suffering opposites, without a distinction in time, relation, or respect, then the soul is many things and not one thing. Plato offers some examples of opposites, such as wanting and refusing, being willing and unwilling, going toward and moving away, and assenting and dissenting.

Plato offers two main examples to help make PO clear. Consider a man standing still, but moving his head and hands.[54] Plato does not go through each of the qualifications, time, relation, and respect. He does not draw a distinction in any of these three categories. Instead, he offers his conclusion. He tells us that there are two different parts. One part is moving and the other part is not. This shows that there is no distinction to be drawn in time, relation, or respect. Since there is no distinction in any of the three

---

[51] *Phaedrus*, 246.
[52] *Republic*, 135c–d.
[53] *Republic*, 436b.
[54] *Republic*, 436c.

categories of PO, we must say that there are two things and not one. The next example concerns a spinning top set on a peg. The circumference of the top is moving around its axis, but the axis is not moving. When we apply PO to the spinning top, we can see that it is moving with respect (*kata*) to its circumference, but not moving with respect to its axis. The example is clear; there is a distinction in one of the three categories of PO. One thing, the top, is moving and not moving in different respects.[55] There is no need to distinguish two things according to PO. In the case of the man moving and standing still, there are two things, not one. In the case of the spinning top, there is one thing doing opposites in different respects. Plato does not offer a distinction in time (*hama*) or in relation (*pros*), probably because they are so obvious. We go toward food when hungry, but pull away from that same food when satiated. We go toward the workplace and away from home. In neither case do we need to distinguish two different subjects. In each case, one thing does opposites at a different time or in relation to different things.

With the exemplary illustrations in hand, Plato turns to apply PO to the soul. It is possible for a person to want to drink and refuse to drink.[56] We can think of a person adrift at sea, dying of thirst. This person can be so thirsty that he wants to drink the saltwater. This person can also know that the saltwater will hasten death. So, the person could refuse to drink. We should note that when Plato refers to the desire for food or drink, he is referring to unqualified hunger or thirst. He is not talking about the desire for a hot drink, a cold drink, or any qualified sort of drink. He is referring to thirst unqualified.[57] The person adrift at sea wants to drink and not to drink at the same time, in relation to the same thing, and in the same respect. Since there is no distinction in any of the three categories of PO, Plato distinguishes two parts of the soul. In this case he tells us that the irrational appetitive (*epithumoi*) desires drive the person to want to drink. The rational (*logistikoi*) desires are desires not to drink.

The second example concerns a man named Leontius, who is walking from Athens to the Port of Piraeus.[58] There is a wall and road connecting Athens to Piraeus. As Leontius walks along, he sees some beheaded corpses.

---

[55] *Republic*, 436e.
[56] *Republic*, 439c.
[57] *Republic*, 437d.
[58] There is a character named "Leontius" in a contemporaneous play (comedy). This character has a sexual desire for pale boys. Possibly Plato is referring to this character, though he does not specify Leontius appetitive desire.

He has the desire to look at the corpses and the desire not to look at the corpses. Plato argues that Leontius has the desire to look and not to look at the same time, in relation to the same thing, and in the same respect. Since there is no distinction in the three categories of PO, we must distinguish two parts of the soul. Plato tells us that Leontius has an appetitive desire to look at the corpses and a spirited (*thumos*) desire not to look. In the third and final example, Plato refers to Odysseus. After 20 years away from home, Odysseus returns in disguise to see his great hall. There he sees the suitors mistreating his home and possessions. Odysseus wants to kill them all right then. Yet, he does not have a plan, and he would surely fail. So, he does not want to kill them all right then. He desires both to kill them and not to kill them, at one time, in relation to one thing, and in the same respect. Plato distinguishes two parts of the soul, the rational and spirited parts of the soul.

Though each example allows us to distinguish just two parts of the soul, through the three examples Plato distinguishes three parts of the soul. He distinguishes the rational part, the spirited part or the angry part, and the appetitive part. As Plato moves from the case of Leontius to the case of Odysseus, he wonders if the spirited part, or the part that gets angry, is simply the appetitive part or the rational part. Sometimes a person goes into a blind rage. In this case the spirited part seems to be a form of irrational appetites. Then again, the spirited part also generates righteous indignation. This type of anger is a response to a perceived injustice. In this case the anger seems to be rational. Why should we think that the spirited part is a third part of the soul? Plato's answer is complicated. He offers the case of Leontius, where the spirited part opposes the appetitive part. He offers the case of Odysseus, where the spirited part opposes the rational part. He also tells us that nonhuman animals have spirit but not reason. Furthermore, children are chock full of spirit but do not have much reason.[59] More subtly, he tells us that spirit is the natural helper of reason and that it only opposes reason when the person has a bad upbringing.[60] Otherwise, the spirited part is the natural ally of reason. When a person thinks that he has done an injustice, he will calm his spirit to endure just punishment. Alternatively, when a person believes himself to have been treated unjustly, he will arouse his spirit to seek justice. This line of argument makes room for examples such as Odysseus, where spirit opposes reason. It is possible for the spirit to oppose reason, but its natural function is as an ally of reason.

---

[59] *Republic*, 441a.
[60] *Republic*, 441a.

In Book IV of *Republic*, Plato distinguishes three parts of the soul. He subsequently tells us that the appetitive part is the largest part of the soul. It is also the most complex part. In Books VIII and IX, Plato distinguishes three parts of appetite. There are necessary appetites. These desires for food and drink must be satisfied to live. These desires are beneficial.[61] There are also unnecessary desires. These desires go beyond what is necessary. These desires go after exotic food and drink. These desires are not beneficial. Finally, there are base or lawless desires.[62] These desires go after food, sex, and drink that are the stuff of nightmares. Fulfilling these desires involves incest, bestiality, cannibalism, and the foulest of murders. So, we have three main parts, or types, of the soul, one of the parts has three parts. So, there are five parts of the soul.

Plato's account of appetite is problematic in a way that his account of the other parts is not. Plato ascribes abilities to appetite that allow it to act on its own. Appetite is able to figure out how to satisfy its desires by setting goals and determining the means to accomplish the goals. It is able to accomplish means-to-end reasoning without the help of reason. It seems that appetite is not irrational, devoid of reason. It seems that Plato has posited a homunculus, a little person, inside the person, by attributing means-to-end reasoning to appetite. If Plato characterizes appetite as a homunculus, he would generate an infinite regress. Since the person has three parts and appetite is a homunculus, appetite must have the same three parts as the person. The appetitive part in the homunculus would then again have three parts, and so on. This is called the Homunculus Problem.[63] We can avoid this problem by noticing that Plato attributes limited and narrow-minded abilities to appetite. These abilities are far from any robust reasoning about the good. They are more like the ability of appetite to move the body in habitual ways even when reason urges otherwise. We have all had the experience of eating a chip, or some other treat, and deciding not to have any more, only to subsequently find that we have eaten more without thinking. Plato points out that we need money to satisfy the appetites. You need money to get food, sex, and drink. You need more money to get better food, sex, and drink. Appetite goes after money to get satisfaction for its desires. There are habitual ways to get money, which involve little more thought

---

[61] *Republic*, 559b.

[62] *Republic*, 571b.

[63] See Julia Annas, *An Introduction to Plato's Republic* (New York: Oxford University Press, 1981), 142.

than did the physical movements necessary to put another treat in your mouth. We can also note that Plato explains actions by referring to the parts of the soul. More specifically, he explains behavior by indicating the dominant part of the soul. This part sets the goal and it uses the other parts instrumentally to achieve the goal. All the parts are active, more or less, all the time. When appetite acts for a goal, by using spirit and reason, one part dominates the others. Yet, all the parts are active all the time, though they do not set the goal of the act. These lines of argument allow us to avoid burdening Plato's account with the homunculus problem.

The account of soul applies to character types. Each part of the soul sets up a view of the good. The appetites take wealth to be the good, because one needs money to satisfy the appetites. The spirited and angry part takes courage and honor to be the good. The rational part takes wisdom and learning to be the good. Plato holds that one of the parts is dominant over the other parts in each person's soul. He puts this as one of the parts taking the other parts as subordinate allies, since he describes conflict among the parts as a civil war within the person. When we consider the three parts of the soul distinguished in Book IV, we can identify three character types. The aristocrat has the rational part of the soul ruling over the spirited and appetitive parts. He is a lover of wisdom. The timocrat has the spirited part of the soul rule over the other two parts. He is a lover of courage and honor. He uses reason and appetite to help him achieve those ends. The oligarch has the necessary pleasures to rule the other parts. He uses reason to calculate how to make money. He uses spirit to honor wealth and wealthy people. The democrat sets the unnecessary appetites as ruler of the other parts. He is a lover of freedom. The tyrant sets the base appetites as ruler over the other parts. He is a lover of the lawless pleasures. Each character type sets a view of the good for itself, by establishing one part of the soul as a ruler of the others.

4.4.5 The State

In *Republic*, Plato argues that everything that comes into being decays.[64] It is inevitable for any constitution that comes to be that it will fracture and change. Plato does not employ PO to distinguish the parts of the state, though he does describe the parts of the state as being opposed to each other. The parts of the state, or factions, form when the ruling class fractures

---

[64] *Republic*, 546a.

in two parts and falls into civil war.[65] The threat to any ruling class does not come from outside the ruling class. It comes from within the ruling class. One cause of the fracturing of a ruling class is from nature, bad breeding, and the decay of all things in the world of becoming. Plato explains the cause of bad breeding through a geometric metaphor. He tells that births are governed by three and four being married with five.[66] This is a reference to the first triangle that can be formed from whole numbers under 10. One side of the triangle is three and the other side is four. Mom and dad get married or joined and this produces an offspring, the hypotenuse five. When the parents are not precisely three and four, they engender irrational offspring. When Plato seems to be talking just about breeding, get your mind out of the gutter, he is actually talking about something deeper, geometry. I have never heard of a child named Five, but it would not be surprising to find one in the Kallipolis. The other causes of the destruction of a political constitution come from the mistaken and imperfect view of the good that each of the four degenerate constitutions adopts. These imperfect views of the good carry internal disharmony and tension. Over time these tensions grow and cause a fracture in the ruling class.

The aristocratic constitution is ruled by the wise and learned part of the state. This constitution starts to fracture because of bad offspring and a lack of attention to education. This leads to a fracture within the ruling class, such that it splits into a ruling class and a military class. The military class, or auxiliaries, grow to value courage and honor over wisdom. At the same time, part of the ruling class comes to value money over wisdom and learning. Because of bad breeding and a corrupt education, the ruling class fractures into three parts. Some rulers remain, but they are countered by two other classes, the military class and the oligarchic class. A civil war breaks out with the timocrats and the oligarchs fighting against the rulers. The war ends when the constitution dissolves and settles between the aristocratic class and the oligarchic class. The aristocratic constitution devolves into a timocratic constitution. Though Plato does not invoke PO to distinguish the fighting factions in the civil war, it is clear that they oppose each other and pull in opposing directions.

The timocratic constitution establishes the auxiliaries or military class as rulers.[67] The timocratic constitution values courage and honor. Given the

---

[65] *Republic*, 545c.

[66] *Republic*, 546c.

[67] Nickolas Pappas offers an insightful discussion of justice and injustice in the state and soul. See Chapters 4, 5, and 8 in *Routledge Philosophy Guidebook to Plato and the Republic* (2nd ed.) (New York: Routledge, 2003).

civil war that brought it to power, the timocratic class will be infected with images of the aristocratic and oligarchic classes. Over time the timocratic class starts to fracture. They come to distrust the wise and to envy the wealthy. As the timocratic class molds education to its view of the good, they value war and strategy over wisdom. They come to see the aristocrats as useless and cowardly. They also come to desire wealth and they start to amass fortunes in secret. As they grow to love money, they hoard their private stashes and spend the money of others. The more the timocratic class comes to value money the more they fracture into opposing parts or factions. As the wealthy part of the timocratic class grows, they come to honor wealth instead of courage and honor. Eventually the oligarchic faction of the timocratic class overthrows the remaining timocratic faction. This part of the timocratic class then modifies the constitution by establishing a wealth requirement to serve in the government. At that point the timocratic constitution has collapsed.

The oligarchic part values wealth over wisdom and courage. Their constitution requires the rulers to be wealthy. This class is so enamored with wealth that they borrow money for speculative ventures and they make loans at high interest. Yet that is not enough, they start to make more and more loans to what we would now call "subprime" borrowers. That is, they loan money to people that they know will not be able to pay back the loans. Why would they do this? (1) They are enticed by the profit to be made. (2) They can take the property of people when they default on the loan. Either way, they amass more wealth. The problem is that many of the oligarchs and others in society become disenfranchised. These former oligarchs have lost all their property and wealth. As this disenfranchised class grows within the ranks of the oligarchic class, they become more numerous than the remaining oligarchs. In fact, the term "oligarch" is derived from the term *holigos* meaning few. There are few who are wealthy and the majority of people (*hoi polloi*) are not rich. Now the oligarchic class has fractured into the wealthy and the disenfranchised. The disenfranchised have nothing that they value left to lose. This class is the democratic class, the class that includes the majority of people. They rise up and mount a civil war against the remaining oligarchs. The democratic class overthrows the oligarchic class, cancels all debts and redistributes the land. When they remove the wealth requirement for rulers, they have successfully overthrown the oligarchic constitution.

The democratic constitution values freedom over wisdom, courage, and wealth. They value the freedom to indulge any of their desires and to do whatever they want at the moment. They take everyone as equally fit to rule. This class imitates all the other classes. They pretend to be aristocrats when they feel like it. They pretend to be timocrats when it suits them. They imitate oligarchs for short periods of time. After saving money, they spend it on drugs, exotic food, exotic sex, and whatever else they want at the moment. The democratic class does not even value ruling over freedom. So, they turn over rule to any class they want. Sometimes the ruling class in the democratic constitution resembles an aristocracy, a timocracy, an oligarchy, and even a tyranny. There are many iterations of the democratic constitution. Sometimes it is a caricature of the aristocratic state:

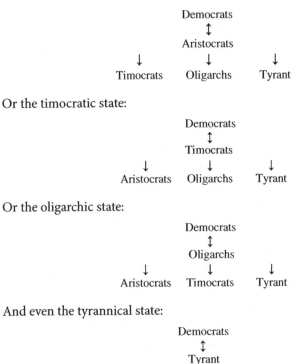

Democrats
↕
Aristocrats
↓   ↓   ↓
Timocrats   Oligarchs   Tyrant

Or the timocratic state:

Democrats
↕
Timocrats
↓   ↓   ↓
Aristocrats   Oligarchs   Tyrant

Or the oligarchic state:

Democrats
↕
Oligarchs
↓   ↓   ↓
Aristocrats   Timocrats   Tyrant

And even the tyrannical state:

Democrats
↕
Tyrant
↓   ↓   ↓
Aristocrats   Timocrats   Oligarchs

As Plato puts it, the democratic constitution is the most beautiful of constitutions because it resembles various constitutions at different times. It is a good place to examine caricatures of all the constitutions.[68] The democratic class are dilettantes, never wholly devoting themselves to anything. They would put a person to death one day and bring him back to life the next. They love freedom so much that they extend it to animals. A horse has as

---

[68] *Republic*, 557c.

much right to walk wherever it wants as any human does. Democracy puts the majority as governors. The majority then allows other factions to take turns ruling.

Before continuing with the account of the democratic constitution, let us take this opportunity to notice a peculiarity of the democratic man. The unnecessary appetites rule in his soul, but they rule by allowing the other parts of the soul to take a turn ruling. His soul is complicated in a way that the other character types are not. There are four iterations of the composition of the democratic man's soul. He is a caricature of the aristocrat:

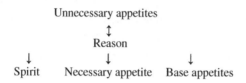

The timocrat:

The oligarch:

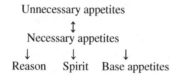

And the tyrant:

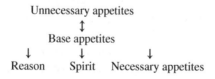

The democratic soul is a caricature of all the other character types. He is an imposter, a dilettante, and a charlatan. Ruling by letting others rule is anarchy. The other constitutions rule directly, but democracy rules indirectly. Democracy never fully rules. It only indirectly rules. Compared to the other constitutions, democracy is anarchy. It does not rule as all the others rule.

The democratic class loves the freedom to do whatever it wants, the freedom to indulge every desire equally. Though they need money to indulge their ever-changing desires, they do not value wealth. Accumulating wealth takes discipline and the democratic class lacks discipline. Their relation to money is different from the oligarchs. Whereas the oligarchs love necessary wealth and pleasures, the democrats love unnecessary wealth and pleasures. They indulge in spendthrift ventures. Their love of freedom allows every desire to take a turn at setting their view of the good. This allows not only the necessary appetites and the unnecessary appetites but also the base appetites to enter the ruling class. The democratic class has no shame. They also have no fiscal restraint. They waste money. They neglect the affairs of the city that are necessary to rule the city properly.

The democratic ruling class fractures into three parts. There is a class that does not want to work, so they do not work. These are the unemployed idlers. There is a class of people who employ good organizational skills. They are the wealthy class. There is a class of people who work with their hands. These are the craftsmen. These three groups within the democratic class start to wage a civil war against each other. As they see their city bereft of funds, ill-governed, and capricious in its court judgments, the people fear that they will lose their freedom. Under these circumstances, they consolidate power into one person who promises to be the champion of freedom. They wrongly think that this one person will secure their freedoms. They hand over rule to this champion of freedom, who is actually a tyrant. In changing their constitution from rule by the many to rule by the one, they overthrow the democratic constitution and become a tyranny.

The tyrannical constitution loves lawlessness or the indulgence of base pleasures. The tyrant does unspeakable things. He kills people on a whim and tortures whomever he wants. He indulges in lawless types of food, sex, and drink. He lies and makes false charges against anyone he wants. He makes constant war in the city, stirring up civil war to deflect attention from his own unspeakable acts. All this creates many enemies in the city, as the people plot against each other and against the tyrant. He reduces the people to slavery in his service. The tyrannical constitution collapses when the enslaved people revolt and kill or exile him. At that point the city can establish a new constitution of one sort or another.

The analogy between the state and the soul is intuitive. It is theoretical and not empirical. Just as each of us has different desires that can come into conflict with each other, the state has different factions that can come into conflict with each other. Just as our desires fight for dominance in thought and action, political factions fight for dominance in the ideology and control of the state. Just as our desires focus on valuing certain objects and outcomes, political factions rally around ideology and outcomes. The analogy is not without some disanalogous features. When a person has conflicting desires and sacrifices some desires for the sake of others, the person is on the whole satisfied. When a person forgoes dessert to achieve weight loss and drops the weight, he is satisfied overall. When one political faction has its desires satisfied, however, it is fully satisfied and the other factions are fully dissatisfied. There is no entity, society, that is overall satisfied. Along similar lines, each person is a concrete and particular object in the world. In contrast, a political faction is an abstract object; it is not a concrete particular. Plato runs the risk of hypostatization in treating abstract objects as if they were physical particulars. Finally, an analogy can only establish a probability that the two analogs are similar. It cannot show that they are the same. This is a challenge for Plato, since he aims to show that justice is the same in the individual and in the state. Finally, Plato runs the risk of committing the fallacy of division, or composition depending on one's perspective. If Plato argues that the person has three parts because the state has three parts, he commits the fallacy of division. If he argues that the state has three parts because the person has three parts, he commits the fallacy of composition. These are some of the challenges for Plato's analogy between the soul and the state. Many of these concerns can be addressed by noticing that Plato only presses the analogy so far. He does not treat them as the same, only similar. These concerns also can be addressed by noticing that the analogy is meant to be instructive, but it does not justify inferences on its own merits. That is, Plato does not use the analogy to justify inferences, instead he uses it illustratively to put the analogs in relation to each other. Plato offers parallel but separate arguments for the analogs.

Republic is focused on distinguishing and defining the virtue of justice. He distinguishes the parts of the soul to help in understanding the virtue of justice. He also distinguishes the parts of the state and the political constitutions to help define justice. Plato argues that it is easier to see justice in a larger thing than in a smaller thing. He holds that the state and the soul are analogous. Since the state is larger than the individual, he suggests that it will be easier to see justice in the state than it will be to see it in the individual.[69] As part of defining justice, Plato examines other virtues. Plato argues that the virtue of wisdom (*sophia*) is found in the rational part of the soul and the aristocratic part of the state. He argues that the virtue of courage (*andreia*)

---

[69] *Republic*, 368e.

is found in the spirited part of the soul and in the timocratic class of the state. The virtue of temperance or self-control (*sophrosyne*) is found in the agreement by the spirited and appetitive to be ruled by reason. In the state, it is found in the willingness of the parts of the state to be ruled by the aristocrats. We have run through the three main parts of the soul and we have not found justice. We find justice (*dike*) by recognizing that each part of the soul has its own proper work. Reason's proper work is to rule, spirit's work is to help reason with verve, and appetite's work is to provide for the necessary desires. Justice is each of these parts doing their own proper work and not meddling in the proper work of others. Turning to the state, we can see that justice occurs when the rulers rule, the military fights, and the tradesmen decide how to make the necessary things. Alternatively, injustice occurs when the timocrats decide how to rule and with whom to fight. Their proper work is to decide how to fight and not to decide with whom to fight. We can see that injustice occurs when the oligarchs decide how to rule, when to fight, and how to fight. Justice is each part doing only its own work.

We made our way through the five forms of the state and the corresponding five forms of the soul:

Characters and Constitutions	Ruling part of the State	Ruling Part of the Soul	View of the Good
Aristocrat	The rulers	Reason	Wisdom and learning
Timocrat	The military	Spirit	Courage and honor
Oligarch	The wealthy	Necessary appetites	Necessary wealth
Democrat	The majority	Unnecessary appetites	Freedom
Tyrant	The one tyrant	Base appetites	Lawlessness

We can now see which constitution and character is best, according to the text. Plato offers three arguments to the conclusion that the aristocratic state is the best and happiest, as is the aristocratic man.[70] He ranks the others according to their goodness and happiness. He puts them in the descending order indicated above. The timocratic form is better than the oligarchic form, the oligarchic form is better than the democratic, and the democratic

---

[70] *Republic*, 580a.

form is better than the tyrannical. Plato's first argument holds that only the aristocrat rules over himself. Only he has the correct conception of goodness and justice. His desires always come from and coincide with an understanding of what is best.

The second argument notes that if you were to ask each of the character types which of the lives is the best, most pleasant, and happiest life, each would say that their own lives have the most happiness (*eudaimonia*). So, there is a dispute. The proper method for settling disputes justly is to yield the decision to a competent judge. The timocrat focuses on the virtue of courage so much so that he is not adequately acquainted with wisdom. He does not know much about wisdom. The oligarch focuses so much on wealth that he does not know much about courage or wisdom. Only the aristocrat knows about wisdom, courage, and temperance. Only he knows about spirit and appetites. Only the aristocrat knows all sides in the dispute, so he alone is the competent judge. The aristocrat judges that his life is the best and happiest.

The third argument is the decisive and final throw. Here Plato points out that to take care of your body and be healthy, you need to eat certain foods in certain amounts. Eating too much or too little or eating the wrong things is not healthy. The aristocrat knows this, but the oligarch does not. Being angry too much or too little, or in the wrong circumstance, is not healthy for the soul. Some character types are prone to eat the wrong foods or too much of them. Some character types are prone to get angry too much or at the wrong times. Just because a person is pleased by something or angry at something does not show that the pleasure and anger are warranted. Some people are pleased by things that they should not get pleasure from. Some people are angry when or to an extent that they should not. The perceptions of pleasures and pains need judgment and understanding. There are true pleasures, pleasures that are good to experience. There are false pleasures, pleasures that are not good to experience. Plato argues that the aristocrat understands the difference between true and false pleasures as well as true and false anger. The pleasure of the aristocrat is pleasure, not pain by some other name. The other character types think they have true pleasure, but they do not. Their pleasures engender pain and destruction to varying degrees. Again, the aristocrat wins the case. His pleasure is true.

5

ARISTOTLE

5.1 Biography and Texts

Aristotle was born in 384 BCE in the city of Stagira in the Macedonian region of northeastern Greece. His father, Nicomachus, was a physician in the court of the Macedonian king Amyntas II, and his mother was Phaestis. Both of his parents died when Aristotle was young. His older sister, Arimneste, and her husband, Proxenus, raised Aristotle after the death of his parents. At 17 Aristotle went to Athens to continue his education. Aristotle studied at Plato's Academy, where he excelled as a student. Many thought that Aristotle would assume the leadership at the Academy after Plato's death (347 BCE). He did not stay on at the Academy, but instead traveled to Assos in Asia Minor. After about three years he moved to the island of Lesbos. In 343 BCE, King Philip II invited Aristotle to Macedonia to tutor his son, Alexander (the not yet great). In 335 BCE, Aristotle returned to Athens and established his own school, the Lyceum. Aristotle had a habit of walking about the grounds of the Lyceum while he lectured on a topic. His school and students were called the Peripatetics, referring to Aristotle's habit of walking and lecturing along the path in the Lyceum. After Aristotle's first wife, Pythias, died, he partnered with Herpyllis. They had children and named one of their sons Nicomachus, after Aristotle's father. This son is most likely the namesake of Aristotle's ethical work *Nicomachean Ethics*. After the death of Alexander the Great, resentment against the Macedonians festered and grew in Athens. Aristotle was a native of Macedonia. He had a close association with the king of Macedonia and with Alexander when he was young. Aristotle

This Is Ancient Philosophy: An Introduction, First Edition. Kirk Fitzpatrick.
© 2024 John Wiley & Sons, Inc. Published 2024 by John Wiley & Sons, Inc.

became afraid for his safety due to the anti-Macedonian sentiments in Athens. Aristotle worried that the Athenians would prosecute him, just as they had with Socrates. Having lived in Athens about 13 years, Aristotle left the city in 323 BCE. In this way, he prevented the Athenians from wronging philosophy again. He went to Chalcis in Attic Greece, on the island of Euboea. He died there the next year in 322 BCE.

We can organize the Aristotelean texts into broad topics based on subject matter. Some focus on logic and others on natural philosophy, metaphysics, ethics, politics, and rhetoric. We will discuss the fine-tuned distinctions among subjects in Aristotle's texts subsequently; for now here is a basic topography:

	Logic and language		
Categories	On interpretation	Prior analytics	Posterior analytics
	Topics	Sophistical refutations	
	Natural philosophy		
Physics	On the heavens	On generation and corruption	Meteorology
On the soul	Sense and sensibilia	On memory	On sleep
On dreams	On divination in sleep	On length and shortness of life	On youth, old age, life and death, and respiration
History of animals	Parts of animals	Movement of animals	Progression of animals
	Generation of animals		
	Metaphysics		
	Metaphysics		
	Ethics		
	Nicomachean ethics	Eudemian ethics	
	Politics		
	Politics	Constitution of Athens	
	Rhetoric		
	Rhetoric	Poetics	

In this chart, we have 17 texts on natural philosophy, 6 works on logic, 2 each on ethics, politics, and rhetoric, and 1 on metaphysics. We have 30 texts listed above. In addition, we have a set of texts called *Fragments*. This brings the total number of texts that we believe to be from Aristotle to 31. We can see that the majority of texts that we have concern natural philosophy, followed by logic, and we have just one or two texts on the other subjects of study. Aristotle's focus on natural philosophy and his attention to observation led interpreters to count him as the first scientist. We reference Aristotle's texts through Bekker page and line numbers. This reference system is named after August Immanuel Bekker, the editor of the Prussian Academy of Sciences Complete Works of Aristotle. There are two works lacking Bekker numbers: *Constitution of Athens* and *Fragments*. All other texts are referenced by Bekker numbers.

Aristotle's works are challenging to read and understand. He makes use of technical terminology, not all of which he makes clear. Aristotle loves to draw distinctions between and among terms, distinction after distinction after distinction. Also, it may be that we do not have any works from Aristotle in the form that he meant for them to be circulated. What we do have seem to be lecture notes and drafts of texts in process, often cryptic in their structure and content. At times these texts are much like notes that one might write to keep one on track through a lecture on a topic. Aristotle's texts seem to assume that you have already read everything he has written. In a text, he makes use of distinctions developed in other texts or sets of texts. In these cases, he often does not reiterate the content of the distinction, when he makes use of it anew. There is a joke among scholars that if Aristotle had just drawn one more distinction, then everything would be clear. Given the texts of his that we have, an interpreter might think that Aristotle was not a skilled writer. We have testimonia from no less than the great Roman orator Cicero, however, telling us that Aristotle wrote dialogues much like Plato. Aristotle's dialogues were reputed to be even subtler than Plato's in their use of language and stylistic composition. All of Aristotle's dialogues are lost to us. We have numerous texts under Aristotle's name that are either spurious or indisputably spurious.[1] We do have 31 texts from Aristotle, but it is not clear if any of them were originally organized as we have them today. Aristotle was a polymath, who wrote on a broad range of

[1] The chart omits many spurious texts. Some texts are "seriously doubted" to be Aristotle's: *Problems*, *Magna Moralia*, and *Economics*. Some texts are without serious advocation for their attribution to Aristotle: *On the Universe*, *On Breath*, *On Colours*, *On Things Heard*, *Physiognomonics*, *On Plants*, *On Marvelous things Heard*, *Mechanics*, *On Indivisible Lines*, *The Situations and Names of Winds*, *On Melissus, Xenophanes, and Gorgias*, *On Virtues and Vices*, and *Rhetoric to Alexander*. See Jonathan Barnes, *The Complete Works of Aristotle*, Vol. I. (Princeton: Princeton University Press, 1991), Contents, and Note to the Reader.

subjects. We have works ranging from *Parts of Animals* and *On the Heavens* to a work *On Divination in Sleep*. Despite the missing texts and the cryptic style of many of the texts, we do have enough texts to get a clear view of Aristotle's philosophy.

5.2 Aristotle's Philosophy

5.2.1 The Subjects

Aristotle's texts tend to follow an organizational pattern. He begins by distinguishing the subject of study for the text. He distinguishes the sciences (*epistemai*) as a broad category of study. The sciences include three subcategories. (1) The *theoretical* sciences focus on what we now call "metaphysics," and his main work focusing on this topic bears the name *Metaphysics*. This topic and title come from the traditional name of the text, which was *After the Physics* or *ta meta ta phusika* in Greek. If we take away the definite articles, *ta*, and put the two remaining terms together, we get *metaphusika* or metaphysics. The idea of interpreters organizing Aristotle's texts was that this text was not really on physics, but on more fundamental concepts that inform physics. So, the work was placed after the physics. Aristotle does not use the term "metaphysics," but instead calls the subject "first philosophy." The theoretical sciences also include the subjects of mathematics and geometry. Here Aristotle focuses on mathematical puzzles, paradoxes, and the incommensurability of certain geometric relations. The theoretical sciences include the subject of physics, the study of natural world from the earth to the heavens. There are also more narrowly focused theoretical sciences, such as the study of biology and botany. Finally, we have the study of the animating force of all living things or the soul (*psuche*). All the theoretical sciences study knowledge for its own sake. (2) The *practical* sciences cover correct and incorrect behavior and actions. Here, we see Aristotle concerned with how we should live, act, think when acting, and what habits we should develop. We do not simply need to know what moral goodness is; we need to learn how to be good. A person can read all he wants on ethics, but behaving correctly requires practice. This subject extends beyond the individual to groups of people. A person can read all he wants on governance, but governing requires practice. The practical sciences include the subjects of ethics and politics. (3) The *productive* sciences focus on the making of artifacts and other products by human hands. These subjects include the making of ships, farms, chariots, and shields. They also include the arts such as poetry, music, and dance. By extension, these sciences include medicine, the making of a healthy body, and rhetoric, the art of persuasion.

There is a fourth category that runs throughout the three sciences, though Aristotle does not formally distinguish it along with the three sciences. (4) *Logic* is the study of argument, and this study of language is useful as a tool for inquiry into every science. Aristotle was the first philosopher to study argument in its own right, the study of the preservation of truth from premises to conclusion. He developed the first system of formal logic, where the form and not the content of propositions accounts for the preservation of truth. He is the first to identify the concept of validity: assuming the premises are true, the conclusion cannot be false. To develop his system of logic, Aristotle identified four types of propositions: two types of universal propositions and two types of particular propositions. Universal propositions are also called major propositions and particular propositions are also called minor propositions. There are four propositions in total.

The four syllogistic propositions		
Universal propositions	**A**	All A are B
	E	No A are B
Particular propositions	**I**	Some A are B
	O	Some A are not B

The A claim is a universal affirmative proposition, the E claim is a universal negative proposition, the I claim is a particular affirmative proposition, and the O claim is a particular negative proposition. Aristotle restricts the number of propositions to just these four propositions. The variables "A," "B," and "C," in the four types of propositions stand for terms.

A syllogism is an argument that has two premises and a conclusion:

The syllogism	*The form*	*The example*
Universal premise	All A are B	All humans are mortals
Universal premise	All B are C	All mortals are fallible
Conclusion	All A are C	All humans are fallible

This inference is valid. If the premises are true, the conclusion cannot be false. It is also sound, since the premises are in fact true. The argument is valid and all the premises are true. Aristotle is the first philosopher to demonstrate that there are valid arguments with in fact false premises. Consider the following arguments:

The syllogism	The form	The example
Universal premise	All A are B	All dogs are cats
Particular premise	All B are C	All cats are immortal
Conclusion	All A are C	All dogs are immortal

If the premises are true, then the conclusion cannot be false. So, the falsehood of the premises does not alter the validity of the argument. The argument is valid because of its form and not the content of the propositions.

There are exactly three propositions in every syllogism and there are four types of propositions. The order of the premises does not make any difference to the syllogism. So, there are 256 possible syllogisms. Of these possibilities, Aristotle counted 24 valid forms from the 256. Today, we have refined this count of valid syllogisms. Aristotle holds that we can infer a particular proposition from a universal proposition. We call this the existential fallacy:

The syllogism	The form	The example
Universal premise	All A are B	All chimeras are fire breathers
Universal premise	All B are C	All fire breathers are dangerous
Conclusion	Some A are C	Some chimeras are dangerous

True as this conclusion may seem to be in Greek folklore, there is not one chimera. In fact, there never was one and there never will be one. If we assume the premise is true, we can see that the conclusion can be false. There are eight forms of syllogism that commit the existential fallacy. We call these forms conditionally valid, on the condition that the particular object referenced exists. When we eliminate the 9 conditionally valid forms from Aristotle's conception of valid forms, we are left with 15 unconditionally valid forms of syllogisms. In the following chart, we have a list of the 4 claims allowed in syllogistic logic and a list of the 15 valid forms. The forms have mnemonic names developed after Aristotle. In the name, a string of vowels gives the form. The syllogism of Barbara, for example, has the letter "a" three times.[2] The argument referenced by AAA uses the first two letters to reference the premises and uses the third letter for the conclusion. The other names and forms use the vowels likewise:

---

[2] The consonants in the names have a function in syllogistic logic.

Name	AEIO	Premise	Premise	Conclusion
Barbara	AAA	All A are B	All B are C	All A are C
Camestres	AEE	All A are B	No C are B	No C are A
Calemes	AEE	All A are B	No B are C	No C are A
Baroco	AOO	All A are B	Some C are not B	Some C are not A
Darii	AII	All A are B	Some C are A	Some C are B
Datisi	AII	All A are B	Some A are C	Some C are B
Celarent	EAE	No A are B	All C are A	No C are B
Cesare	EAE	No A are B	All C are B	No C are A
Ferio	EIO	No A are B	Some C are A	Some C are B
Festino	EIO	No A are B	Some C are B	Some C are not A
Ferison	EIO	No A are B	Some A are C	Some C are not B
Fresison	EIO	No A are B	Some B are C	Some C are not A
Dimatis	IAI	Some A are B	All B are C	Some C are A
Disamis	IAI	Some A are B	All A are C	Some C are B
Bocardo	OAO	Some A are not B	All A are C	Some C are not B

The 15 valid syllogistic forms

These 15 valid syllogistic forms are timeless contributions by the founder of logic.

5.2.2 Doxography

Another feature of Aristotle's compositional style is that he reviews the opinions (*doxa*) of others. Usually this is in the second section of his texts. We call the approach doxography, which is the combination of *doxa* or opinion and *graphe* or writing. Aristotle is one of our main sources on the early Greek philosophers. The doxography that he offers is of great philosophical and historical value, as is his criticism of the early Greeks. The method that Aristotle employs, doxography as an integral part of a text, has been retained in contemporary scholarly practice.

We need to take what Aristotle says about his predecessors with some scrutiny. We can neither dismiss his characterizations as inaccurate nor accept all that he says as true. We need to compare what he says about the early Greeks to all else that we have in the historical record. There is no simple calculus, oh wait there is no complex calculus, to establish the credibility of Aristotle's characterizations of his predecessors. There are historical features that lend credence to his claims. Aristotle was a student of

Plato and Plato was an associate of Socrates. There is no doubt that Aristotle heard much from Plato and that Plato heard much about the early Greek Philosophers. Other people in Athens had their own history with early philosophical views. This puts some pressure on Aristotle to keep to what is known about the early Greeks in his time. Yet, when you read Aristotle's account of the early Greeks, they all seem to be trying to say what Aristotle ends up saying. Aristotle uses the early Greeks to specify his efforts to account for a particular subject. We often get Aristotelian versions of the predecessors. Aristotle was a man of his own mind. As much as he loved his predecessors, especially Plato, he loved the truth more. This independence might explain why he did not inherit the Academy.

5.2.3 The Four Causes

Aristotle offers an account of the four causes in *Metaphysics* V.2 and *Physics* II.3. The four causes are four different answers to one question, What is this? The question can be interpreted in a number of ways. As a question about the cause of an object, it is a question about what caused the object to be. With this question, Aristotle is not simply asking what something is, since hylomorphic analysis can answer the question interpreted this way. He is asking for a cause of it being what it is and this requires an explanation of it being what it is.

Suppose we encounter a bronze statue of Socrates and ask, What is this? We can answer this question by citing its *material cause* of being, the material out of which it is made. Here we answer that the object is bronze. We can answer the question with the object's *formal cause*, the shape of the object. Here we answer that it is a likeness of Socrates or in the shape of Socrates. We can see that the material and formal causes are closely related to the method of hylomorphic analysis. The four causes go beyond hylomorphic analysis. We can answer the question with the object's *efficient cause*, the source of it coming to be what it is. Here we answer that the object is a statue produced by or fabricated by an artisan. We can answer the question with the object's *final cause*, that is, for the sake of which the object is. We can think of the "sake for which" as the end, the goal, or the *telos* of the object. Here we answer that the object is a depiction of one of the great philosophers. There are four answers to the question, "What is this?" when directed at a statue of Socrates. It is a hunk of bronze, made by an artisan, as an image of Socrates, to represent one of the great philosophers.

In *Physics*, Aristotle employs the four causes to study artifacts. Yet, his aim is to apply the method of analysis to the entire natural world from the earth to the *Kosmos*. The four causes explain how something came to be what it is. A major focus of this explanatory model is to account for change. The early Greek philosophers focused on material causes. Some of them offered accounts that took one element as primary substance and then explained the other elements in terms of a primary element. Aristotle adopts a materialist and empiricist approach to the world in his philosophy. His materialist commitments reach back through the early Greeks. He accepts that matter is a non-generated, eternal substance. He accepts that what-is does not come into being and does not pass away. Aristotle refers to earth, air, fire, and water. These material things combine to make other material things. But the four material things are not basic elements. Instead, earth, air, fire, and water are names for material things that yoke the features of hot and cold, wet and dry. The features are the underlying stuff of the material world:

Element	Hot/cold	Wet/dry
Fire	Hot	Dry
Air	Hot	Wet
Earth	Cold	Dry
Water	Cold	Wet

These features combine and separate to form various material bodies. For instance, they combine in a certain way to make bronze. Turning to living bodies, the material features combine to make flesh and blood. The formal cause is closely related to the final cause, and the shape is closely related to the sake for which the object is. Sometimes they are the same. The formal cause of a human being is a rational animal and the final cause of a human being is to be a rational being. The efficient cause of a human being is a human being. Living things are the cause of living things. Aristotle does not have an explanation for the first living thing. Today we reject Aristotle's inclusion of the final cause in the study of nature. We do not ask what the final cause of a human being is. We do not ask what the final cause of the earth or the cosmos is. We do not think of nature as having a *telos*, an aim, or a purpose.

5.2.4 Hylomorphism

A third part of Aristotle's texts is his philosophical perspective. In *Categories* and *Metaphysics*, Aristotle distinguishes different meanings of the term "substance" (*ousia*), being, or what-is. There is a strict or primary use of the term "substance." In Chapter 5 of *Categories*, there are at least three features of primary substances:

1. They are each numerically one thing.
2. They are the subject of predicates, but they are not predicated of other things.
3. They are capable of accepting and losing contraries, such as light and dark.

Primary substances are individual objects, "a this," such as a particular person or a particular horse.[3] Consider a particular man, Socrates. He is numerically one, he is not predicated of other things, and he can take on the qualities of being light or dark. Secondary substances are predicates of primary substances. For instance, Socrates is an animal, is a man, is white, is short, and has other predicates. Aristotle distinguishes predicates that signify a simple qualification from predicates that signify a substance qualification.[4] The predicates that apply in a *simple qualification* can change without a change in the primary substance being what it is. The predicate white is a simple qualification. Socrates can take on or lose simple qualifications without a change in what Socrates is. A *substance qualification* is a predicate that applies to a primary substance being what it is. A substance qualification is a predicate that cannot change without a primary substance ceasing to be what it is. Socrates' genus and species are substance qualifications of him as a primary substance. Socrates cannot cease to be an animal or a man without ceasing to be Socrates. The substance qualifications are more informative about the primary substance than are the simple qualifications. Socrates is of the genus animal and the species man. The species is nearer to the primary substance than the genus. It is more informative to say that Socrates is a man than it is to say that Socrates is an animal. Aristotle notes this distinction and restricts the proper range of secondary substances. Secondary substances are the genus and species of a primary substance. The species is more a secondary substance than the genus. Though *Categories* distinguishes primary substances from secondary substances, it does not specify, as much as we might hope, what a substance is.

In Book VII of *Metaphysics* (aka Book *Zeta*), Aristotle discusses primary substances in more detail. He notes that within the existential use of the

---

[3] *Categories*, 5.
[4] *Categories*, 5.3b20.

verb "to be" (*einai*) we refer to different sorts of things. In other words, we say that different sorts of things exist. We say that plants and animals exist. Earth, air, fire, and water exist. Points, lines, and other geometric objects exist. We say that mathematical objects exist and that Forms exist. Aristotle offers a series of categories of things that exist. He refers to physical bodies (e.g., animals), natural bodies (e.g., water), geometric bodies (e.g., line), mathematical bodies (e.g., 1), and Forms (e.g., goodness itself). We say that objects of these different sorts exist. So, we call objects of various sorts substances.

Metaphysics is an account of what-is, or substance. Substance is being. Aristotle's *Metaphysics* is an account of being in itself, or an account of the being of being. *Metaphysics* is "first philosophy." Aristotle names features of substance, but never collects all the requisite features in one place. He does offer exemplars, which we will use. Substance is thought first and foremost of bodies, animals, plants, their parts, and artifacts.[5] Since we refer to different sorts of substances, it is not clear exactly which features must apply. He does tell us that a substance is one thing. It is distinct. It may be separable actually, as oil is to water, or conceptually, as animal is to Socrates. A substance is a subject unto itself, it is not a predicate of other things. It can take on contrary predicates without becoming a different substance. A thing is or is not a substance, there are no degrees. So, one substance cannot be more a substance than another substance. A substance does not have a contrary. The substance of a thing is what makes that thing what it is. It is the essence of it, after all accidental qualities are removed. A substance is primary to what a thing is. It comes first in a thing's definition. It is conceptually first in our knowledge of it, and it is temporally first of a thing. Aristotle argues that there are three main contenders for primary substance: Matter (*hyle*), Form (*morphe*), and Hylomorphic (*hyle* and *morphe*) combinations of matter and form.

We will begin with Aristotle's consideration of matter, form, and compound as primary substances in Book VII (aka Book *Zeta*). Matter is the what-is of the early Greek philosophers. Many of them searched for the underlying physical stuff. For some, it was water, air, *apeiron*, or atoms. Aristotle considers matter as primary substance. Let us consider a bronze statue of Socrates. If we melt it down to bronze, it loses its form. It is not a statue, let alone one of Socrates. Matter is one thing. It underlies other

---

[5] *Metaphysics*, 7.2.

things. It is a subject of predication. It seems to be being, or primary substance. On the other hand, matter is a predicate of other things, e.g., the statue is bronze. Matter is not an individual animal, plant, or artifact. When we take the form out of the matter, we are left with bronze. Aristotle urges us to strip away the other features that the matter has. Conceptually separate the length, breadth, height, and other generators of predicates of the bronze. We are left with an indistinct pile, lump, blob: Let us call it a *heap* of bronze. The bronze on its own is not an individual "this." So, the raw matter, the heap, is not a substance.

Plato argued that the form was prime substance. For him, being is the form of the circle itself and the just itself, and so on. The world of becoming is not a harbinger of truth; it is an invitation to see the meaning and essence of substance. In Book VII, Aristotle agrees that form has features of substance. The form is the essence of the statue of Socrates. It is the being of that artifact. When it loses that form it ceases to be what it was, a statue of Socrates. The form is essential to it being a statue of Socrates. An *essential* feature must be for the thing to be what it is. An *accidental* feature can change while the underlying subject remains one same thing. The matter is not essential. It is accidental, since the statue could be made of silver, gold, wood, or any other suitable material. The form is a universal that applies to many different instances. Socrates, Thales, Parmenides, and Heraclitus were human beings. So, the form is predicable of many subjects. The form is common among many subjects, but the matter is distinct. So, the form is not an individual "this." When we conceptually distinguish the form without matter, we see that it needs a primary substance to be an actuality. Without the individuals being a human being, or a wooden chair, or a bronze statue, the form is a potentiality and not an actuality. It is not some this, until there is some particular embodied this. So, the form it is not a substance.

In Book VII, Aristotle considers the hylomorphic compound as substance. The bronze statue is a subject of predicates and it is not a predicate of other things. It is an individual this and it underlies other features. It can take on contrary qualities, such as hot or cold. The compound does not have a contrary. The compound has many features of substance and it seems that we have identified the compound as a primary substance. Yet, Aristotle does not take this position in Book VII. Primary substance is to be the most basic stuff and the most primary stuff that is. The compound does not seem to be the primary stuff. It is a combination of matter and form. It has an essence. It has constituent features. So, the hylomorphic combination is not substance.

Book VII does not conclude that any of the three candidates for substance is a primary substance. The matter fails to be a this. The form fails to be an individual. The hylomorphic compound fails to be a primary substance. None of the other candidates for substance in Book VII end up being the primary substance. Book VII is a challenging text, to say the least. Readers of the text in English might think that if they could read it in Greek the text would become transparent. No such luck. The text is difficult in any translation and in its original language.

In Chapter 6 of Book VIII (aka Book *Eta*), Aristotle takes up the search for substance again. The compound is a unity, not like a heap, but a unity beyond the parts.[6] When we combine oil and water in a vessel, we have two material things that retain their features in the compound. The hylomorphic compound is something yet again beyond its parts. The cause of the unity of a hylomorphic compound is the form being embodied in matter. The form is not a this in a this (matter). The matter is an actuality, but it also has the potentiality to take on the form. In this way, the form is a potentiality that is actualized when the hylomorphic compound comes to be a unity. The definition of the bronze sphere has two features, matter and form, but these features are not two things. As Aristotle puts it, the proximate matter, the particular piece of bronze, and the form, the shape of a sphere, are one and the same.[7] This line of reasoning helps to remove the concern in Book VII that the compound is not primary because it is a combination of two features. In Book VIII, the compound is a unity of two features: an actuality and a potentiality. In this way, a hylomorphic compound is a primary substance.

Aristotle's theory of hylomorphism is the analysis of primary substance into a combination of matter and form. The formula of the essence of any primary substance is form and matter. When we encounter a substance and say, "What is this?" we can define the substance as a combination of two features. An iron ax is a certain shape made of iron. Here we make reference directly to its form (ax) and its matter (iron). The subject, iron ax, takes on the form as its subject and the matter as the predicate. The compound is able to function in certain ways. The function of an ax is to chop wood. The shape of the ax and the matter of an ax combine to allow the unity to function. The material used to make the ax must be of a suitable sort to embody the function of the form. You can make an ax out of different kinds of metals. A plastic ax looks like an ax but does not function as an ax. A plastic ax is an ax homonymously. When we turn to animate beings, Socrates, for example, we say that he is a compound of soul and body. He is a rational animal in this

---

[6] *Nicomachean Ethics*, 1045a10.

[7] *Nicomachean Ethics*, 1045b18.

proximate flesh and blood. The soul is not in a body as a thing in a thing, any more than the ax is in the iron. Hylomorphic analysis also applies to the parts of substances. We can analyze the parts of a substance as a combination of matter and form. A hand, for example, functions to grasp objects. The hand has a form and matter that unite to allow the substance to function in a certain way. If we were to come across a severed hand on the side of the road, we might call it a hand. Yet, is it has lost its function. So, it is a hand homonymously. The early Greeks tended to focus on the matter at the expense of the form. They tended to hold that matter is the primary substance. Plato took a contrary approach in holding that the form is the primary substance. Aristotle's account of hylomorphic analysis unifies two approaches into a method that allows us to define all primary substances as a unity of matter and form.

5.2.5 Voluntary Action

It is important to distinguish voluntary actions from involuntary actions. We do voluntary actions. Involuntary actions are caused by force, compulsion, or ignorance. These events happen to us. Aristotle indicates the importance of the distinction. We praise and blame voluntary actions, and we pity and forgive involuntary actions. This distinction is important in ethics, to account for the justice and injustice that we do. It makes all the difference in a moral judgment to blame or forgive. The moral concerns coincide with legal concerns. If you act voluntarily, then you are legally to blame. If not, then not.

In Chapter 1 of *Nicomachean Ethics* III, Aristotle distinguishes voluntary and involuntary acts. If the act is voluntary, then the person could have done it or not. A voluntary act is up to the person. It is done by the person. To act voluntarily, a person must know what he is doing. Aristotle lists the features that a person must know when he is doing something. If he acts under compulsion or with ignorance, then he acts involuntarily. A person can be ignorant of many things when taking action. Aristotle offers a list of what a person can be ignorant of; who he is, what he is doing, what or whom he is acting on, what instrument or tool he is using, what end, goal, or *telos* he acts to actualize, and how he is doing it.[8] There are times when a person tries to help but is ignorant of certain facts. A person might mistake poison as medicine when giving care to someone. A person might reach down to save a drowning man, but punch him in the face, knock him out, and drown the poor guy. The person trying to help was ignorant of how he was doing it. A person might

---

[8] *Nicomachean Ethics*, III.1.1111a3.

mistake a practice spear for a combat spear. If the person acting was ignorant that the object was a combat spear and that he had no reason to think that it was a combat spear, then he was ignorant of the instrument.

A person can be ignorant of numerous facts in the context of his action. Aristotle also distinguishes different types of ignorance. A person can act in ignorance, through ignorance, or both in and through ignorance. To act *in ignorance* is to act ignorantly. A drunk person or an angry person acts ignorantly at the time of action. To act *through ignorance* is to be ignorant of one of the features in the list that Aristotle offers. A person could drink what he knows to be alcohol and subsequently act ignorantly. He knew that the drink was alcoholic. So, he acted in ignorance but not through ignorance. His act is voluntary, since he knew the object on which he was acting. Alternatively, a person could drink what he thinks is not alcohol. He might subsequently become drunk and act in ignorance. In this case, he acted through ignorance and in ignorance. This act is involuntary. We can say that actions done in ignorance can be voluntary or involuntary. Actions done both in ignorance and through ignorance are involuntary. Actions done through ignorance are involuntary.

Aristotle does not stop at the distinction between the voluntary and the involuntary. He distinguishes different involuntary acts. There are acts made under compulsion or force. It is not clear how far the soul goes to endure torture and other forms of compulsion. If a person's family is ransomed, he might do shameful things to gain their safety. He might do things that no one would otherwise do. Aristotle offers the example of the ship captain. In a storm, he might throw his cargo overboard to save the ship. Except for these circumstances, no captain would throw the cargo off of the ship. Within the category of involuntary actions, there are these mixed actions. The person voluntarily does an act because of circumstances. Without the circumstances, he would not have voluntarily acted.

5.2.6 Knowing and Doing

Aristotle discusses the soul in *De Anima* (aka *On the Soul*) and the *Nicomachean Ethics*. The soul is the form and actuality of the body.[9] There are two main parts of the soul: the rational and the irrational. There are three aspects of the soul: the rational, the appetitive, and the nutritive.[10] Reason is the rational part of the soul. The nutritive part of the soul is irrational. The appetitive part is predominantly irrational, but it has a bit of

---

[9] *De Anima*, 412a22.
[10] *Nicomachean Ethics*, 1.13.

reason in it. It can hear and obey the commands of reason. It can be trained or persuaded to follow and obey reason.[11] There is another part of the irrational soul, the spirited (*thumikos*) or angry part.[12] The appetite is concerned with bodily desires. The spirited part is concerned with courage, honor, and reputation. One way that Aristotle distinguishes the spirited part from the appetitive part is by holding that the spirited part has more of a share in the rational part of the soul than does the appetitive part, since the spirited part is more obedient to reason than is the appetitive part. Aristotle distinguishes four parts of the soul, by mixing the rational and irrational parts. We have a part that is wholly rational, reason. We have a part that is wholly irrational, nutrition. We have two parts that are predominantly irrational, but they have some sort of rational part in them: spirit and appetite.

Part of soul	Aim of desire
Rational	
Reason	Wisdom and learning
Rational/irrational	
Spirit	Courage, anger, and reputation
Appetite	Pleasure and money
Irrational	
Nutrition	Autocratic bodily needs

Aristotle distinguishes intellectual excellence from practical intelligence. The intellect is exercised in theoretical science, which seeks knowledge for its own sake. Practical intelligence seeks production, activity, and the arts. In theoretical science, we contemplate that which cannot be otherwise, in practical affairs we contemplate variable affairs.[13] In a jab at Plato, Aristotle says that in ethics we do not aim to know what moral goodness is, we aim to know how to be good.[14] We use the word "knowledge" with reference to theoretical propositions, as when we know that two and three sum to five. We use the word to reference activities, as when we know how to play the lyre. This difference can be found in our distinction between knowing *that* something is the case and knowing *how* to do something. Theoretical knowledge is one and done, you do not need to keep calculating the sum to improve or enhance your knowledge. Practical knowledge requires practice, you need to practice playing the

---

[11] *Nicomachean Ethics*, II.13.1102b30.

[12] *Nicomachean Ethics*, 1102b.27.

[13] *Nicomachean Ethics*, 6.1139a9.

[14] *Nicomachean Ethics*, II.2.

lyre to come to know how to play the lyre. This requires that you develop a habitual interaction with the lyre. When playing the lyre well becomes a habit, you know how to play the lyre well. The character of a person is his habitual relation toward certain behaviors. Children are able to gain theoretical knowledge at a young age.[15] It takes time, study, practice, and habit to engage in practical affairs well. Children do not know military strategy, ethical activity, or political leadership.

Aristotle explains the actions and behaviors of animals through a practical syllogism. He is not attempting to describe what the animal is thinking when acting. He is trying to explain the action. When the animal eats food, he explains it by attributing a desire to the animal and a perception of the animal. Pigs have a standing desire to eat pig-chow and as it turns out almost anything is pig-chow. The pig walks around desiring to eat pig-chow. We can attribute the following desire to the pig: All pig-chow is to be eaten. The standing desire is a universal premise. Sometimes the pig sees, smells, tastes, or perceives some pig-chow. We can attribute the following perception to the pig: This object is pig-chow. The perception is a particular premise. When the two premises come together, the pig acts to eat the chow. The explanation of human behavior is more complex and subtler than the explanations of the pig's behavior, on a good day. Human beings have a rational faculty. There are theoretical syllogisms and there are practical syllogisms:

	Theoretical syllogism	*Practical syllogism*
Universal premise	All humans are mortal	All sweets are to be eaten
Particular premise	This person is a human	This object is a sweet
Conclusion	This person is mortal	Eat this

Aristotle explains human behavior by attributing a syllogism to a certain sort of desire and perception in the person. Some practical syllogisms that explain an act are attributed to the rational faculty:

Rational practical syllogism
All healthy food is to be eaten
This is healthy food
Eat it

---

[15] *Nicomachean Ethics*, 6.8.1142a15.

We can do the same for the spirited part:

Spirited practical syllogism

All courageous acts are to be done

This is a courageous act

Do this

We have already seen the appetitive practical syllogism that desires to eat all sweets and perceives a sweet. He eats the sweet.

5.2.7 Virtue

Aristotle warns us to expect only as much precision from a subject as is fitting for the subject.[16] In mathematics, it is fitting to expect exactitude. In ethics, we should not have expectations of exactitude. Just as what is healthy for one person might not be healthy for another person, ethics deals with variations. Aristotle will speak in general about virtue. Ethics is the study of the good life. The goods that we seek in ethics are goods that we choose for their own sake, intrinsic goods. Other good things are sought for the sake of something else, extrinsic goods. Happiness (*eudaimonia*) is the most general intrinsic good. It is properly said of a person or a life at the end of life.[17] The virtues are intrinsic goods too. We seek these things for their own sake. The function of a human being is to be a rational animal. For us to flourish we must follow reason as it guides us to embody the virtues. A happy life is a life of actualizing our human capacities; the result is human flourishing.

Aristotle argues that moral excellence is in our passions, our faculties, or our dispositions.[18] Excellence is not found in our passions, since we are not called good because we feel anger, fear, appetite, and other passions. Moral excellence is not found in our faculties, since we are not praised or blamed for our capacity to feel the passions. So, moral excellence is found in our dispositions (*hexis*) or states in relation to our passions. We are praised and blamed for being properly disposed toward feelings of anger, fear, appetite, and other passions. To feel anger to the right extent, means that we must be disposed toward it neither too much nor too little. The anger must

---

[16] *Nicomachean Ethics*, 1.2.1094b12.

[17] *Nicomachean Ethics*, 17.1098a18.

[18] *Nicomachean Ethics*, II.5.

be directed toward the right things, people, and at the right time. Moral excellence is being disposed toward our passions to the right extent, at the right time, and for the right reasons.[19] The right reasons for acting are the reasons that a man of practical reason has for acting. The man of practical reason deliberates and chooses the virtuous act for its own sake. Moral excellence is a disposition toward choosing the mean in passions, with neither excess nor deficiency.[20] Virtue is a mean disposition between excess and deficiency. Though all virtues are mean dispositions, not all mean dispositions are virtues. The mean disposition toward adultery is not a virtue, since adultery is not a virtue.

Having offered a general account of virtue as a mean between two extremes, one of excess and one of deficiency, Aristotle turns to show that the particular virtues are dispositions to a mean. He goes through each virtue:

Deficiency	Mean/virtue	Excess	Domain
Insensibility	**Temperance**	Overindulgence	Food, sex, and drink
Cowardice	**Courage**	Rashness	Fear and confidence
Illiberality	**Liberality**	Prodigality	Small sums of money
Pettiness	**Magnificence**	Vulgarity	Large sums of money
Unambitious	**Pride**	Vanity	Small honors
Pusillanimity	**Magnanimity**	Vainglory	Large honors
Lack of Spirit	**Patience**	Irascibility	Anger
Understatement	**Fidelity**	Boastfulness	Truth
Cantankerousness	**Friendship**	Obsequiousness	Relationships
Boorishness	**Friendliness**	Buffoonery	Discussion
Shamelessness	**Modesty**	Shyness	Shame
Spitefulness	**Righteous indignation**	Envy	Indignation

Through his discussion, Aristotle notes that the Greeks do not have words for some of these dispositions. For example, they do not have a word for some of the excessive or deficient dispositions, such as underindulgence. They do not have a word for some of the virtues, such as friendliness. This might incline a reader to think that the virtue is not really a mean

---

[19] *Nicomachean Ethics*, II.6.
[20] *Nicomachean Ethics*, II.6.1107a1.

between two extremes. It is important to remember that Aristotle is offering a conceptual account of the virtues.

Consider the virtue of temperance, a mean disposition toward the objects of touch and taste. Temperance is a disposition to choose the mean in relation to food, sex, and drink. A person who is disposed toward overindulgence goes to the excess and the person disposed toward underindulgence goes to the deficiency. Suppose that 10 pounds of food a day is too much and that 2 pounds a day is too little. The arithmetical mean is 6 pounds of food each day. If we expect Aristotle to tell us exactly how much food each of us should eat, we are mistaken. Ethics does not admit of this sort of exactitude. Six pounds of food a day might be too little for a person under a rigorous training regimen. Six pounds a day might be too much for a person not in training. Aristotle distinguishes the arithmetical mean from the relative mean. The *arithmetical mean* is the numerical midpoint between two extremes and this midpoint is the same for everyone. The *relative mean* is the mean relative to each of us and this is different for different people. Each of us must determine for ourselves what amount is too much food and what amount is too little. Each of us must find the mean relative to us. When a person is training, more food is the mean amount of food. When not training, less food is the mean. How much food is the mean amount of food is different for different people and is different for the same person at different times.

When we consider the virtues themselves, Aristotle argues that they are not equidistant between the two extremes. Some virtues are closer to one extreme than the other. Temperance is closer to underindulgence than it is to overindulgence. Aristotle explains why this is the case. When all of us, or almost all of us, are naturally disposed toward one of the extremes, the virtue is closer to the other extreme. The extreme toward which we are all naturally disposed is more opposed to the mean. To be *more opposed* is to be farther away from the mean.[21] So, temperance is more opposed to the excess than the deficiency. Aristotle argues that courage resembles rashness more than cowardice. So, courage is more opposed to cowardice, the deficiency, than it is to rashness, the excess. The cause of this is found in the virtue itself. When a virtue resembles or is more like one extreme, then the other extreme is more opposed to the mean. So, we have two causes of a virtue being more opposed to one extreme or the other. One cause is in us and the other is in the virtue itself.

We can now see that virtue is a disposition toward choosing the mean relative to us. Aristotelian virtue is complex and subtle. Consider the virtue

---

[21] *Nicomachean Ethics*, II.8.1109a1.

of temperance. Suppose a person deliberates about his consumption of food and ends his deliberation by choosing (deciding) to have one plate of food at the local all-you-can-eat buffet. Suppose that he is at the buffet and that he has eaten his plate of food. If this person finds that he desires more food, thinks it would be pleasant, and finds abstaining from the food painful, then he does not have a firm and fixed disposition toward the virtue of temperance. Today we tend to think that as long as he abstains from the second plate of food, he has acted virtuously. Virtue is not so easy, according to Aristotle. We can see how well a disposition toward virtue is established in us by noticing whether we find doing the virtuous act painful. Aristotle is not simply concerned with doing the virtuous act but also concerned with doing it as a virtuous person would do the act. The virtuous person would find abstaining from the second plate of food pleasing and not painful. The virtuous person does not even desire to act otherwise. In Aristotle's ethics, it is possible for a person to choose to forgo the second plate, but desire the second plate and eat the second plate without abandoning his choice.

Recall Aristotle's model of action explanation. The universal premise is the choice (*prohairesis*). The particular premise is a perception (*aisthesis*), thought (*nous*), or imagination (*phantasia*).[22] Let us suppose that the person at a restaurant desires a second plate of food. He does not have a firm and fixed disposition toward virtue. So, he is not virtuous. There are two possibilities for him: he can act according to his choice or contrary to it. If he resists the temptation for the second plate, then he is morally strong or continent. If he does not resist his desire for the second plate and eats a second plate, then he is morally weak or incontinent. The continent person and the morally incontinent person face desires that conflict with their choice. A vicious person chooses to overindulge, or underindulge, and does so. The vicious person does not choose well, instead chooses either the excess or the deficiency.

Persons	Choice	Desire	Action
Virtuous	Chooses the mean	No conflicting desires	Acts with choice
Continent	Chooses the mean	Conflicting desires	Acts with choice
Incontinent	Chooses the mean	Conflicting desires	Acts against choice
Vicious	Chooses the excess or deficiency	No conflicting desires	Acts with choice

[22] *On The Soul*, III.3.428a1.

Aristotle offers some advice or general rules to follow that will help us hit the mean.[23] (1) Always be on guard against pleasure and pleasant things. The allure of pleasure influences one to judge poorly. Pleasure leads us to do shameful and wrong things. (2) Notice the areas where you struggle to be virtuous. These areas are different for different people. One person might struggle to be patient, because he has a natural tendency to lack spirit, the deficiency. This person should err on the side of irascibility. In this way, he will have a better chance of hitting the mean. (3) Avoid the extreme that is more opposed to the mean. When consuming food, sex, or drink, err on the side of insensibility. When going into battle, err on the side of rashness. Following these three rules will help a person establish a fixed disposition toward virtue.

When interpreters discuss Aristotle's ethical theory, they ground their discussion in the *Nicomachean Ethics*. Our preceding discussion of Aristotle's ethics focused on *Nicomachean Ethics*. We have an additional ethical text from Aristotle, *Eudemian Ethics*. There are 10 books in the *Nicomachean Ethics* and 8 books in the *Eudemian Ethics*. These two works are joined at the hip. There are three books in common between the works. Books V, VI, and VII of *Nicomachean Ethics* are the same books as Books IV, V, and VI of *Eudemian Ethics*. The *Eudemian Ethics* is thought by most interpreters to be a work of lesser quality than the *Nicomachean Ethics*. As a result, it is not studied as much as the *Nicomachean Ethics*. There are important differences between the texts. Some virtues are mentioned in one of the works but not in the other. Some topics are argued for or contextualized differently in the two works. Despite the widespread neglect of *Eudemian Ethics*, it is worth noting it as a valuable addition to Aristotle's ethical theory.

5.2.8 Politics

Aristotle considers politics as necessary for ethical development. Politics sets the context for education and the development of the virtues. Ethics seeks the good for each human being and politics seeks the good for groups of human beings. Political structures are not an imposition on the ethical life of a person. They are an outgrowth and necessary context of ethical life. Political organization allows for the full expression of certain virtues, such as courage, magnanimity, and friendship. By nature, human beings are

---

[23] *Nicomachean Ethics*, II.9.1109a20.

political animals.[24] Just as ethics seeks the good for each person, politics seeks the good to a higher and greater degree.[25] In this way, politics encompasses the goods of ethics and goes beyond them to address the highest good for human beings.

Aristotle's discussion about politics is informed by his survey of theoretical works on political constitutions. Positions in Plato's texts are often rejected in Aristotle's discussion of theoretical constitutions: for example, *Politics* II.3 and 5 reject Plato's account in *Republic*. Yet, Aristotle is more concerned with the practical aspect of political science. Aristotle sent his students out to collect constitutions from cities around Greece. He gathered over one hundred functioning constitutions. These informed his discussion of political constitutions. These documents help Aristotle detail enormous varieties of constitutional subtypes and detail the historical pitfalls of various types. His account of the collapse of different types of constitutional arrangements has an empirical character that Plato's discussion lacks. Aristotle is not so interested in the best theoretical constitution. He is interested in finding the best constitution in practical application. For Aristotle, a constitution is the structure of offices in the state. The constitution sets the end, aim, or *telos* of the state.[26] The basic political arrangement is found in the family. Collections of families form a village and collections of villages form a community. Families and villages are not large enough, according to Aristotle, to be self-sufficient. A community is large enough to form a self-sufficient political organization. Such a community is the state, and it is the actualization of the political structure *in* the family to its fullest degree.

For Aristotle, the political structure starts at the family and finds its full expression in the state. Aristotle grounds his account of the political structure in nature. Man and woman come together and procreate not by choice but by nature.[27] In Aristotle's account of nature, there are active and passive objects. Aristotle takes the man as active and the woman as passive. The active and passive relationship of man and woman is expressed by Aristotle as the relationship between a master and a slave.[28] This is the relationship of a director and a person being directed. Though Aristotle describes the marital relationship this way, he distinguishes women from slaves. He argues

---

[24] *Politics*, I.1.1253a6.

[25] *Politics*, I.1.1252a5.

[26] *Politics*, IV.1.1289a15.

[27] *Politics*, I.2.1252A29.

[28] *Politics*, 1.3.1253b15.

that women, like men, have reason but that reason is not authoritative over their actions. As for slaves, Aristotle distinguishes slaves by convention (*nomos*) and slaves by nature. Slaves *by convention* or law are spoils of war and as such they are the rightful property of the victor.[29] Slaves *by nature* are people of limited mental capacities.[30] These slaves are not able to care for themselves. They need to be directed by another person, or else they will not survive. Aristotle mentions that there is an ongoing debate about the legitimacy of slaves by convention. He argues that the opponents deny the legitimacy of such slavery, but support the legitimacy of war and victors possessing the spoils of war. So, he rejects their counterarguments.

Turning to the state and the political constitutions, we saw that Plato offers five main types of political constitutions. Aristocracy is the best followed by timocracy, oligarchy, and democracy. Tyranny is the last and the worst. Aristotle notes some of the same constitutions as Plato. He discusses kingships, oligarchies, democracies, and tyrannies. He goes into great detail about the various forms of governments under these main headings.[31] Yet Aristotle offers a novel approach to characterizing and classifying the constitutions. He argues that some constitutions function for the benefit of the rulers and others function for the benefit of the ruled.[32] The function of the state is to help the people in the state flourish in their distinctly human capacities. So, the constitutions that function for the benefit of the ruled are better than those that function for the benefit of the rulers. He also distinguishes constitutions that have rule by one person, rule by a few people, and rule by many people. The distinction between rule by the few and rule by the many is a distinction between rule by the rich and rule by the poor. We can plot these distinctions as two axes and represent them in a table:

	Good constitutions: benefit of the ruled	Bad constitutions: benefit of the rulers
Rule by one	Kingship	Tyranny
Rule by few	Aristocracy	Oligarchy
Rule by many	Polity	Democracy

---

29 *Politics*, I.6.1255a5.
30 *Politics*, I.5.1254b22.
31 *Politics*, IV and VI.
32 *Politics*, III.7.1279a29.

There are three good constitutions: rule by one, rule by few, and rule by many.[33] Each good form has a corrupted constitution as its counterpart. A corrupt king is a tyrant, a corrupt aristocracy is an oligarchy, and a corrupt polity is a democracy. Aristotle names some Greek city-states as exemplars of certain constitutions. The Constitution of Crete is the best example of a kingship. Sparta (Lacedaemon) is the best aristocracy. Carthage is the best polity. Magistrates should not be able to make money in any form of constitution.[34]

The bad constitutions order from the worst at the top to the best of the worst at the bottom of the chart above. Tyranny is the worst constitution.[35] Tyranny suffers from all the problems of oligarchy and democracy, adding to them its own problems. Oligarchy is the second worst. Tyranny and oligarchy are the most short-lived of all constitutions.[36] Democracy is the best of the bad forms of government.[37]

We can see that the kingship is the extension of the family writ large in one person for the entire constitution. It is not likely that one person can do that job well. There are many different features of the constitution and many competing interests. A person would need to be superhuman to judge well all of these competing interests. You might get lucky and find a person fit for the job, but Aristotle thinks that the odds are not on your side. Another challenge for a kingship is that it does not allow people to participate in the constitution. This deprives people of the opportunity to actualize their capacities in political participation. Aristotle reminds us that in the *Nicomachean Ethics* he established that the happy life allows for the flourishing of our capacities. This flourishing is available to all freemen, as they seek excellence in the mean. In the constitution, the opportunity to flourish in our natural capacities should be available to as many as possible.[38] The kingship deprives people of the opportunity to actualize political virtues. When people are not involved in the functions of the constitution, people come to distrust the government and to see the government as an impediment to their happiness.

---

[33] *Politics*, III.18.
[34] *Politics*, V.8.1308b32.
[35] *Politics*, V.10.1311a9.
[36] *Politics*, V.12.
[37] *Politics*, IV.2.1289b4.
[38] *Politics*, IV.11.1295a.36.

The aristocracy broadens involvement in the constitution. In this constitution the few best families govern. This form of government expands the participation in governing the constitution. Yet, in an aristocracy, the majority of people do not participate in governing. This leads to distrust. It also places the majority of people as being ruled. They are not freemen, but rather subjects of a ruling class. This leads to a relationship of master and slave between them, not a relationship of freemen in friendship with each other. There is another problem with kingships and aristocracies. Aristotle holds that politics and economics are intertwined. Better put, economics is a part of politics. The term "economics" comes from the Greek term (*oikonomia*) for household management. Since politics starts in the family, for Aristotle, and economics is part of household management, economics is part of the politics. One of the greatest threats to any constitution is a lack of a strong economic middle class. Large divisions between the rich and the poor inevitably bring factions and conflict into the state. The aristocratic constitution does not engender a strong middle class. The few in the ruling class will tend to be rich and the majority in the ruled class will be poor.

Aristotle points out that the polity (aka constitutional government) is not accounted for by political philosophers.[39] The polity remedies or lessens the major challenges for the kingship and the aristocracy. The polity expands participation in the constitution more than the other good forms. This allows the greatest number of people to flourish in both their ethical life and their political life. Aristotle argues that a large group of people judge matters better than a single person.[40] An individual person or some few rulers are more liable to corruption than a large group. A polity allows for a strong middle class. By broadening participation in politics, the large group participating in the constitution can guard against the consolidation of wealth in the hands of the few. The polity can make economic opportunities available to the largest group. This leads to the stability of the constitution. Since the polity expands participation in the state, allows the greatest number of people to flourish in their capacities, judges matters better than other constitutions, and has the strongest economic middle class, it is the best constitution.

Aristotle distinguishes two ways of identifying the best constitution: an absolute best form and a relative best form.[41] The *absolute* best constitution

---

[39] *Politics*, IV.7.1293a41.

[40] *Politics*, III.11.1281a40.

[41] *Politics*, IV.11.1296b9.

is established in the abstract, in theory. It does not make reference to the particular people forming the constitution. The *relative* best constitution is practical and it takes the particular people forming the constitution into account. Aristotle argues that the best relative form of government is the one best suited to the people being governed. In some cases, a democracy might be a better fit for the populace than an oligarchy.[42] We can see that a polity requires broad participation in the constitution. This assumes that the people founding a polity are up to the task. If a group of people are founding a constitution and not many of them are educated well, they might better form a kingship or an aristocracy. Aristotle makes the same point about the laws. There is no one set of laws that applies equally to all constitutions. The particular laws must match the type of constitution. Though we can say which constitution is the absolute best constitution, we cannot say that any one of the constitutions is the relative best constitution.

---

[42] *Politics*, IV.2.1289b20.

6

THE SUBJECTS OF PHILOSOPHY

There are three main philosophers in the Golden Age of philosophy: Socrates, Plato, and Aristotle. Socrates does not leave us any writings and, from all evidence, did not write philosophy. He walked around Athens and spent time in the marketplace (*agora*) talking with whoever would be willing. He focused on a narrow range of topics, with ethics being his primary concern. He wanted to know how to live well. This led him to focus on the virtues, such as wisdom, courage, temperance, and justice. He also discussed political philosophy, insofar as his interactions with the state involved contexts for him to embody the virtues. Despite the early Greek philosophers' interest in natural philosophy, Socrates had no interest in the subject. He touched on the subject of epistemology, by challenging other people's claim to knowledge and by questioning the limits of his own knowledge. Metaphysics was not of interest to him, as he favored action-guiding knowledge over abstract knowledge.

It might seem that Socrates claimed to know nothing. This is not true. His attempt to disprove the oracle's claim that there was no one wiser than Socrates in Athens led him to question those who thought themselves wise. This process showed Socrates that these people did know some things, but they thought they knew many things that they did not know. He surmised that a wise person knows the difference between what he knows and what he does not know. The people who thought themselves wise did not know the difference. Socrates did know the difference, since he did not claim to know about such things as politics, art, and military generalship. His questioning often shows that he knows certain things. The speech of the Laws in *Crito* reveals numerous commitments that Socrates had about his

This Is Ancient Philosophy: An Introduction, First Edition. Kirk Fitzpatrick.
© 2024 John Wiley & Sons, Inc. Published 2024 by John Wiley & Sons, Inc.

relationship to the state, such as the state was dearer than his parents. In *Crito*, Socrates also argues that no one should do wrong or return a wrong for a wrong. Elsewhere, Socrates claimed that all wrongdoing is ignorance and that all learning is recollection. These are just some of the explicit commitments that Socrates avows.

Socrates makes a lasting contribution to the history of ethics through his rejection of Homeric ethics. To embody the Homeric virtues a person must be well-born, good looking, courageous, held in high repute, and able to defend those under his charge. The Homeric virtues are publicly demonstrable, results oriented, and grounded in a view of natural virtues. Socrates' debate with Callicles in *Gorgias* is a dramatic portrayal of the contempt with which the naturally well-endowed Homeric hero views Socrates' account of virtue. Callicles sees Socrates as ugly, socially useless, cowardly, and unfit. He accuses Socrates of turning the natural virtues upside down to benefit himself and hobble his betters. Socrates urges us to look inward to the care of our souls and not to care what the majority thinks. He urges us to be temperate, even if we have the resources to indulge. He urges us not to do wrong to others in retaliation for the wrongs that they have done to us. His interloculars often misunderstand what he is saying or think that what he is saying is absurd, because he often uses familiar terms in unfamiliar ways. His approach to ethics is nothing short of revolutionary.

Perhaps even more valuable than his positive claims are his disproofs of claims that we thought we knew. The aporetic Socratic dialogues are instructive, by showing us what a certain virtue is not and by guiding us to think about the virtue in a different way. We learn from Socrates that a person who already thinks he knows has nothing to learn. His interloculars reveal much about their thoughts and themselves in the way that they react to being shown that they do not know what they claimed to know. Many of them get angry with Socrates and attack him personally. Many of them simply walk away, showing that they really do not care about knowing the truth. Socrates' interactions with the Sophists are revealing, by showing that the Sophists cannot teach what they claim to teach. These dialogues show that the wealthy who pay large sums to the Sophists are exchanging drachmas for snake oil. It is no surprise that Socrates made many powerful enemies.

Socrates' most lasting contribution to philosophy is possibly not in any of his positive views or in his refutations of the views of others. The Socratic method, *elenchus*, is probably his most lasting contribution to philosophy. The method requires us to define the key concepts that we seek to know and to test the definitions that we propose. It requires us to set our egos aside, to be humble in our claims to knowledge, and to be unceasingly corrigible and self-reflective. It is instructive to consider how many terms we use without being able to precisely say what they mean. Vagueness is a feature of language in many contexts. Yet, when we speak about important things, when we praise and blame behaviors, we should expect to be clear in the meaning of the terms we use. The method reveals how sloppy we often are when discussing matters of the highest import. Confronting our own ignorance takes courage and a commitment to learn.

Plato expands the range of subjects that Socrates entertained. He directly addresses issues in political philosophy, metaphysics, and epistemology. He offers our first text devoted to epistemology, *Theaetetus*. His account of the soul offers insights into different forms of desire and the function of desire in explanations of actions. The account of the soul is enlarged to generate an account of political factions and their relations to different political constitutions. His account of political constitutions in the *Republic* puts democracy as the penultimate worst form of government. Only tyranny is worse. Meanwhile, Sparta's form of government turns out to be second best. Only an aristocracy is better. His account of politics flies in the face of commonly held Athenian beliefs. Unlike Socrates, Plato offers an account of actions done in the face of conflicting desires. In this account, Plato distinguishes judgments of goodness from desire and thereby makes room for an explanation of moral weakness. His ethical system directly challenges the views of Homer. He does not find the Homeric heroes to be morally admirable. He argues that these heroes behave in immoral and undignified ways. He urges educators to avoid using many of the stories about the Homeric heroes. He rejects the gods of Homer, insofar as the Homeric gods lie, cause evils for men, or make war. Plato's challenge to Athenian democracy and to the Homeric epics were direct challenges to Athenian values. There is no doubt that Plato, as Socrates, made powerful enemies.

Plato's distinctive contribution to metaphysics is his theory of forms. He distinguishes the world of becoming from the world of being, the world of opinion from the world of truth. His account synthesizes the Heraclitean focus on flux with the Parmenidean focus on timeless, unchanging truth. The theory shows how and to what extent each position is accurate, according to Plato. When we perceive a round object, we perceive an imperfect circle. This experience can lead us to contemplate the circle itself. According to Plato, physical objects are imperfect harbingers of a perfect, timeless reality. This reality always is, it never came to be, and it will never cease to be. The forms are timelessly true. They give meaning to our experience in the world of becoming. Without forms, Plato thinks, nothing in the world would mean anything. The immortality of the forms gives them the primary feature of divinity. Our ability to contemplate the forms shows that we are in some way kindred to the divine. The Myth of Er at the end of *Republic* shows that our souls can participate in the form of justice and that the *Kosmos* participates in the form of justice. The myth invites us to harmonize our souls with the whole of the *Kosmos*. This is a lofty pursuit to be sure. The theory of forms urges us to move beyond the senses, to focus on our understanding, and to embody goodness itself insofar as it is possible for us.

Aristotle distinguishes almost every major area of inquiry that we have today. He spent much of his time working on biology and the physical sciences. He presented a genus and species framework to distinguish a hierarchy of plants and animals. In this model, each animal possesses the capacities of the lower animals and is distinguished by its peculiar capacity or difference. For instance, human beings are animals with the peculiar capacity for reason. His work on ethics revolutionized the relationships between virtue and vice. Formerly, philosophers thought of virtue as being at one end of a spectrum and vice at the other end. Aristotle places virtue as a mean between two forms of vice, one of excess and one of deficiency. His account of politics is grounded in actual political constitutions from across Greece. He expands on Plato's five forms of political constitutions, by distinguishing constitutions that function for the good of the rulers from constitutions that function for the good of the ruled. This taxonomy allows Aristotle to distinguish a hitherto overlooked form of government, a polity or constitutional democracy. Aristotle's concept of human flourishing urges us to develop our peculiar human capacities to their fullest. This concept enlivens the ethics and its outline of happiness. It also reaches through to enliven his account of politics as an opportunity for us to flourish. Political constitutions offer an even larger context in which to flourish and be happy. The four causes, material, efficient, formal, and final, offer a framework to explain what something is. The causes allow us to explain what something is made of, how it came to be what it is, why it has the shape it has, and what larger purpose it serves.

Aristotle's account of substance and his theory of hylomorphism is his distinctive contribution to metaphysics. Aristotle offers a detailed account of the material world by going beyond the basic elements of the early Greek philosophers to reference the underlying features of those elements. He offers an account of change in the material world that shows an underlying substratum that persists throughout change. He takes the forms from Plato's other world and requires them to be embodied. In this way, Aristotle synthesizes the philosophical perspectives of the early

Greek materialists and the Platonic forms. Substance is a form in matter. This is the referent of "being" in the fullest sense of the term. Hylomorphic analysis is applicable to both inanimate and animate physical objects. It is also applicable to the parts of animate and inanimate physical objects. According to Aristotle, there is no substance in the world that cannot be understood through hylomorphic analysis. Just imagine what we would see if we had more than Aristotle's lecture notes. The Golden Age of philosophy distinguishes the subjects of philosophy and codifies the scope of the subject. Socrates focused his concerns narrowly. Plato, however, discusses many areas of philosophy, although he does not formally distinguish them. Aristotle distinguishes all areas of philosophy. These subjects remain today as the subject of philosophy.

Metaphysics is the study of being, what-is, or substance. The Golden Age gives us two main theories, formalism from Plato and hylomorphism from Aristotle. By distinguishing the subject, they help us look back to early Greek philosophy and appreciate the innovations in the subject made then. From the early Greeks, we have material accounts of what-is or being. We also have the Parmenidean Constraint, the fact that nothing comes from nothing. What-is is an eternal and unlimited whole. Plato argues that ideas are the reality of the world.

Epistemology is the study of knowledge. Plato raises a basic problem for knowing anything. He argues that to know something the person must believe, it must be true, and he must be justified. The problem is that we cannot account for what it is to be justified without also assuming that we know. Aristotle talks about knowing in different ways. We know how to play the lyre in a different way than we know that two and two is four. Of theoretical knowledge, we know a proposition when it is an intuition or derivable from an intuition. An intuition is a base-level proposition held to be true not derived from argument. These are the building blocks of knowledge. The propositions, for example, that "each thing is identical to itself," or that "everything is or is not," or that "propositions are either true or false," are not the result of inference from premises. These are intuitions. The concept of intuitions allows Aristotle to avoid an infinite regress. Take any proposition; if that proposition is justified by some other proposition, then we can ask what supports that other proposition. If it, in turn, is justified by some other proposition, then we ask what justifies the other proposition. And so on. Without intuitions, it seems that our knowledge is never justified.

Ethics is the study of normatively right thought and action. The Golden Age focuses on virtue ethics, where moral goodness is a virtue. Socrates focused on this subject to try and determine what are the virtues and what is a virtuous life. Plato continues by analyzing the soul or its parts as instruments of virtue. When a person sets up a certain view of moral goodness as the ruler of his soul, he adopts a certain character. The aristocratic character differs from the timocratic, for example, because of the different views of goodness that the two have. Plato's ethics distinguishes the virtuous character types from the vicious. Aristotle finds virtue in the mean. He argues that virtue is human flourishing, the actualization of our peculiarly human capacities. For him, this flourishing is the happy life.

Politics is the study of the normatively right constitution or government. The subject extends to issues of leadership and the handling of offices in a government. Socrates encounters real politic and questions his obligations to the state and his fellow citizens. Plato considers political constitutions in an abstract or ideal form. He identifies five constitutions. He argues that the aristocratic constitution, like the aristocratic man, is the best constitution. Aristotle focuses on existing constitutions in relation to the ideal forms. He argues that a constitutional democracy or polity is the best constitution. Aristotle was not a citizen of Athens, and he could not participate in government. Yet he, and not Plato, selected a version of democracy as the best constitution.

Logic is the study of argument. An argument has two parts, the premises and the conclusion. The premises are offered in support of the conclusion. Aristotle is the first to distinguish deductive arguments from inductive arguments. He argues that deductive arguments move from the universal to the universal or from the universal to the particular. Inductive arguments move from the particular to the universal. He is the first to distinguish the form of a proposition from its content. He abstracts from the content to the form. The proposition "All men are mortal" refers to men and mortality. The proposition also has a form: all A are B. There are an infinite number of propositions that have this form. Aristotle accounts for four forms of propositions.

	Affirmation	*Negation*
Universal	All A are B	No A are B
Particular	Some A are B	Some A are not B

When we put these propositions into deductive arguments, we get the form of the argument. Here is a deductive argument, the so-called syllogism of Barbara.

Syllogism		
Premises/conclusion	*Content*	*Form*
Universal premise	All men are mortal	All A are B
Particular premise	All mortals are embodied	All B are C
Conclusion	All men are embodied	All A are C

Aristotle noticed that if these premises are true, regardless of whether they are in fact true, then the conclusion cannot be false. This necessity is analogous to physical compulsion. It does not matter what the content of the argument is. A valid argument is one where if the premises are true then the conclusion cannot be false. All arguments that have this form are valid and there are an infinite number of such arguments. Plato focused on the arguments from the Sophists and the Eleatics. He considered the content of the argument. So, to evaluate the arguments he had to go through them one by one. Aristotle's method allows him to evaluate the validity of the form of an argument and thereby account for an infinite number of instances of that form. Of course, we want more than validity from an argument. We want the premises to be, in fact, true. An argument that is valid and has all true premises is sound. Induction is useful in forming general conclusions based on limited observation or experience. The more observations and experiences we have, all of which support the same conclusion, the more likely that the conclusion is true, if the premises are true. Inductive arguments get stronger and stronger the more evidence we can collect in favor of the conclusion. Logic sets the rules of how to think about a subject, not what to think about that subject. It is a useful tool for supporters of any stripe on a topic. It is an invaluable tool in the study of every subject.

The Philosophy of x is a study of the theoretical commitments of any area of inquiry. There is a theory in all that we voluntarily do. The farmer can account for why the farm is managed the way it is. There is a theory underlying any pursuit. The theory accounts for why the pursuit is done the way it is. In this way, philosophy can study any subject. In the sciences, we can turn to math and physics. The conclusion of the formal education ends in a doctorate of philosophy, also called a PhD. This title applies to all academic subjects, though professional and vocational subjects tend to have other designations. To this day, we graduate the highest degree in the study of any subject to philosophy. Plato examines philosophy in different disciplines, education, music, military, math, and medicine. The Golden Age of philosophy organizes and expands the subject of philosophy after the early Greek philosophers. It sets the subjects of study in philosophy to this day.

Part III

HELLENISTIC PHILOSOPHY

7

CYNICISM AND EPICUREANISM

7.1 Alexander's Death

The Hellenistic period of philosophy begins with the death of Alexander the Great in 323 BCE. Aristotle died one year later in 322 BCE. The reason that we trace the historical period back to Alexander, and not Aristotle, is that Alexander conquered from Greece to western India, Macedonia to Egypt. Alexander died suddenly at 32 years of age. When he died, he did not name a successor. He apparently said that the strongest should rule the empire. This led to infighting among the various regions of the short-lived Alexandrian Empire. The successors of Alexander were his generals and friends. These generals were called the *Diadochi* (successors). They fought a series of wars for the territory covered by Alexander's Empire. The generals fought among themselves for power and control of land. There were three main regions. Antigonus ruled in his homeland, Macedonia. His region was called the Antigonid Empire. Ptolemy ruled in Egypt, establishing the Ptolemaic Empire. Seleucus ruled over what had been much of the Persian Empire, now called the Seleucid Empire. This region went from Asia Minor at the Aegean Sea to the western part of India. The early Greek-speaking world stretched from Asia Minor to Southern Italy and up to Macedonia. The expansion of the Greek-speaking world to Persia and Egypt gave a broad reach to the Greeks. The beginning of the Hellenistic period ended the Golden Age of philosophy.

When Alexander conquered a region, he established some homogeneity and stability in its governance. He expanded the reach of Greek ideas. Practically, the Alexandrian Empire was an extension of the Greek ideal in

This Is Ancient Philosophy: An Introduction, First Edition. Kirk Fitzpatrick.
© 2024 John Wiley & Sons, Inc. Published 2024 by John Wiley & Sons, Inc.

ethical and political thought. This was the potential realization of the ideals of Greek political thought, including that of Plato and Aristotle. The expansion of the Greek-speaking world led to the expansion of Greek thought and culture into Persia and Egypt. Greeks could now travel from Southern Italy to Egypt and to Persia while remaining in a persistent form of city governance and linguistic coherence. This greatly enhanced the range of travel, trade, commerce, and culture of the Greeks. For about 100 years, the Hellenistic empires facilitated the expansion of Greek architecture, philosophy, commerce, and culture. The Hellenistic empires also led to a geographical expansion of the Greek language. As the language expanded, non-Greeks found incentives to learn it. This expansion of people speaking Greek led to a more accessible form of Greek. The Attic Greek of Plato and Aristotle is grammatically complex and difficult to speak correctly. To make it easier for non-Greeks to learn Greek, the Attic form of Greek was replaced by a grammatically simpler form of Greek, *Koine* Greek or common Greek. This is the form of Greek used by Roman writers and used in the New Testament.

As the Diadochi waged wars among themselves and against other threats, the large political and economic Alexandrian Empire began to fragment and falter. What had been an expansive network of cities that were politically, linguistically, and culturally integrated now became the more isolated regions and empires of the Diadochi. The loss of manpower and the depletion of wealth from wars undermined the governance, defense, and maintenance of the cities. The empires of the Diadochi faced threats both from within their borders and from beyond. Over time the homogeneous and interconnected Alexandrian Empire fractured and failed to fulfill the ideals of the city-state. As the empire collapsed, the larger political structures failed the people. The political structures decayed during this time of rapid change. The fighting among the three main empires: the Antigonid, the Seleucid, and the Ptolemaic Empires, undermined the larger political structures of the Alexandrian Empire.

Individuals living in the collapsing empire saw less trade, less political infrastructure, and changing social structures. Working to care for yourself, your family, and your friends became more difficult. Engaging in politics became even more dangerous than it was in the Golden Age. This led the philosophical systems to change focus. Rather than focusing on the grand systems of metaphysics, epistemology, ethics, and political philosophy that we saw in Plato and Aristotle, the focus turned inward to the governance of oneself. The focus of philosophy turned to the care and maintenance of the individual person. This refocusing turned inward to the care of the self and soul. These topics harken back to Socrates, largely skipping over the great philosophical systems of Plato and Aristotle. In fact, each of the major schools of thought in the Hellenistic period locates the origins of their philosophy in Socrates, some schools more directly than others.

The end of the Golden Age of philosophy and the inception of the Hellenistic empires marks the beginning of the fall of the ethical and political ideals of Plato and Aristotle. The great schools of the Academy and the Lyceum are largely replaced by schools of thought or philosophies that focus more narrowly on living well. The main schools of thought in the Hellenistic period do not rival the philosophies of Plato or Aristotle in their breadth of concerns, their subtlety of thought, and their complexity. Yet this is not a condemnation of Hellenistic schools of thought. Plato and Aristotle still remain today as two of the greatest philosophers who have ever lived. What we do see in Hellenistic philosophy are schools of thought that mix the ideas of their predecessors in unique and provocative ways. These philosophies reach back to the early Greek philosophers and Socrates. They offer practical advice on living well that resonates powerfully in the contemporary world. Most notably, today we see a dramatic rise in the popularity of Stoicism as a school of thought fit to help us deal with the stress and uncertainty of contemporary geopolitical changes. There are websites that will give you Stoic wisdom every day. Cynicism has also seen a resurgence, though not under that name. It tends not to be noticed that over recent decades there have been revivals of naturalist, minimalist, and unconventional ways of living. The Cynics stress self-sufficiency. They offer an austere, self-sufficient, and unconventional way of life. This ethos tends toward minimalism in possessions, in desires, and in entanglements. The date marking the end of the Hellenistic period is not as clear as its beginning. In some ways, it depends on the lens through which one is looking. Scholars locate the end of the Hellenistic period at different events. Some place it at the Roman conquest of central Greece after the Achaean war in 146 BCE. More commonly, the end of the Hellenistic period comes in the fall of the Ptolemaic Empire in the battle of Actium in 31 BCE.

7.2 Cynicism

7.2.1 Antisthenes

To start we need to go back before the death of Alexander and Aristotle. Antisthenes (*c.*, 446 BCE to c. 366 BCE) was a close associate of Socrates. He is named in Plato's *Phaedo* as being present when Socrates drank the hemlock and died. Let us recall that Socrates was indicted by Meletus, with help from Anytus. Antisthenes was responsible for exiling Anytus from the city and for Meletus being executed. He did not start as an associate of Socrates. He began by being a student of Gorgias and devoted himself to rhetoric. Eventually, he met Socrates and became his associate. His association with Socrates shows great devotion. He lived in Piraeus, the port city to the south of Athens. This means that he walked about five miles each way each day to associate with Socrates. He was closer in age to Plato and Xenophon than he was to Socrates. Antisthenes wrote many texts on a wide variety of subjects. Apparently, there were 10 volumes of his texts, with topics ranging from physics to rhetoric. Other topics include moral goodness, various particular virtues, and law. He wrote so much and on such varied topics that some critics urged him to write less or more narrowly. We have a few fragments from Antisthenes, but we do not know how many works he wrote. Still, he was reputed to be a prolific writer. His use of rhetoric gave him a reputation for being a persuasive writer.

Antisthenes is mentioned in Plato's *Phaedo*, but he is also mentioned in Xenophon's *Symposium* (aka *Banquet*). We learn more about him from Xenophon than we do from Plato. In *Symposium*, (III.4) Callias, the host of the drinking party, offers the useful knowledge that he possesses. Socrates asks him to offer the most valuable knowledge that he possesses. Callias claims that he can make people better, he can improve them. Antisthenes asks if Callias teaches a manual craft or justness (*dikaiosune*). Callias says he teaches justness and turns to the attendees to let them go first.[1] Eventually, Antisthenes' turn comes round. Socrates calls on him to explain how wealth is his greatest possession, when everyone knows that you do not have much money. Antisthenes argues that wealth and poverty are not to be found in property, possessions, silver, or gold. Wealth is found in the soul (*psuche*).[2]

Antisthenes is not referencing wealth. He is referencing our relation to our desires for money and possessions. Money allows us to satisfy our desires for food, sex, and drink. Antisthenes desires food, but not gourmet food. He is satisfied equally with water or the exotic wine Callias is serving. He enjoys both and will not go on to desire exotic wine. He is satisfied with a basic coat that keeps him as warm as Callias' expensive coat. He is satisfied with basic bedding and sleeps as soundly as anyone. When he wants sex, he goes to find an available and willing woman. Usually, these are

---

[1] Xenophon's *Symposium* II.4.
[2] Xenophon's *Symposium* IV 34.

women whom other people do not desire. When the sex is finished, Antisthenes is as satisfied as anyone. One of the greatest things about his wealth, he says, of soul is that if someone robbed him of his money, he would not be troubled. Also, he is willing to loan money to a person who needs it. By controlling his desires for money, he can focus on virtue. Possibly the best thing about his wealth is that he has the leisure to do what he wants when he wants. He is not bothered with concerns about business or making money. He can go where he wants when he wants. This allows him to spend time with Socrates. Socrates shared his wealth with Antisthenes. That is how he became wealthy. Antisthenes can in turn share his wealth with others. Callias comments that Antisthenes is also wealthy in a way that frees him up from government control and commands. We can add that Antisthenes is freed from the customs of the city. He follows his natural desires and satisfies them in simple ways. Antisthenes claims that he has the most wealth, because wealth is a pleasurable soul. He can share his wealth with others, without depleting his own wealth in the least.

Antisthenes argues that most people accumulate objects and property. The objects come with ongoing obligations. He does not spend money at the market buying various exotic goods, buying things for the sake of collecting them, or buying things to enhance his reputation. He procures only what he needs, and he needs little. It does not take much to find water, food, clothing, and shelter. If you want luxurious water, food, clothing, and shelter, it is going to cost you. You will have more money, but you will have more obligations. These obligations will lead you to act in vicious ways. The majority end up spending all their time trying to acquire stuff, add to that stuff, and seek a never-ending task toward getting the next thing. This is true of food, sex, and drink, and it is also true of honors and reputation. Way beyond what we need is the connoisseur and the collector. In a word, this is a consumer. He argues against the consumer, collector, and connoisseur.

He says that the desire for money leads people to do vicious things. There are many people with a lot of money and possessions that think they are poor. These people do vicious things to get and maintain their lifestyle and possessions. The desire for wealth leads brothers to fight over inheritances. It leads people to steal. It leads public officials to leverage their family and their state, sometimes losing everything. The desire for money and for all the things in the appetites gives strong inducements to do vicious things. Antisthenes' wealth safeguards him from all those inducements. Antisthenes has cleverly turned wealth from a contributor of vice to a safeguard for virtue. In Xenophon's *Symposium*, Antisthenes holds that he can teach virtue by teaching people to have a pleasant soul or justness. This makes them wealthy.

Diogenes Laertius (*fl.*, 3rd CE) writes about Antisthenes 500 years later than Xenophon. He says that Antisthenes claimed that Plato was conceited and pompous. There is no doubt that Antisthenes and Plato went in different directions from their interaction with Socrates. Antisthenes was not shy about expressing his opinions. He was humorous and caustic. Diogenes Laertius also reports many works by Antisthenes, but we have none of them. This does not mean that they did not exist, but it does temper our understanding of Diogenes' report. He also offers many anecdotes about Antisthenes. It is challenging to determine the veracity of the anecdotes. These tales tell of Antisthenes' philosophical perspective and his personality.

Antisthenes adopts Socratic beliefs and a Socratic way of life, but not wholesale. Like Socrates, he does not think that moral good is pleasure. He holds that the moral goodness is a virtue, which is a sufficient condition for happiness (*eudaimonia*). He agrees with Socrates in holding that virtue is a sufficient condition for happiness. He also shares Socrates' practical focus on ethics. Virtue is demonstrated through thoughts and actions. He disagrees with Socrates in holding that virtue can be taught. If you observe his way of life and converse with him about his reasons for doing what he does, you can emulate his way of life. For Antisthenes, virtue is a weapon that cannot be taken away, and wisdom is a bulwark against vice. He thinks that having a bad reputation is better than having a good one, since the people holding you in bad repute commit vicious actions to gain and maintain their wealth. Having a pleasant soul, for Antisthenes, requires self-sufficiency, virtue, and wisdom. Antisthenes is the first Cynic (*kunikos*), a term which means "doglike." There are two main reasons to attach the term to Antisthenes. The first reason is that he spent time at the gymnasium of the Cynosarges, the name which means "white dog." The other reasons are that his way of life resembled a dog's life and that he used his sharp tongue to rebuke people as dogs bark at passersby.

7.2.2 Diogenes of Sinope

Diogenes of Sinope (404–323 BCE) became a student of Antisthenes through a series of events. Sinope is on the Black Sea. It was a powerful city, acting as a trade route between Asia Minor and Europe. Diogenes' father was involved in the economics of Sinope. Either his father and Diogenes together or Diogenes alone debased the coinage. Once the debasement was discovered, either his father and Diogenes together or Diogenes alone left Sinope. He went to Athens, where he became an associate of Antisthenes. Antisthenes was not keen to have students, but Diogenes doggedly pursued Antisthenes. Diogenes was more eager to spend time with Antisthenes than Antisthenes was to spend time with Diogenes. In one story, Antisthenes used his staff to ward off Diogenes. In response, Diogenes offered his head and told him that no wood was a match for his persistence. He would continue to go headlong into his study of Antisthenes' way of life. Diogenes was a devoted Cynic.

The first Cynic ridiculed Plato, and Diogenes followed in grand style. He said that Plato's lectures were not worth the time and that Plato was vainglorious. He accused Plato of defining a "human" as a bipedal animal. Diogenes is said to have presented a chicken to Plato and proclaimed that he had a human in his hand. This and the other anecdotes are difficult to verify. Still, the reported interactions between Diogenes and Plato are instructive of Diogenes' beliefs and his way of life. The philosophical content of all legitimate anecdotes is our focus.

Diogenes Laertius reports that Diogenes of Sinope rejected Plato's forms. The story goes that Plato is talking about "tablehood" or the idea of a table. Diogenes is said to have replied that he sees no "tablehood," only a table. Plato responds by saying that Diogenes has the eyes to see the table but he lacks the understanding to comprehend the meaning of "tablehood." Diogenes is challenging Plato's view that to understand the particular object one must understand the universal object. For Diogenes, the meaning of the table is in its contribution to having a pleasant soul. He knows its contribution, so he does not need to know the form. He is focused on the practical knowledge that he needs to live well. Knowledge of abstractions is of less importance than the knowledge of physical objects. Diogenes was focused entirely on living well, not on theories about living well. He said that he does as music trainers do; he sets the note a little higher so when the chorus tries to hit the note he set, they hit the true note. This anecdote makes the same point as Aristotle's suggestion on hitting the mean. Aristotle argued that if we err on the side of avoiding the extreme that is more opposed to the mean, we have a better chance of hitting the mean. The passage also implies that Diogenes knows that his behavior is a bit more extreme than is necessary to hit the mark. This means that one could become wealthy from Diogenes (learn from him) and live in a less extreme way. Doing so might hit the true note and not the note that Diogenes placed above the true note. He spends no time on metaphysics. He focuses on ethics. He harkens back to Socrates and Antisthenes. He is described as Socrates gone crazy.

He embraced hardship and lived without creature comforts. He had a cloak, which he used as bedding. He lived in a large water jug. He lived on the streets of Athens with the dogs at the shrines and in the marketplace. He had no house, no stockpile, and no other significant possessions. He aimed to rid himself of all unnecessary objects. When he saw that he could drink out of his hands instead of using a cup, he rid himself of the cup. Today, we would call him "jobless," "homeless," and "a public nuisance." Diogenes' way of life, Cynicism, is by choice. Though Socrates had a home, Antisthenes followed by abandoning a home, and Diogenes abandoned almost all possessions. Diogenes seeks out hardship. He asked for things from statues to practice being rejected. He withstood the cold without complaint. He purposefully brought hardship on himself. He does not think that money is a good or that pleasure is a good.

Diogenes thinks that the good life is found in a natural (*phusis*) life and not a conventional (*nomos*) life. He distinguishes between the two parts of the *phusis* vs. *nomos* debate that was so frequent in dialogues between Socrates and the sophists. Let us recall that the sophists tend to think that *phusis* is the measure, but Socrates holds that *nomos* is the measure. Diogenes goes back to nature, but not back to the Homeric idea of the good person. Diogenes goes back to nature by living as he does and by openly rejecting the norms of the city. He seems to test the taboo norms. He masturbated in public. He had sex in public. He ate food that was offered to the gods at a temple. Just think, one could be walking to the marketplace and be verbally accosted by Diogenes. One might be subject to the sight of Diogenes engaging in sexual satisfaction. One might go to the temple and make an offering only to find Diogenes eating the offerings or sleeping on the steps. You might think that the Athenians despised him. They did not, since they erected statues of him and revered him. He must have done what he did in a way that was convincingly philosophical. He must have been able to justify his outrageous behavior, testing of taboos, and accosting city dwellers, or the Athenians would have exiled or killed him. If Socrates corrupted the youth, then we need a stronger term for what Diogenes did to the youth through his associations. Anyone could have argued that Diogenes destroyed the youth by his influence. No one drafted an indictment. He was honored after his death.

7.3 Epicurus and Epicureanism

Epicurus (341–271 BCE) was born on Samos, an island off the coast of Asia Minor in Ionia. Samos was wealthy with much trade and a reputation for luxuries. His father, Neocles, was an Athenian citizen. After Alexander the

Great died, the Athenian settlers were forced to leave Samos. Neocles went to Colophon, a city on the Ionian mainland north of Samos. When Epicurus was 18 years old, he went to do his military and civil service in Athens. After his service in Athens, he joined his father in Colophon. There he started teaching. He later went north to the island of Lesbos in the city of Mytilene to establish his own school. From there he went to Lampsacus near Troy, north of Lesbos on the mainland. There he also founded a school. At the age of 34, he returned to Athens and founded his school south of Athens' city walls between it and Piraeus (*c.* 307/6 BCE). He stayed there and taught in his "Garden" for the rest of his life. He died in 271 BCE, handing the Garden and house over to Hermarchus to continue the school.

Epicurus started his studies in philosophy at the age of 14. Apparently, he was dissatisfied with his schoolmaster's inability to explain "chaos" in Hesiod's works. So he turned to philosophy for answers. Other reports tell us that Epicurus was a schoolmaster before turning to philosophy. Either way, Epicurus turned from traditional schooling to study philosophy to find answers to cosmological questions. He possibly turned first to Platonism in Samos through an association with Pamphilus. He then turned to the works of Democritus the atomist, possibly through an association with Nausiphanes. Eventually, he denounced the teachings of Nausiphanes. Over time, he added to his focus on atomism and focused also on ethics. His efforts in founding schools in Mytilene and Lampsacus must have had some success; they emboldened him to do likewise in Athens. There were already two major schools of philosophy in Athens, Plato's Academy and Aristotle's Lyceum, and the city was the center of Greek philosophy. When Epicurus founded his school, the Academy was headed by Plato's third successor, Polemon. The Lyceum was headed by Theophrastus at the time, though it did close for a year in 306 BCE. Epicurus' return to Athens to establish a rival school of philosophy was audacious.

The school that he founded, the Garden, was unlike the other two schools of philosophy in Athens. It probably did not offer a curriculum to be learned or lectures to be studied. Epicurus was a prolific author. We have a few letters that he wrote to his mother and his friends. We also have his "Principal Doctrines," a list of 40 central doctrines. Thanks to the discovery of the Herculaneum papyri in the eighteenth century, we also have the charred remains of fragments from Epicurus' text *On Nature*. Lucretius' *On the Nature of Things* is our most valuable secondary resource. Yet the letters and *Principal Doctrines* that we have are invaluable, since Epicurus wrote them himself, and they hold a summary of his philosophical views. It is rare for us to have such documents from any ancient Greek philosopher, and they compensate somewhat for the absence of his voluminous other writings. Despite his expansive writings, it is unlikely that the Garden consisted of a close study of Epicurus' texts. Instead, the Garden was a meeting place for friendship and conversation. The school stood physically outside of Athens. Epicurus urged withdrawing from politics and civic life. This location represents a physical and conceptual separation from the politics and civic interactions of Athens. This is shocking, since so much of Athenian philosophy and identity was found in their political organizations and their participation in civic affairs. As a citizen of Athens, Epicurus' rejection of civic affairs was antithetical to Athenian values. His school was radical in other ways. He allowed anyone to spend time in the Garden. He admitted slaves and women to the Garden. Though he was not the first to admit women (Plato's Academy was also reputed to have admitted some women), he was the first to admit slaves. The egalitarian nature of admittance into his school represented a rejection of Athenian norms. Spending time in the Garden with friends discussing philosophy does sound like a pleasurable experience. Epicurus loved his followers and they loved him.

Before we turn from Epicurus' biography to his philosophy, let us confront the term "Epicurean" in its contemporary connotations. Contemporarily, the term refers to hedonistic indulgence of all sorts. An Epicurean feast involves overindulgence of food. An Epicurean lifestyle involves wild indulgence in sensual pleasure of all kinds, food, sex, and drink to start with. This impression of Epicurean philosophy goes all the way back to its founding in the Garden. Back then there were accusations of overindulgence, sexual orgies, and pleasure-seeking in all its forms. Even a cursory examination of Epicurus' philosophy shows that this contemporary impression and the ancient rumors are not accurate. Though Epicurus is a hedonist, his philosophy aims at imperturbability or *ataraxia*. The pursuit of certain sorts of pleasures is a means to achieve a condition of well-being. There were other philosophical approaches to hedonism available at the time. The Cyrenaics were hedonists. Their founder was Aristippus, an associate of Socrates. For the Cyrenaics, the pleasure at hand was worth more than the distant pleasure. One particular point of contention concerned the import of physical pains in relation to mental pains. The Cyrenaics took physical pains as more valuable than mental pains. Epicurus took mental pains as more valuable than physical pains. The Cyrenaics did not think that happiness (*eudaimonia*) was an ethical good; they sought pleasure in its most immediate expression as a moral good. Epicurus did not think that maximal immediate pleasure was a good. Epicurus offers a tripartite division of philosophy into the subjects of *physics*, *canon*, and *ethics*. They do not study dialectic, since they take it to be unnecessary. The physics (*phusis*) part of his philosophy is his atom-istic account of nature. His physics also covers metaphysics. He adopts the Parmenidean Constraint that nothing comes from nothing and he violates Parmenides' monism by holding that there is a void.

7.3.1 Physics, Canon, and Ethics

7.3.1.1 Physics

The *physics* (*phusis*) adopts and innovates the atomism of Leucippus and Democritus, though Epicurus might have denied that Leucippus existed. Atomism holds that there are only atoms and void. Atoms (*atomos*) are what-is and void is what-is-not. The term "*atomos*" means uncut, uncuttable, or indivisible. Epicurus' atoms are unchangeable. There are an unlimited (*apeiron*) number of atoms, though there is a limit to the size of them. There cannot be an atom the size of the universe that is not big enough for us to perceive with our senses. Yet the objects we do perceive are comprised of atoms, and the compound objects have some things in common with atoms. The atoms are composed of matter. Atoms have magnitude, but they are not comprised of anything that can come apart. The void is unlimited (*apeiron*) in the expanse. Epicurus argues that there must be a void, since otherwise there would be no space in which the atoms can move. If all space were full of atoms, there would be no motion. Epicurus' physics does not just cover physics, it also covers metaphysics. Atoms do not contain a void and there are no atoms in a void. A void is the space between the atoms. The atoms are always in motion. Epicurus is concerned with setting a minimal size. He holds that the atoms have spatial parts, but the parts are indivisible. These parts are the minima of measurement. He aims to avoid the paradoxes generated by the infinite divisibility of space.

The atoms are grouped together into objects that display themselves as images. They become entangled with each other such that like atoms become entangled with like atoms. Epicurus puts it this way, "when by hit-ting (*tunkhosi*) they are entangled."[3] The first meaning of the term "*tunkhosi*" is to hit, but its secondary meaning is to meet by chance. So Epicurus may mean that the atoms become entangled by chance. Aristotle uses the term "*tunkhosi*" with reference to "luck." The basic concept is that the event did not happen as planned. Aristotle's concept of luck does not instantiate

---

[3] My translation, Diogenes Laertius, *Lives of Eminent Philosophers*, R.D. Hicks trans. (Cambridge: Harvard University Press, 1931), X.43.

randomness into the *Kosmos*; it refers to a person engaging in a task but having another task come unexpectedly. When we apply Epicurus' concept to the *Kosmos*, it refers to events that are not planned or determined. With just atoms and a void, it is tempting to think that Epicurus adopted a deterministic system. He does not say that the *Kosmos* is determined. His use of the term "*tunkhosi*" allows for, but does not require, non-determined events. Epicurus holds that when like atoms become entangled with like atoms, they are contained in an object large enough for us to perceive. Some atoms are of a certain sort to form a "film" (*tupos*), image, or idol around collections of atoms. The film contains atoms that are like each other. Through collisions in the void, like atoms sometimes go into a particular film. At times, atoms leave that film. The atoms move at the speed of thought, colliding by chance with other atoms.

The atoms have the primary qualities of shape, weight, and size. These properties do not change. Properties of the atoms that seem to change, such as motion, color, smell, flavor, sound, and temperature, are not features of the atoms themselves.[4] The changeable properties arise from the entangled compound. Epicurus mentions the secondary properties of smell, color, sound, and taste. The qualities of the compound objects are accidental properties that change through time. Sensation accurately perceives these accidental properties and their changes over time. There is no absolute reference to the direction of the motion of an atom. Up and down are relational references in a *Kosmos* considered in a certain orientation. Epicurus holds that there is not just one *Kosmos* in the infinite void; there are infinitely many *Kosmoi*. Atoms move with equal speed, whether heavy or light, in the void. The void offers no resistance. An atom could travel an infinite distance in any direction. The atoms travel at different speeds and motions because they collide with each other or become entangled. Their weight does not alter their velocity. Even when entangled they can achieve great speed by oscillating rapidly. Objects vary in weight because the atoms are of different weights. Different atoms have different densities.

7.3.1.2 Canon

The *canon* (*kanonikos*) accounts for epistemology through perception. The "*kanonis*" is a ruler and it metaphorically refers to a standard of measure. His canonic philosophy offers an account of the standard of measure. The

---

[4] Diogenes Laertius, *Lives of Eminent Philosophers*, R.D. Hicks trans. (Cambridge: Harvard University Press, 1931), X.55.

standards of truth are sensations (*aistheseis*), preconceptions (*prolepseis*), and feelings (*pathai*). In sensation, there is no rational element. Reason depends entirely on sensation. There is no memory in sensation. *Sensations* are the stripped-down experience of atoms colliding with the body. So all sensations are real events and true. There are no exceptions. When we have two different sensations from the same sense organ, we cannot use one of them to refute the truth of the other. They are equally true. When we have two sensations from two different sense organs, we cannot use one of them to refute the other. They are equally true. The concern for Epicurus is that if we pick one sensation to refute another, the standard of truth cannot be a sensation. We have sensations of color, odor, taste, sound, and solidity. These qualities are not in the atoms. They are in the aggregate arrangement of the atoms in the film. They arise from the relation between the effluences of atoms from the object to the sensory organ of the perceiver. Epicurus insists that the sensations are true, not because they are features of the atoms but because they are facts about the relation of the sense organ and the effluences of the object. If we reject some sensations, we will have undermined the truth of sensation as a measure of truth. No sensation has any less credence than any other. In fact, all that we experience, think, opine, dream, or imagine is from sensation.

Preconceptions are right opinions or apprehensions formed by the memory of repeated presentations of an object. We often see men, for example, and we come to have a preconception of the universal idea of man. In this way, we can see a man as a member of a universal class that covers all men. The objects denoted by universal terms, such as man, horse, or cow, are learned by the preconception of the many individual objects through repeated experience. When we judge that a certain object is a man, we are making a judgment about the relation between the preconception and the sensed object. The opinion that an occurrent object is a man is a judgment that the object is an instance of a preconception of man. Opinions about the relation between a preconception and an occurrent object must be confirmed to determine the truth of the opinion. In this way, opinions about preconceptions in relation to an object must await confirmation. The opinion may be true or false, though the preconception is always true. The opinion is true when confirmed and false when disconfirmed.

The feeling is amalgamated into two types: pleasure and pain. From pleasure and pain, we can choose to pursue an object or avoid it. No feeling can undermine the truth of another feeling. No sensation or preconception can undermine the truth of a feeling. All feelings are true and on an equal footing with sensations and preconceptions. The canon forms the measure of truth through sensations, preconceptions, and feelings. All these sources of truth are equally legitimate. One sensation cannot undermine another, nor can a sensation undermine the truth of a preconception or the truth of a feeling. The same relation holds for preconceptions and feelings. All three members of the canon are true. Falsehood enters only in our opinions and judgments about the sources of truth.

7.3.1.3 Ethics

The *ethics* (*ethos*) of Epicurus' tripartite division offers an account of choice (*airesis*). Here we move from the physical and metaphysical account in the physics, through the epistemological account in the preconceptions, to a normative account in the ethics. Now Epicurus addresses what is good or bad, what is choice-worthy or not. Sensation determines the choice, he thinks, since we are entirely dependent on sensation. Our preconceptions and feelings are determined by sensation. Our thoughts, opinions, and judgments are determined by sensation, pursuit, and avoidance. We go after or flee actions and objects as we are informed by sensations, preconceptions, feelings, opinions, judgments, objects, and actions. The sensations, preconceptions, feelings, opinions, and judgments are the proximate causes of choice. Epicurus is a hedonist; he holds that pleasure is the moral good. Every preference should aim to secure health and a tranquil mind. The aim is to rid oneself of pain and fear.

Epicurus holds that there are two main types of desires: natural and empty. There are two types of natural desires, natural and necessary natural. The natural desires are unnecessary, since all they add is a variety of pleasures and not an increase in pleasure. The necessary natural desires are required by the body to live, to be happy, or to be rid of want. The only time we should seek pleasure is when we are in pain by the need for necessary natural desires. Epicurus holds that pleasure is both the ruler (*arche*) and the end (*telos*) of a good life. Pleasure and the aversion to pain are the objects of every choice. Not every pleasure is a choice that is worthy for Epicurus. Any pleasure that involves or entails a greater amount of discomfort should be avoided. Though Epicurus holds that all pain is bad, some pain involves or entails a greater amount of pleasure. Some pleasures damage health and are not to be chosen. Overindulgence in alcohol is pleasurable in the short term but damaging to health in the long run. Getting treatments at the doctor is often painful, but such treatments enhance health. Some pains enhance health and are to be chosen. So not all pleasures are to be chosen and not all pains are to be avoided. The goal is to gain independence from external objects. When we are thirsty, water satisfies us fully. When we are hungry, basic food satisfies us fully. Epicurus urges us to satisfy our pains of hunger through objects that are easy to get and ready at hand. We are to avoid empty pleasures, such as exotic drink or food, because they involve hardship to procure and lead to more pain in their absence. If one insists on fine wine when thirsty, one brings on more pain than the pleasure involved in quenching one's thirst. Common foods that are readily available give as much pleasure as expensive and exotic foods. We should train our desires to go after simple and inexpensive food and drink. This also frees us from the fear that we might not be able to procure the exotic items.

The Cyrenaics were hedonists that sought to get as much pleasure as possible. They indulged in all pleasures, but prized the physical pleasures. They also hold that bodily pains are worse than mental pains. They do not admit that there are mental pains. Epicurus rejects their approach. He holds that there are two different types of pleasures. He calls the pleasures of the body active (*kinesis*) pleasures. He calls the pleasures of the mind static (*katastema*) pleasures. He holds that static pains are worse than active pains. Pleasure is not a positive state that we should pursue. The good life is not a life of piling up as much pleasure as possible. For Epicurus, pleasure is just the absence of pain in the body and mind. The Epicureans sought a sober life and freedom from mental anguish. Living this way instills prudence (*phronesis*). This virtue is the basis of all other virtues, such as honor and justice. So pursuing necessary natural desires ends the pain of want, allows for prudence, and leads to the other virtues. We can now see why the Epicureans sought to not fall in love, to not marry, or to not have children. All these things require attachments to external objects and involve more pain than pleasure. Friendship is important, not in itself, but as a means to protect against bad fortune in the future. Friendship also allows one to look back on time spent together and gain pleasure from such memories.

There are two primary causes of mental pain, the fear of cosmic events and the fear of death. The fear of cosmic events is alleviated by the atomic account of the *Kosmos* and by recognizing that for many physical events, there is more than one explanation. People often fixate on a particular explanation when others are equally justified by observations. Epicurus urges us to allow for multiple explanations for phenomena when the plain facts are not decisive for one over the other. When we fixate on a single possible cause of phenomena, we often descend into fear and hopelessness. There may be several causes of phenomena and several explanations. By recognizing that phenomena can occur from several causes, we can better achieve a tranquil mind. Many natural philosophers imply that the *Kosmos* is determined. Epicurus thinks that this causes fear in people, since they think that they are powerless to alter their fate. Epicurus responds that there is chance (*tukhe*) in the *Kosmos*. He does not mean that we can make every effort to live well and have it all undone by chance. He means that our actions are not determined; they are free. Chance allows for free action and makes living well within our power. Since our actions are free, we are subject to praise and blame.

The atomic account of the *Kosmos* also offers freedom from the fear of death. Epicurus' famous saying that "Death is nothing to us" has a nice play on words.[5] The phrase means that death is of no concern to Epicurus. The saying also aptly describes what Epicurus thinks death is: it is nothing. When the atoms that make the body disperse at the time of death, the person no longer has sensation or thought. The person ceases to exist, though the atoms continue to exist. After death, there is no longer a person to sense. Death is a state of nothingness. So there is nothing to fear since death is not a state of being for the person.

There is a singular goal of Epicurus' ethic. We are to reach a state of imperturbability (*ataraxia*). The root of the term "*tarache*" is trouble, disorder, or confusion. The alpha privative at the start of the word means "not." So the term means not troubled, disordered, or confused. It is tempting to think of *ataraxia* as indifference, since to no longer be troubled by anything seems to entail that one no longer cares about anything. Epicurus cares about certain things very much, though he does not care for physical objects overmuch. His atomism frees him from superstition and fear of cosmic events and death. His sensations, preconceptions, and feelings guide him to the truth. He is content with whatever food is easy to procure, feeling as satisfied as anyone eating more exotic food and drink. He spends his time conversing with friends in the Garden. Epicurus is strict about the basic beliefs of his philosophy. He is strict in directing how a person values the objects in the world and how he interacts with objects. It takes more effort to try to achieve *ataraxia* than it does to maintain it. It aims to be engaged and mindful but is effortless.

It was customary to put the canonic part with the physical part. The canonic part was to offer the yardstick of interpretation and the physical part was to offer the account of atomic compounds coming to be and perishing. Epicurus would like to derive his ethics from his physics, or to derive his ethics from both his canon and physics. The relation between physics

---

[5] Diogenes Laertius, *Lives of Eminent Philosophers*, R.D. Hicks trans. (Cambridge: Harvard University Press, 1931), 124.

and ethics, however, is not necessary in any way. The canonic subject of philosophy is meant to establish the connection between physics and ethics. Since the relation between them is contingent, establishing a necessary relation is an overly ambitious task. The justification for the ethical system cannot be established from the other two parts of his system; it must come from within the ethical part itself.

Epicurus had a set of master (*kurios*) maxims that he urged his students to memorize. Diogenes Laertius offers 40 of them.[6] In these maxims, we find many of the key ideas that we already encountered in our discussion of the physics, canon, and ethics, for instance, the claim that death means nothing to Epicurus and that pleasure is just the removal of pain. There are some notable claims in the maxims. They make it clear that one goal of Epicurus' philosophy was to free people from superstition about the *Kosmos* and the gods. There is no such thing as justice or injustice without covenants between people. Justice is found in what is mutually beneficial to both parties. Injustice is not bad in itself. It is bad only for its consequences. Laws that do not serve the expediency of both parties are not just. Turning to pleasure, there is no increase in pleasure after the pain of want is removed. So fine foods are no more pleasurable than basic foods. All that fine foods add is variation in pleasure and not a greater amount of pleasure. Turning to sensation, if you reject all sensations, you have no standard for judgment, in which case you have no basis to determine that a judgment is false. If you reject any single sensation, then you reject one sensation on the authority of another. If you are correct, then sensation is not authoritative. So, Epicurus holds, you will undermine the legitimacy of all sensations.

7.3.2 Lucretius as Epicurean

We are fortunate to have Diogenes Laertius' record of Epicurus' letters. The letters are a summary of Epicureanism from the founder himself. They represent his teachings in the garden, where friends conversed soberly with friends. Everyone was welcome, rich men, poor men, enslaved men, and women. All were welcome. His Garden was not a drunken orgy, as some at the time claimed. On the contrary, it was a place of moderation, simple pleasures, and friendship. The other main source of Epicurus' beliefs is an Epicurean explaining Epicureanism. Lucretius offers an account of

---

[6] Diogenes Laertius, *Lives of Eminent Philosophers*, R.D. Hicks trans. (Cambridge: Harvard University Press, 1931), 139–154.

Epicureanism in *De Rerum Natura*. Lucretius (*mortem*, 50 CE) predates Diogenes Laertius (c. 200 CE) by well over a 100 years. In Lucretius' writings, we have a more developed trinity in the physics, canon, and ethics. Epicurus puts his own twist on atomism, and Lucretius puts his own stamp on our understanding of Epicureanism. We start his account of Epicurean physics, and then we examine the canon and the ethics.

7.3.2.1 Physics

Physics is the first topic that Lucretius discusses in detail in his poem. He offers a deeper account of the *Kosmoi* and the *apeiron* of the void. He moves between the physics and the canon without distinction between the two. In this way, they come to form one topic. Lucretius argues that the void is confirmed by the different weights of objects that occupy the same amount of space. A certain size piece of iron and the same size piece of wood have different weights. The wood is lighter because, the Epicureans argue, it has more void in it than the iron. The one is more densely packed than the other. There is no time in the *Kosmos*; it is sensed through perception. Epicurus was clear to say that there is no absolute orientation of the *Kosmoi*. For Epicurus, all references to direction are purely relational. Up and down and east and west are not objective features of the *Kosmos*. So there is no worry that all the atoms will fall to some lowest point in the *Kosmos*. There is no lowest point. Instead, the atoms hit each other as they happen to hit each other, and they become entangled in the same way.

Lucretius has a different account. Lucretius is the only source to integrate the "swerve" to Epicurus' account of the atom. Other later writers mention and assume the swerve, but do not explain it. Lucretius says that, according to Epicurus, as the atoms fall downward through the void, they go straight down. Epicurus does say that the atoms fall downward in a *Kosmos*. Along their way, Lucretius makes innovations in Epicureanism by claiming that atoms swerve from their path at undetermined times and places.[7] The concern is that if all the atoms fall through the void straight down as if they were drops of rain, there would be no collisions among the atoms. If there is no collision, then there is no "blow" or wind to cause the

---

[7] Lucretius, *De Rerum Natura* or *On the Nature of Things*, W.H.D. Rouse trans., revised by Martin Ferguson Smith (Cambridge: Harvard University Press, 1992), Bk. II, ii.217–219.

beginnings of the *Kosmos*, in which case no compounds of atoms would have come into being. The swerve is very slight, just so much as to make the atoms go sideways.

The Epicureans employ empirical arguments conducted through sensation, preconceptions, and feelings. Their favorite form of argument is the indirect argument. A direct argument offers reasons for an affirmative conclusion. An indirect argument establishes its conclusion by assuming the negation. Here we show that the opposite of our thesis entails a contradiction. The contradiction shows that anything follows from the assumption. Here is the form of the argument to conclude *p*:

Premise 1	~*p*
Premise 2	If ~*p* then *q*
Premise 3	If ~*p* then ~*q*
Premise 4	*q* and ~*q*
Conclusion	*p*

There is an intuitive way to derive the contradiction. The argument assumes the opposite of what it concludes. It shows that if the assumption is true, then a certain proposition (*q*) is entailed. It also shows that if the assumption is true, then not *q* follows. The argument has now derived a contradiction, *q* and not *q*. So the assumption not *p* must be false. The argument concludes *p*. This is the basic form of an indirect proof.

The Epicureans, for example, argue to the conclusion that nothing comes from nothing. They support this view by assuming that the opposite is true. Suppose that something can come from nothing. It follows that anything can come from nothing. It follows from these two premises that anything could come to be at any time or place. So an apple tree could come from an acorn, or the apple tree could just come to be from nothing. Yet this conclusion is in clear contradiction with the facts. We do not find that things just come to be or that living things make different living things. So something cannot come from nothing. To put it another way, nothing comes from nothing. In more formal terms, if something can come from nothing, then anything would come from anything or nothing at any time or place. Anything does not come from anything at any time or place. So something cannot come from nothing. The indirect proof of the Epicureans is a circumlocution. It is more complicated than *modus tollens*. It reduces the alternative position to the absurd. There is a more detailed account of the argument. It holds:

Argument	Form	Example
Premise 1	~p	Something can come from nothing
Premise 2	If ~p then q	If something can come from nothing, then anything can come from anything at any time
Premise 3	If q then r	If anything can come from anything at any time, then we sense objects coming from nothing
Premise 4	r	We sense objects coming from nothing
Premise 5	~r	We do not sense objects coming from nothing
Premise 6	~r and r	We do not sense objects coming from nothing and we do sense objects coming from nothing
Conclusion	p	Something cannot come from nothing

The first premise, not p, assumes the negation of the goal p. The second and third premises establish conditional implications from the not p assumption. Premise 4 is a sub-conclusion from premises one through three. Premise 5 is a fact, for the Epicureans, of sensation, perception, feeling, opinion, and judgment. The implications of not p generate a contradiction. So p must be true. The Epicureans employ this form of argument on a broad range of topics.

7.3.2.2 Canon

Lucretius offers reasons to think that nature exerts power by invisible means. The wind moves objects without being seen. Sound carries without the object making the sound or the sound being seen. Odors work in the same way. Clothes hung outside collect dew, though no water was visible. A ring on the finger smooths and wears down imperceptibly from one moment to the next. Many plants grow imperceptibly but slowly. These are all reasons to hold that nature functions through unseen atoms. Time is a feature of our sensations and not the *Kosmos* itself.

The mind and spirit are bodies of the finest, smallest, smoothest, and roundest atoms. The mind is located at the head and the spirit is in the chest. We should not take the locations of the mind and spirit too narrowly, since they both spread through the entire body. The mind functions as intelligence and understanding. The spirit functions through fear and confidence. They are interlaced in the body and they move the body immediately. The mind and spirit differ, but it is not clear how they differ. At times, Lucretius shifts from mind and spirit as if they are interchangeable. They are similar in the shape, size, and swiftness of the atoms. Though they differ, they are bound together and have one nature. They are similar in their interaction with the body. Lucretius distinguishes the mind from the spirit in a way that makes it difficult to disentangle the two. The mind is atoms that have the qualities of water and honey. The water feature of the mind is in the ability to move throughout all the parts of the body, through the blood, muscles, and smallest parts of the body. It permeates everywhere in the body. The mind is also like honey in its internal stickiness or cohesion as a conglomeration of atoms. The mind spreads through the body as water saturates what it contacts, and the mind holds together like honey. The spirit permeates every part of the body, all the veins, blood vessels, and extremities of the body. It is more like air, breath, or vapor. So we have water, honey, heat, air, and vapor. The spirit is like heat and air, but the mind is like water and honey. Lucretius holds that the spirit animates the body and the mind dictates movement in the body. Though Lucretius says that mind and spirit do not have weight, he cannot be consistent in holding this. All atoms have weight.

Lucretius holds that the mind has four parts. We just saw breath, heat, and air. We need another part, he argues, since none of the parts, alone or together, can account for sensation, thought, and feeling. Lucretius tells us that heat and breath are the initiating features of spirit and mind in a body. He says that when these parts leave the body and the last air is breathed out, the body is dead. The missing part accounts for sensation, thought, and feeling. This part has no name, but it functions to produce sensation, thought, feeling, and movement in the body. Other authors attest to this fourth element and to its namelessness.

We saw that Epicurus is an atomist, and since there are only atoms and a void, he explains perception by reference to atoms. The atoms from objects collide with our sensory organs and cause a sensation. As atoms move out of films, they strike our eyes, nose, or any of the other senses. Small atoms strike our minds in sleep, such that dreams are caused in the same way as hearing. All sensation is caused by the collision of atoms. Even our thoughts of the gods are caused by the extremely fine atoms of the gods. Epicurus holds that the gods live in the rarefied void among the *Kosmoi*. The soul, likewise, is corporeal. It is fine atoms dispersed through the entire frame. Epicurus holds that non-corporeal things cannot act on corporeal things. If the soul is non-corporeal, it cannot act or be acted upon. Yet the soul does act and is acted upon. So the soul is corporeal. The mind is an additional part with finer atoms than the soul. It moves the body with the most directness and speed. Epicurus holds that you can lose part of your body without losing any part of the soul or mind.

The gods are entangled atoms of the finest shape, matter, and size. They dwell between the *Kosmoi* in undisturbed tranquility. The effluences from them cause perceptions in us of them, often in dreams. The gods do not interfere with human events. They do not cause harm to the *Kosmoi*. They are eternally blissful and undisturbed by Kosmic events. They are composed of the finest atoms. These atoms strike us constantly, but we perceive them only when we are asleep or tranquil. The impressions of the gods are real events caused by the impact of their atoms on our minds. These faint effluences from the gods are as real as the sensory experiences, the preconceptions, and the feelings we have. Epicurus and the Epicureans accept the reality of the gods, but they place the gods as bystanders among the *Kosmoi*.

7.3.2.3 Ethics

The swerve serves another function in Lucretius' account of Epicurus' atomism. If atoms are determined to fall straight down according to nature, then all atoms would pile up at the bottom and all events would be determined by nature. Lucretius argues that this determinism would doom Epicurus' atomism to the deterministic regress of cause. There would be no freedom of movement, no freedom of choice, and no freedom of action. There would be no room for moral responsibility and so no need for ethics. The swerve adds freedom of movement to all living things, Lucretius argues. Freedom of action extends not just to human beings but also to other animals, such as horses. For human beings, the freedom of movement starts with the mind, then moves to the heart, and then spreads to the entire body. Without freedom of the mind and freedom of choice, all movements of the body would be determined. We can see, Lucretius says, that many people are simply led on by their bodily desires and by the force of nature. The freedom of choice in assenting or not to a desire is made possible, he argues, by the swerve that occurs at no determined direction and no determined time. It occurs in the mind through voluntary action.

Lucretius takes on a difficult task. He needs to show that the atomic swerve functions to account for voluntary action. The Latin term translated as "swerve" is *clinamen*, meaning "swerving" or "turning aside." The Greek term that corresponds to it is *klino* meaning to bend, slant, turn, or turn aside. The prefix *para* can combine with *klino* to make *parenklino*, meaning to incline sideways. Lucretius argues that the swerve makes free action possible. He refers to actions done as "*voluntarius*," which translates as "voluntary," "willingly," or even "of free will." Lucretius says that the swerve happens at uncertain times and places, just a little bit, and is so slight that you could just barely call it a change in motion.[8] He shortly thereafter refers to the mind. He claims that the swerve occurs without fixity, but as one's mind moves one. It helps to put the function of the swerve in context. In physics, it provides the justification for the collision of atoms. It does so by introducing an indeterminist movement of atoms. In ethics, the swerve functions to introduce free action through choice. There is no point in urging people to choose this over that if there is no freedom of choice. After all, if there is no freedom of choice, then whether you choose this or that is determined. The lack of freedom of choice undermines the main assumption of ethics: namely, it is possible for you to choose in a way that engenders a better life. The goal of Epicurean philosophy is *ataraxia*, and this would be pointless without freedom of choice. This makes the swerve, or some other justification for free choice, essential to Epicurean philosophy.

---

[8] Lucretius, *De Rerum Natura* or *On the Nature of Things*, W.H.D. Rouse trans., revised by Martin Ferguson Smith (Cambridge: Harvard University Press, 1992), 2.216–224.

8

STOICISM AND SKEPTICISM

8.1 Stoicism

8.1.1 The Stoics

Zeno (c. 334–262 BCE) is the founder of Stoicism. He was from Citium on the island of Cyprus in the eastern Mediterranean. As the story goes, when Zeno was in his early 20s he was in Athens at the ancient equivalent of a bookstore.[1] He came across the *Memorabilia of Socrates*, by Xenophon. After reading the scrolls and becoming fascinated with Socrates, Zeno asked the shop owner where he might meet a man like Socrates, and the owner pointed him to Crates of Thebes. Crates was an understudy of the Cynic Diogenes of Sinope. In this way, Zeno became the pupil of the Cynic Crates. As a Cynic, Crates expected Zeno to live the life and perform socially embarrassing actions. Zeno was unwilling to fully embrace the Cynic's way of life. It seems that Zeno retained his modesty and would not embody the socially shameful lifestyle of the Cynics. He then associated with Stilpo of the Megarian school. The Megarian school was about equidistant between Athens and Thebes. The school was established by Euclides of Megara, an associate of Socrates. After Euclides, Ichthyas became the primary figure of Megarian philosophy and later Stilpo was the central figure of the Socrates-inspired Megarian school. Zeno also associated with Xenocrates of Chalcedon, who was the director of Plato's Academy from about 339 BCE to 314 BCE. Zeno spent about 10 years

---

[1] Diogenes Laertius, *Lives of Eminent Philosophers*, R.D. Hicks trans. (Cambridge: Harvard University Press, 1931), VII.3.

This Is Ancient Philosophy: An Introduction, First Edition. Kirk Fitzpatrick.
© 2024 John Wiley & Sons, Inc. Published 2024 by John Wiley & Sons, Inc.

studying with Stilpo and Xenocrates. After about 20 years of studying with two movements inspired by Socrates, the Cynics, and the Megarians, and a movement still following Plato's philosophy at the Academy, Zeno went his own way.

Zeno spent his time at the painted stoa (*stoa poikile*) or the stoa, for short. There he paced back and forth, as he developed a distinctive school of philosophy. A stoa is a colonnade or portico, an outdoor covered structure dedicated to some god, achievement, or tradition. There were a number of stoa among the municipal buildings and the law court. The painted stoa was among the buildings that centered on the courthouse. Its central locale meant that just about anyone who had business or court proceedings in Athens was in proximity to it. Socrates had previously associated with people just to the side of the municipal complex. At the start, the followers of Zeno were not called "Stoics." They were named eponymously as "Zenonians." As the philosophy found popularity, it expanded beyond one man. Subsequent leaders of the school emerged. Cleanthes (c. 330–232 BCE) led the school, as did Chrysippus (c. 279–206 BCE). As the movement broadened and the philosophy developed, the term "Zenonian" was too restrictive. The movement was better designated by the place where the associates met, the stoa, and thus they came to be known as Stoics.

8.1.2 Stoic Philosophy

Stoic philosophy is divided into three main subject areas: physics, logic, and ethics. Zeno was the first to propose these divisions, followed by Chrysippus.[2] The subjects are more broadly conceived than their contemporary connotations. The subject of physics (*phusis*) includes the study of all physical things, matter, plants, animals, gods, and metaphysics. So, the subject of physics ranges over natural science, theology, and metaphysics. The subject of logic (*logos*) includes not only informal and formal logic but also dialectic, grammar, semantics, syntax, rhetoric, and epistemology. The subject of ethics (*ethos*) covers both normative and applied ethics. Different Stoics list the topics in different orders of priority. Some Stoics name more than three subjects, ranging up to as many as six subjects. Cleanthes, for instance, names the subjects of dialectic, rhetoric, ethics,

---

[2] Diogenes Laertius, *Lives of Eminent Philosophers*, R.D. Hicks trans. (Cambridge: Harvard University Press, 1931), VII.39.

politics, physics, and theology.[3] It is likely that the additional subjects are simply specifications under the three primary headings. We should not take the divisions among the subjects as marking three distinct or isolated topics. The Stoics offer analogies and similes to describe the relations among the different subjects. Some Stoics say that philosophy is like an animal. Physics is like the soul of the animal, logic is like the bones, and ethics is like the flesh.[4] Alternatively, the subjects of Stoicism are like an egg. Physics is like the yolk, ethics is like the white, and logic is like the shell. Alternatively, Stoicism is like a fertile field. Physics is like the soil. Ethics is like the crops, and logic is like the encircling border or fence. Some Stoics begin with logic and move to physics before teaching ethics. Other Stoics begin with ethics and still others begin with physics.[5] Though taking the subjects in a certain order might be didactically advantageous initially, it would not be a sustained approach. The subjects are interrelated and mutually reinforcing. They form a unitary whole. After an initial introduction to Stoicism, the subjects would not be studied independently or in isolation. They would be studied as an organic whole. We must start somewhere. We will work through the subjects beginning with physics, then logic, and ethics, building on the subjects as we go.

8.1.2.1 Physics

We begin with metaphysics. The basic category distinguishes something (*ti*) from non-thing. Plato's universals are non-things. They are not things in any sense of the term. There are different sorts of somethings. Within the category of something are nonphysical things, other things, and physical things. Under the category of nonphysical things are the sayable, void, place, and time. Under the category of other things are fictional objects and geometric objects. These things do not exist, strictly speaking. Instead, they subsist (*huphistasthai*) or stand under existent things. They are something, in some sense, though they are not physical things. The void, for example, surrounds the *Kosmos* but it is not a physical thing. Centaurs, for example, exist as objects of thought, though they do not physically exist.

---

[3] Diogenes Laertius, *Lives of Eminent Philosophers*, R.D. Hicks trans. (Cambridge: Harvard University Press, 1931), VII.41.

[4] Diogenes Laertius, *Lives of Eminent Philosophers*, R.D. Hicks trans. (Cambridge: Harvard University Press, 1931), VII.40.

[5] Diogenes Laertius, *Lives of Eminent Philosophers*, R.D. Hicks trans. (Cambridge: Harvard University Press, 1931), VII.41.

Under the category of physical things are the substrate, the qualified, the disposed, and the relatively disposed. The substrate names substance, being, or existence at its most basic level. The qualified physical things are physical things that take on different qualities. A lump of clay can be molded into the shape of a dog and then remolded into the shape of a horse. The clay dog is a qualified physical thing. The disposed physical things are dispositions of qualified physical things. A person is disposed to walk, understand, or know. The Stoics take the disposition of qualified things to be physical things. The relatively disposed seems to reference relational qualities between or among things, such as being to the right of something or being on top of something. The following chart presents the various *somethings* from left to right.

Prime Genus	Subgenus	Species			
Something	Physical	Substrate	Qualified	Disposed	Relatively disposed[6]
	Nonphysical	Sayable	Void	Place	Time
	Neither	Fictional objects	Geometric objects		

The Stoics reject the Platonic ontology that places universals as the most fully existent things. Though universals are not-something, the Stoics can refer to them as linguistic features of propositions. In this way, universals count as features of language, without also being Platonic ontological substances. They also posit certain things as physical that we would take as nonphysical, such as virtue, knowledge, dispositions, and relations. They posit these things as physical since they can cause physical events.

There is some variance in what would count as a substrate verses a qualified physical something. If we reference primary matter as the substrate, then clay would be a qualified category. If we reference a clay dog, then clay would be the substrate, and the dog would be the qualification. There is a similar variance between the qualified and the disposed. "Understanding" is a qualification of the soul, but the soul is itself a qualification of breath. In this way, understanding can considered to be either a qualified physical thing or a disposed physical thing. This is reminiscent of the same

---

[6] This chart is based on the chart in Long and Sedley, *The Hellenistic Philosophers* (New York: Cambridge University Press, 1987), vol. 2, 163.

phenomena in Aristotle's distinction between genus and species. Dog is a species under the genus of animal, but animal is a species under the genus of living things.

The Stoics hold that there is both mind (*logos*) and nature (*phusis*). They claim that God imbues himself in seminal moisture and breath from which the *Kosmos* comes. He is the "designing fire," the soul, and the logos of the *Kosmos*. He creates the four elements: earth, air, fire, and water. He directs the formation of the world and the eternal life cycle of the *Kosmos*. Though God always is, the world as we know it now is in constant change. Since the Stoics hold that the four elements come to be, the elements cannot be eternal matter. The world goes through a rationally directed cycle from creation through moisture and breath, to organization among the elements into the world, to conflagration and recreation. God is not a bystander of the *Kosmos*. He is an ever-present material and rational agent throughout the *Kosmos*.

For the Stoics, the mind is an *active* force in the *Kosmos* and matter is a *passive* force. Cleanthes held that fire alone has generative or active abilities. Chrysippus added air to the generative elements.[7] He holds that hot breath is generative element. As the Stoics innovated within the canonic principles, they came to hold that fire and air are active elements. Earth and water are passive elements. Though earth and water are passive, they are infused with fire and air. The four elements are not primary matter. The more basic features are hot (fire), cold (air), wet (water), and dry (earth). The concept of breath is subtler than that of hot air. The hot fire is mixed with the cold air and wet water. Breath is a tensioned circle that moves in and out. It is a process that mixes different elements in a cyclical process of expansion and contraction. They apply this process to God, *Kosmos*, soul, and body. We can see that the Stoics blend elements of earlier philosophers. Breath is the oldest meaning of soul (*psuche*). They take mind and connect it to breath. They connect breath to soul, and they connect soul to mind. It is circular in the same way that the *Kosmos* is circular in its cycles.

In opposition to the Epicureans, the Stoics do not think that there is a minima in the measurement of matter, of space, or of time. For the Stoics, there is no minimal division. They admit that, practically, there is a minima in our measurements and in our ability to understand. Nonetheless, they hold that matter, space, and time are infinitely divisible. Some divisions

---

[7] Long and Sedley, *The Hellenistic Philosophers* (New York: Cambridge University Press, 1987), vol. 2., 287.

involve physical things (matter) and others involve mental things (space and time). The Stoics argue for a physical continuum. They do not hold that there is an infinite amount of matter in any slice, or infinite space between two locations, or an infinite amount of time between two timestamps. Consider Zeno's argument for infinite divisibility. If things were infinitely divisible, then there would be no difference in size. We could not say that this something is bigger than that something. Yet, some things are bigger than others. So, things are not infinitely divisible.[8] Epicurus placed void between atoms, and so he did not posit physical contact among atoms. The Stoics hold that there is direct contact among the material mixtures. Any slice that we might make is arbitrary and infinitely divisible for the Stoics. The slice is not infinite in the amount of matter, space, or time.

God or gods cause the *Kosmos*. It comes from fire, grows into a world, and returns to fire. The cycle of the *Kosmos* creation repeats eternally. It repeats in exactly the same way, in every detail, in every cycle. The determinism in Stoicism is extreme. Not only is everything in the *Kosmos* determined by the gods, but everything is also determined to happen repeatedly eternally. The ensouled beings in the *Kosmos* are themselves causes of motions, actions, and events. The *logos* directs the material world, the soul directs the body. In some small way, a human being is a *Kosmos* unto himself, within the *Kosmos*. The Stoics distinguish *preliminary* causes from *auxiliary* causes.[9] The Stoics allow for multiple causes of an event. Fate, or gods, set the events writ large in the world, but other causes are operative in the details. Multiple causes can overlap. The distinction between causes and the positing of multiple causes allows the Stoics to posit "co-fated" events.[10] The determinism of the *Kosmos* is that *Kosmos* is the best that anything can be. There is a range of motion for the soul of human beings that allows them to be preliminary or auxiliary causes of events. In the widest reference, gods are the preliminary cause. In the explanation of actions and events, however, the Stoics invoke the person as a preliminary cause or an auxiliary cause. This is meant to allow for both a determined *Kosmos* and voluntary action.

---

[8] Long and Sedley, *The Hellenistic Philosophers* (New York: Cambridge University Press, 1987), vol. 2., 303.

[9] Long and Sedley, *The Hellenistic Philosophers* (New York: Cambridge University Press, 1987), vol. 2., 342.

[10] Long and Sedley, *The Hellenistic Philosophers* (New York: Cambridge University Press, 1987), vol. 2., 343.

The void is nonphysical and does not exist. It is said to *subsist*. The void surrounds the *Kosmos*. As the *Kosmos* expands and contracts from its center through its cycles, it expands into the void. The void is infinite (*apeiron*). When it expands into the void it occupies what was the void fully. At that point, the somethings have a place, and there is no void in that place. The Stoics do not place void among physical things, they place it on the outside. So, they hold that the *Kosmos* is a plenum full of somethings, which are not atoms moving through a void. What-is is God, a mindful physical organism in an eternal cycle throughout the *Kosmos*. In addition to God, other souls have a source of movement in them. They can act and direct a *logos* from themselves. The individual *logos* is free to act or not. It can accord with the *kosmic logos* or not. Still, there is nothing that happens against the *kosmic logos*.

8.1.2.2 Logic

The subject of Stoic logic is important both for its place in Stoic philosophy as a whole and for its historical innovations in the subject. Stoic logic is divided into two main branches, dialectic and rhetoric. *Dialectic* is the study of what is true, false, and neither.[11] There are two subjects under dialectic, the subjects of discussion and language. The study of language is an analysis of subjects, predicates, and propositions. This also includes the study of informal fallacies. Dialectic is concerned with the things that are signified by language and the language that does the signifying. *Rhetoric* has three main subjects, "deliberative, forensic, and panegyric."[12] So, it is the study of the creation of arguments: the words in arguments, the delivery of arguments, and the analysis of the parts of a speech.[13] To these subjects, some Stoics add epistemology or "the canons" (*kanones*) and definitions. Logic is not simply a tool used in the analysis of physics and ethics; it is more importantly an essential part of Stoic philosophy. Logic connects words, arguments, thoughts, and the objects of thought together into an integrated whole.

---

[11] Diogenes Laertius, *Lives of Eminent Philosophers*, R.D. Hicks trans. (Cambridge: Harvard University Press, 1931), VII.42.

[12] Diogenes Laertius, *Lives of Eminent Philosophers*, R.D. Hicks trans. (Cambridge: Harvard University Press, 1931), VII.43.

[13] Diogenes Laertius, *Lives of Eminent Philosophers*, R.D. Hicks trans. (Cambridge: Harvard University Press, 1931), VII.43.

The impressions lead to thoughts, the thoughts to speech, and the speech expresses the *logos*. The Stoics argue that nonhuman animals have external speech, but no internal speech. Human beings, in contrast, have both internal speech and external speech. Impressions (*phantasia*) are mental imprints like those made in wax.[14] Impressions are the focus of our conscious awareness. We can assent or not to impressions. Sensation (*aisthesis*) is a broad term that applies to the sense organs themselves, the mental apprehension of the sensations from the sense organs, and the application of mental impressions to the senses. So, sense impressions are both physical and mental phenomena. Sense impressions come in degrees of clarity and distinctness.[15] A person can assent or not to a cognitive impression. When one assents to a cognitive impression one has a cognition (*katalepsis*). Sensory impressions are the genesis of thought and speech. This helps us identify the empiricist commitments of Stoicism.[16] As an epistemological bridge between physics and ethics, logic plays an essential part in connecting the physical world to the mental world and the ethical implications therein.

The Stoics include thought and judgment in the subject of logic, since both these play a part in determining what is true. Strictly speaking, the Stoics hold that thoughts and judgments, or mental impressions, are not the sorts of things that can be true or false. "Sayable" (*lektos*) means what can be picked out, or what can be said. As such, they include the sorts of things that can be true, false, or neither. Propositions are the things that can be true or false. By distinguishing the signifier from the signified, the Stoics can distinguish the language from the objects referenced by the language. This relation engenders a *correspondence* theory of truth. Accordingly, a proposition is true if it accurately signifies something in the world. Alternatively, a proposition is false if it does not accurately signify something in the world. There are other uses of speech, such as questions, commands, and prayer, that are neither true nor false.

Stoic logic starts with the analysis of terms, distinguishing terms that can stand as the subject from those that cannot. Here they develop an account

---

[14] Diogenes Laertius, *Lives of Eminent Philosophers*, R.D. Hicks trans. (Cambridge: Harvard University Press, 1931), VII.45.

[15] Long and Sedley, *The Hellenistic Philosophers* (New York: Cambridge University Press, 1987), 239.

[16] Long and Sedley, *The Hellenistic Philosophers* (New York: Cambridge University Press, 1987), 125.

of the five linguistic cases, nominative, accusative, genitive, dative, and vocative. They also distinguish the tenses, present, future, imperfect, and perfect. We retain these designations to this day in our grammatical analysis of languages. The Stoics then move to distinguish certain types of simple propositions, including negation, denial, privation, affirmation, definitive, and non-definitive. An example of the *negation* is "It is not day," and an example of a *double negation* is "It is not not-day." A *denial* has a negative subject; for example, "No one is walking." A *privative* proposition has a negated predicate; for example, "This man is unkind." An *affirmative* has an affirmation in the subject and predicate; for example, "Dion is walking." A *definitive* has a demonstrative pronoun as the subject; for example, "This man is walking." A *non-definitive* has an indefinite pronoun as the subject; for example, "Someone is walking."[17] We can see that these distinctions indicate different states and relations in and between the subject (nominative case) of a proposition and the predicate (accusative, genitive, dative, and vocative cases).

The Stoics then move to an account of complex propositions. They distinguish seven different complex propositions. They identify the conditional, the conjunction, the disjunction (exclusive), the negation, the inferential, the causal, and the more-or-less. The *conditional* has a protasis and an apodosis; for example, "If it is day, then it is light." The *conjunction* is a compound linked with "and"; for example, "It is day and it is light." The *disjunction* employs the term "or," and it is always interpreted as exclusive for the Stoics; for example, "It is day or it is night." The *negation* denies a state of affairs; for example, "It is not day." The *inferential* complex proposition gives a reason to hold that something is the case; for example, "Since it is day, it is light." The *causal* complex proposition claims that because something is the case something else is the case; for example, "Because it is day, it is light." Finally, the *more-or-less* complex proposition claims that something is more the case or less the case; for example, "It is more day than night." The four most important complex propositions, given historical hindsight, are the conditional, the conjunction, the disjunction, and the negation. It seems that the simple propositional negation is the same as the complex propositional negation. It is clear, however, that the Stoics thought of the complex negation as adding the negation in front of the proposition;

---

[17] Diogenes Laertius, *Lives of Eminent Philosophers*, R.D. Hicks trans. (Cambridge: Harvard University Press, 1931), VII.70.

for example, "It is not the case that it is day."[18] Yet, if they do not take the complex negation this way, they cannot distinguish it from the simple negation. The Stoics are specific about the conditions under which the propositions are true or false, but they also include nonlogical features in considering the truth functions of the propositions.[19] We cannot say that they developed truth-functional logic as we know it today, but we can say that they developed an account of the truth functions of certain propositions.[20] They offer a truth-functional analysis of the conditional, the conjunction, the disjunction, and the negation.[21]

The Stoics then move to arguments. The Stoics make an important break from the Aristotelian term "logic." Aristotle focused on terms and analyzed their function in four types of propositions. So, he had just the following four types of propositions: All A are B, No A is B, Some A is B, and Some A is not B. The Stoics do not focus on terms as the building blocks of argument forms. Instead, they focus on propositions as the building blocks of arguments. This is a revolutionary turn. It instigates what we now call "sentential logic." Despite their important differences with Aristotelean logic, the Stoics work with syllogistic arguments. These arguments only have two premises and a conclusion. The Stoics distinguish arguments by their forms, which they call "moods":[22]

Form Name	Example	Valid Form/Mood
Modus Ponens[23]	If it is day, then it is light. It is day. ∴ It is light.[24]	If p then q; p; ∴ q
Modus Tollens	If it is day, then it is light. It is not light. ∴ It is not day.	If p then q; not q; ∴ not p

(Continued)

[18] Diogenes Laertius, *Lives of Eminent Philosophers*, R.D. Hicks trans. (Cambridge: Harvard University Press, 1931), VII.80.
[19] Diogenes Laertius, *Lives of Eminent Philosophers*, R.D. Hicks trans. (Cambridge: Harvard University Press, 1931), VII.74.
[20] A.A. Long, *Hellenistic Philosophy* (Berkeley: University of California Press, 1986), 142.
[21] Long and Sedley, *The Hellenistic Philosophers* (New York: Cambridge University Press, 1987), 211.
[22] Diogenes Laertius, *Lives of Eminent Philosophers*, R.D. Hicks trans. (Cambridge: Harvard University Press, 1931), VII.76.
[23] These are the contemporary names for the arguments.
[24] The symbol "∴" indicates the conclusion.

Form Name	Example	Valid Form/Mood
Negated Conjunction	Not both it is day and it is night. It is day. ∴ It is not night.	Not both p and q; p; ∴ q[25]
Exclusive Disjunction	Either it is day or it is night. It is day. ∴ It is not night.	Either p or q; p; ∴ not q
Disjunctive Syllogism	Either it is day or it is night. It is not night. ∴ It is day.	Either p or q; not q; ∴ not p

They offer these five argument forms, claiming that all arguments can be reparsed into one of the five forms. The Stoics account for additional argument forms. They allow for chains of argumentation. After a propositional syllogistic conclusion is derived, it can be used in subsequent argument, or the premise of that argument can function in a subsequent inference. All subsequent inferences would be reparsed into one of the five forms. In dialectic, these forms are presented in dialogue. One person asks for the assent to the first premise. The two then debate and refine the premise to agree on a premise. Once that is established, they move to the second premise and seek agreement. With the two premises in place, they draw the conclusion(s).

The Stoics inherit the concept of validity from Aristotle. So, the Stoics distinguish the truth of the premises and conclusion from the validity of the argument. They hold that an argument with in fact false premises can be valid. They find validity in the form of a propositional argument. They express validity as the truth functions of the conditional. They employ both logical and empirical considerations to the truth of a conditional. The logical considerations affecting validity are limited to the assumed truth of the premises. Yet, the Stoics also consider the factual truth of the premises. This is an attempt to understand the truth functions of the conditional. The Stoics treat the conditional with a false protasis and a false apodosis as false. This analyzes the conditional as false because the protasis is false. The conditional is challenging, however, since it is true whenever the protasis is false.

---

[25] We can rewrite this form using De Morgan's Law: Either not p or not q; p; ∴ not q.

The only time that it is false is when the protasis is true and the apodosis is false. Their examples make it clear that validity is a relation between premises and conclusion, such that whenever the premises are true the conclusion is not false.

The informal fallacies function in dialectic to alert interloculars about how to challenge the truth of premises and inferred conclusions. The informal fallacies come about by defects in the language and the semantics of the premises, not the form of the propositions. The informal fallacies identified by the Stoics have provocative names, The Veiled Argument, The Horned Argument, The No-Man Argument, The Mowers Argument, and The Heaper Argument.[26] The Horned Argument refers to an example; "You lost your horns?" Since one has no horns, both "yes" and "no" seem to be correct answers. The Heaper Argument refers to chains of argumentation that trade on vagueness and ambiguity. Bit by bit the argument goes astray. We do not have detailed accounts of all the fallacies. We are missing many texts in the historical record. The importance of distinguishing informal errors from formal errors is an important distinction that goes back to Aristotle. The Stoics make use of this distinction in dialectic to stop the chain of argumentation from an interlocular, either at the premise or the inference. When a person engages in dialectic, one should be on guard for the fallacies in dialogue.

8.1.2.3 Ethics

Stoic ethics has received the most attention in the contemporary philosophical and popular discussions of the topic. We have so many texts on ethics and such complete texts from the late period of Stoicism, that it makes sense that the current discussions tend to focus on ethics. The Stoics give sage ethical advice, in quotable quotes. The quotes can function as a self-help guide to ridding oneself of fear, anxiety, and disharmony. Stoic ethics can function in this way, but it is so much more. Different Stoics divided the subject of ethics into different topics. Chrysippus offers these topics:[27]

---

[26] Diogenes Laertius, *Lives of Eminent Philosophers*, R.D. Hicks trans. (Cambridge: Harvard University Press, 1931), VII. 44.

[27] Diogenes Laertius, *Lives of Eminent Philosophers*, R.D. Hicks trans. (Cambridge: Harvard University Press, 1931), VII.84.

Stoic Ethics: Chrysippus' 8 Topics	
1. Impulse	5. The end
2. Good and bad things	6. Primary value and actions
3. Passions	7. Proper functions
4. Virtue	8. Encouragements and discouragements

The topics are major subjects in Stoic ethics. Impulse is the motion in action of the soul. Good and bad things are the things that contribute to virtue. Passions are excessive emotional states. The topic of virtue distinguishes virtue and vice. The end concerns the harmonization of the individual *logos* with the *logos* of the *Kosmos*. Value and actions apply the physics and logic in action. The proper functions are the duties we have as children of parents, parents, members of a family, and all the functions that come with life in a community. Encouragements and discouragements cover the training of our assent to impressions. Many other Stoics are said to have followed Chrysippus by distinguishing these same topics. Some Stoics add an additional topic, *indifferent* things, neither beneficial nor harmful.[28]

Chrysippus clearly innovated these topics, since the earlier Stoics, Diogenes tells us, held a more austere division of topics. There are things that benefit our strivings toward virtue and things that harm our striving toward virtue. Seneca tells us that the Stoics distinguish three main topics in ethics. The first concerns assessing the value of each thing. The second concerns the acquisition of control and balance of impulse. The third concerns harmonizing the impulses, actions, and self.[29] Epictetus divides the topic into three: (1) desires and aversions, (2) proper function, and (3) infallibility in acts of assent. He tells us that the first topic is the most important. The reason is that it concerns passions or strong emotions. The second topic is second in importance. It concerns harmonizing our pursuit and avoidance with our duties or proper functions. The third topic comes after attending to the first two. This topic involves training oneself to virtuously assent to sensory and cognitive impressions. For example, when you have a sense impression of an attractive person but the person is forbidden, do you assent to the impression? When your friend inherits a lot of wealth, do you envy your friend? *Assent* is the acceptance or rejection of a judgment of

---

[28] Long and Sedley, *The Hellenistic Philosophers* (New York: Cambridge University Press, 1987), 354, section 58a.

[29] Long and Sedley, *The Hellenistic Philosophers* (New York: Cambridge University Press, 1987), 344, section 56B.

an impression. It is the rational part of the opposition between *logos* and matter, the active and the passive. A person is a microcosm of the active and the passive in the *Kosmos*. Training ourselves to assent properly to impressions comes only after addressing desire and aversion in relation to our proper function.

There is no single taxonomy of Stoic ethics; it differentiated into the early, middle, and late periods. The tripartite division is useful, since it allows us to organize the numerous topics into broader headings. Along these lines, we can distinguish the broad topics of desire, duty, and assent. The additional topics fall under these three topics:

Stoic Ethics: Topics	
Desire	Impulse
	Passion
	Good and bad things
	Indifferent things
Duty	Primary value and actions
	Proper functions
Assent	Encouragements and discouragements
	Virtue
	The end

This organization allows us to go through the topics as they might be presented in learning the subject of Stoic ethics and when training oneself in virtue. The following discussion moves through the three broad topics in order.

8.1.2.3.1 Desire

The Stoics distinguish different stages in the life of every animal: early, middle, and late.[30] From the start of life, the Stoics argue, the initial impulse of every plant and animal is self-preservation and a consciousness of its own bodily constitution. Nature ties the animal to itself by interlacing the mind with the body. By placing self-preservation as the first impulse, the Stoics reject pleasure as the first impulse. For the Stoics, the body is the appropriate home of the individual mind and the animal cannot be alienated from the body. In a human being, the impulse toward consciousness of

---

[30] Long and Sedley, *The Hellenistic Philosophers* (New York: Cambridge University Press, 1987), 347, section 57b.

the body and self-preservation develops through the stages of life. Initially a human is similar to other animals. As a human being develops, the consciousness and *logos* develop. As reason develops, it sets the rational direction for the person. In a mature human being, reason comes to supplement the initial impulse toward self-preservation. Just as the plant or nonhuman animal can live in harmony with nature by following its natural impulses, the human being can live in harmony with nature by following reason. The impulse is the natural motivating drive; it aims toward things that benefit self-preservation and away from things that harm. This concern is focused on the individual, but it naturally spreads to offspring. Then concern widens, but lessens, to the broader family, the community, and to a much lesser extent to the whole of humanity.

A *passion* (*pathos*) is an excessive impulse. Passions can occur when a desire is frustrated or when one encounters an object one is trying to avoid. Passions, such as envy, jealousy, lamentation, sorrow, tumult, and confusion, interfere with or prevent one from following reason. Since following reason is virtue and wisdom, one's relation to passions is of the utmost importance. The English term "passion" refers to a strong occurrent emotion. The Greek term applies to such states, but for the Stoics it is more specific. It applies to physical and mental impulses that are excessive in relation to the naturally directed impulse. For humans this is the reason or the *logos*. A person can go after what one desires too much, too fast, too hastily. A person can avoid what he desires to avoid too much, too fast, and too hastily. Either way, the person is desiring in excess of what is natural. This can happen with both physical desires and mental judgments. Passions can cause impulses that are irrational. The Stoic concept of irrational desire is not grounded in a distinction among the parts of the soul. It is grounded on the relation between the desire and the proper natural desire.

The *primary passions* that come to a person are appetite (*epithumia*) and fear (*phobos*). Appetite desires to go after what appears to be good and fear desires to avoid what appears to be bad. The *secondary passions* of pleasure and distress are set in reference to the primary passions. Pleasure is the fulfilling of an appetitive desire or the avoidance of a prohibited object. Distress is a failure to fulfill a desire or encountering an object one is trying to avoid. The desires of appetite are an expansion of impulse and the desires of fear are the contraction of impulse. We have three passions to be avoided: appetites, fears, and other excessive desires. The Stoics name three correlating good emotions. Wishing is a rational appetitive desire and it is the counterpart of appetitive passion. Caution is rational avoidance and it is the counterpart of fear. Joy is reasoned enjoyment and it is the counterpart of pleasure (*hedone*). Wishing, caution, and joy are impulses possessed by the virtuous or wise person. The Stoics broaden the scope of wishing, by extending it to friendship, genuine well-wishing, affection, and respect. They expand the scope of caution, by extending it to include reverence and modesty. They expand joy to include delight, amusement, and cheerfulness. Wishing and caution are counterparts to the primary passions and joy is a counterpart to one of the secondary passions. We are missing a counterpart for distress.[31] Apathy (*apatheia*) can fill this gap, since the wise Stoic does not suffer distress. The Stoics distinguish this kind of apathy from the apathy in callousness and relentlessness. The Stoic sage is apathetic but not uninterested or unengaged.

The Stoics hold that good things are beneficial. Bad things are harmful. Nature directs the benefit of plants and animals through their natural impulse of self-preservation and bodily awareness. A person has reason to determine what is the beneficial life. The Stoic move from the benefit of self-preservation to the benefit of a life directed by reason is challenging to square. The benefit of self-preservation is empirically obvious. The benefit of a life directed by reason is always open to dispute. Either the person is preserved or not, but there are always rational arguments for and against the benefit of anything. Bad things are impulses and passions that harm a person. These things are referenced in judgments that are not from rational directives. The Stoics offer a novel definition of the good and the bad by identifying them with the beneficial and the harmful.

The Stoics add to the list of good and bad things, there are also indifferent things. These things are neither good nor bad. The list of indifferent things is worth noting, since many of these things are thought to be good or bad outside of Stoic philosophy:

Indifferent Things	Thesis	Indifferent Things	Antithesis
Life	Strength	Death	Weakness
Health	Wealth	Disease	Poverty
Pleasure	Reputation	Pain	Dishonor
Beauty	Noble birth	Ugliness	Ignoble birth

---

[31] Diogenes Laertius, *Lives of Eminent Philosophers*, R.D. Hicks trans. (Cambridge: Harvard University Press, 1931), VII 116.

This list of indifferent things includes objects that are taken to be good by other philosophical systems. Though Stoicism does not count these objects as good, it does not count them as bad either. Stoicism takes them to be indifferent to goodness. The first topic to notice is the rejection of pleasure, the aim of Epicurean philosophy. They also reject some of the traditional Greek requirements of virtue, beauty, strength, reputation, and noble birth. They also reject a narrow-minded naturalism by rejecting life, health, and pleasure as the good. We could place the indifferent under one of these topics, or add it to Chrysippus' list, to get nine total topics. Indifferent things do fit nicely as an addition to the topic of good and bad things. This addendum would give us the good, the bad, and the indifferent.

8.1.2.3.2 Duty

The subject of duty is established through an examination of values and actions together with proper functions. The Stoics establish their values with reference to the *Kosmos*, which has both a material and rational element. The rational element adds a normative aspect of the *Kosmos*, as a counterpart to the material aspect. The Stoics hold that value is in nature. A valuable life is lived in agreement with the *logos* of nature. The Stoics hold that some things have negative value, that is, the things that are contrary to nature and not in agreement with nature. There are other things, indifferent things, that are neither in agreement with nature nor against nature. The Stoics place indifferent things between the things of value and the things of disvalue. We should go after valuable things, ignore indifferent things, and avoid disvaluable things. The valuable things differ in degree, some valuable things are more valuable than others. This is true also of the disvaluable things. There is no degree of difference among the indifferent things. All things agreeing with nature are to be taken hold of, or accepted, apprehended, and undertaken (*lambano*).[32] The apprehension is a recognition of the value set by the *logos* of nature and an undertaking to act accordingly.

"Proper function" is a translation of *kathekon*, which can also be translated as "arriving at agreement with certain other persons or things." The Stoics are concerned with coming into agreement with nature. So, proper function concerns one's place in the kosmic order. The concept extends to all things. The nonliving things, the objects that have no movement, are determined by nature to be in agreement with nature. Living things have a

---

[32] Long and Sedley, *The Hellenistic Philosophers* (New York: Cambridge University Press, 1987), 356, section 58 J.

principle of motion in themselves. So, they can act on their own accord. Many plants and animals are in natural social environments, some find themselves in more solitary environments. Most living things live in community with others and in some kindred relation with others. Nonrational beings are offspring and have offspring. They are neighbors and set into a fated natural order in the *Kosmos*. The nonrational living beings are directed by and live in accord with the kosmic *logos*. Their proper function can be determined by their place in the world and in the lifecycle. The first directive for nonrational beings is to stay alive. Other functions naturally follow, to enhance the ability to stay alive and to create life. The connection to oneself and to one's family are proper functions of a living being.

It is more complicated with rational beings. They have a moving principle in themselves, and they have *logos*. Just as the *Kosmos* has reason, a rational being has reason. The kosmic logos is as good as it can be. There is nothing better than what it embodies. A rational being has natural and kindred relations. Reason adds layers to the natural directives of nonrational living beings. These relations can spread more broadly through reason. Proper functions are right actions and they are unconditionally obligatory. These acts are virtuous acts. Actions against proper function are vicious acts and they are forbidden. These acts include treason, theft, and actions against parents. There are some acts that are intermediate, since they are not unconditionally obligatory. These acts include getting married, serving in the government, and conversing with others at some particular time.[33]

There are also proper functions that come from a person's title or profession. Some of our roles are universal, they come from being rational and different from all other nonrational beings. Other roles are particular to the individual. Cicero argues that there are four roles (*personae*). The first role is universal to all human beings.[34] It comes from our rational ability. Live according to reason. The second role is from our different capacities, strengths, weaknesses, and liabilities. This is an individual role. Cicero urges people to pay careful attention to the roles that fit their nature. By nature, different people are suited for different tasks. A person should not seek to achieve a goal that is beyond their nature. Each person should know

---

[33] Long and Sedley, *The Hellenistic Philosophers* (New York: Cambridge University Press, 1987), 59B.

[34] Long and Sedley, *The Hellenistic Philosophers* (New York: Cambridge University Press, 1987), 66D.

their peculiar natural temperament and their own dispositions. Take up tasks that agree with one's nature. The third role comes from the happenstance of events. These are unpredictable circumstances that place a person in a certain role. One person has access to wealth and opportunity from birth; another does not. One person wins an election; the others do not. These roles come by chance. The fourth role comes from the duties that we take on ourselves by choice. Some people practice philosophy, others law, others practice other virtuous endeavors. The fourth acts are intermediate between obligatory and forbidden. Once the intermediate acts are done, they carry an obligation for the person to function in a certain way. As we take on these additional intermediate functions, we expand the range of obligatory actions. The Stoics warn us to avoid taking on these obligations as much as possible.

8.1.2.3.3 Assent

The subject of assent includes the topics of encouragements and discouragements, virtue, and the end. We will take these in turn. The encouragements are found in the core doctrines, sayings, and precepts. We are fortunate to have the works of Epictetus at all, since he did not write and distribute works. Epictetus was born to a slave and lived for some time as a slave. His student, Flavius Arrian, did not just give us a synopsis of Epictetus' *Discourses* and the *Enchiridion* (*The Manual*) but also transcribed them. The *Manual* gives us a series of *logoi*, sayings, or precepts. Epictetus relied largely on Chrysippus' contribution to Stoicism in crafting the *Manual*. The precepts in the text are terse and dense in their encapsulation of Stoic philosophy. The text begins by distinguishing the things that are under our control from the things that are not under our control. The things that are under our control are up-to-us. They include a conception, a choice, a decision, and any other volition. The things that are not up-to-us are our physical bodies, the possessions that one has, and the office one holds. These things are not up-to-us. The Stoics apply themselves only to what is under their control. There is nothing hindering a person from employing reason, *logos*, to direct judgment and choice. There are no things but impediments to obtaining things that are not up-to-us.

He continues by focusing on conception (*prolepsis*). We can judge external impressions and circumstances as we choose. He stresses that we can see eternal struggles as removed from our concern. We can dismiss the success or not of our endeavors. We can only control how we undertake the duties that we have. After mastering our first and second roles, we encounter the roles that are by chance and by choice. He urges us not to be bothered by splashing in the public bath, not to disturb ourselves about losing a competition, and not to trouble ourselves when losing a child. These things were not yours from the start. They came from nature and go back to nature. We should say that we give back to nature what we enjoyed in the time together. The only thing that one possesses fully is the *logos*, through conception and choice. It is up-to-us. We should wish to have what is occurring, instead of wishing to have everything that we wish for. We can find our masters in the external things that we allow to disturb us. He urges us to think of ourselves as actors playing roles in our lives; much of the story is not written by us.[35] What is written by us is all that is of concern. The Stoics cut to the quick: all your suffering is self-inflicted. No sensation is painful unless you judge it as unwanted. Pain, suffering, hardship, and all other forms of struggle are generated by each of us, implemented by each of us on ourselves, and suffered by each of us from ourselves. Stoicism offers an attractive perspective on life, by urging us to care only for what is up-to-us. We should only assent to judgments that are in agreement with Nature and up-to-us. In this way, we cannot lose when entering a contest, a competition, or an election. Control over judgment produces invincibility.

Marcus Aurelius Antoninus was a Roman emperor from 161 CE to 180 CE. He offers an introspective account of living a Stoic life in the *Meditations*. As emperor he takes on many type three and type four roles. Though he is a Stoic, he makes use of broad and eclectic sources. He invokes the ideas of Democritus, Heraclitus, Socrates, Plato, Antisthenes, and Epicurus, to name a few. This leads him to reference ideas that are not Stoic. Nonetheless, he adopts and reiterates a thoroughly Stoic perspective. The *Kosmos* is matter and mind in an eternal cycle. A human being, accordingly, is flesh, breath, and reason.[36] The length of life does not determine the value of the life lived. The value of the life lived is in its accord with Nature. We are to employ reason to direct our lives, just as reason directs the *Kosmos*. Virtue or vice is found in the relations among our judgments, voluntary actions, and the *logos* of nature.

Turning to the Stoics generally, we can say that virtue is life in accordance (*homologia*) with nature. The Stoics hold that there is virtue or vice. There

---

[35] Epictetus *Discourses Books 3–4, Fragments, The Encheiridion*, W.A. Oldfather trans. (Cambridge: Harvard University Press, 1928), 497, section 17.

[36] Marcus Aurelius, *Marcus Aurelius,* C.R. Haines trans. (Cambridge: Harvard University Press, 1999), 27, II.2.

is nothing in between. The virtuous standard is the Stoic sage. All other people are striving toward virtue or not. There is a sense in which we can improve in our striving toward virtue, but there is no virtue to be had on the road to virtue. All who are not the Stoic sage are not virtuous. "Virtue" when applied to a person, for the Stoics, is a got-it verb. As with knowing, you have it or you don't. A person who has all assent in accord with Nature is virtuous. This is very rare. The refusal to apply the term "virtue" to anyone seeking virtue comes from the belief that there is one *logos*, and until a person achieves it the person lacks it. It is always something to be sought, and for almost everyone it remains something just beyond one's grasp.

The end, or goal, of life is happiness (*eudaimonia*) or living well (*eu zen*). Happiness and living well are acts according to reason, which is also to act according to nature.[37] Zeno describes happiness more generally as flowing well through life.[38] As parts of nature our individual happiness is the same as the happiness of the *Kosmos*. This state for us is not pleasure, it is not sensation, it is not a feeling, and it is not the traditional four virtues. It is a concordance of our individual minds with the mind common in all of Nature. It is difficult to reconcile the English word "happiness" with a state of imperturbability and not suffering. The English term connotes a positive state rather than a privation. The Stoics offer something different. In this way, the relation between being well with the gods and imperturbability is easier to understand. This is a calm state that is embodied in a life concordant with nature.

8.2 Skepticism: Pyrrhonians and Academics

8.2.1 History

Classical skepticism comes in two main branches, the Pyrrhonians and the Academics. Between these two branches, there are four main periods. The first period marks the beginning of skepticism with its founder Pyrrho of Elis (c. 360–275 BCE). In this period, skepticism focused on moral and practical concerns. The second is academic skepticism, beginning with Arcesilaus of Pitane (c. 315–241 BCE). This period comes from the leaders

---

[37] Marcus Aurelius, *Marcus Aurelius,* C.R. Haines trans. (Cambridge: Harvard University Press, 1999), 171–173, VII.17.

[38] Long and Sedley, *The Hellenistic Philosophers* (New York: Cambridge University Press, 1987), 63C.

of Plato's Academy, during the New Academy or Middle Academy. The third is the Pyrrhonian revival, beginning with Aenesidemus (c. 100–40 BCE). This period focuses on systematizing the skeptical dialectic. The fourth comes during the Roman Empire and it culminates with Sextus Empiricus (c. 160–210 CE). This period catalogs skepticism with a focus on their disputes among themselves and the other Hellenistic philosophical movements.

The term "skeptic" comes from the Greek term "*skepsis*," meaning speculation, inquiry, or doubt. The early skeptics did not call themselves by that name. Arcesilaus was the first to use the term with reference to the philosophical movement, and he applied it anachronistically to the Pyrrhonists. The skeptics were also called "*zetetic*" (seekers or inquirers), "*ephektic*" (suspending judgment), "*aporetic*" (at a loss or doubting), or Pyrrhonian.[39] In what follows, we will use the term "skeptic" and discuss the four periods in turn.

8.2.2 Pyrrhonism

We do not have texts from Pyrrho, the founder of skepticism. Diogenes Laertius offers some anecdotes about Pyrrho that are illustrative of his reputation. Apparently Pyrrho makes his way around town without making judgments about his environment. He does not adopt judgments and thereby alter his movements. Fortunately, his associates follow him around to make sure that he does not walk off a cliff, fall in a hole, or get hit by a cart. It is not that Pyrrho wanders aimlessly; he conducts his daily business and sees to his general affairs. He holds that there was no such thing as the honorable or the dishonorable, the just or the unjust. For Pyrrho life is guided only by custom, convention, or law (*nomos*). He lived according to his conception of custom, though not as most people live. It seems that he lived without committing to any judgments. He suspended his judgment. Pyrrho was not a theoretician, dialectician, or logician, and he did not focus on developing a philosophical system. He aimed to live with tranquility and austerity.

Timon of Phlius (c. 315–225 BCE) was a student of Pyrrho. Timon formalizes skepticism more than Pyrrho. He urges us to distinguish three factors: (1) reality, (2) judgment, and (3) the consequences of judgment.

---

[39] Sextus Empiricus, *Outlines of Pyrrhonism*, R.G. Bury trans. (Cambridge: Harvard University Press, 1933), 11, I.7.

Concerning reality, it is not possible to distinguish it, measure it, or make it determinate. He holds that it is impossible to determine reality. Judgments about reality come from sensation. We do not know that our sensations are transparent to reality, indicative of reality, or avenues into reality. We judge in customary ways. The way that things seem to be are not insights into reality. So, when we ask if the way things seem to be according to judgment is true, we cannot assent to a claim of truth. We have no reason to judge that something is true or false. Reality escapes us. Impressions can be judged to be this or that. Judgments allow us to determine that every sensation is controverted by a contrary sensation. There is no objective perspective from which to view the relation between impressions and reality. Since, reality and judgment do not correspond, we must suspend judgment. The Pyrrhonians hold that "it is no more this than that," or "no more" for short.[40] The contrary judgments are equipollent. The skeptics are not dogmatists (*dogmatikoi*); they do not adhere to a set of claims about reality. The third factor is the consequences of judgment. The consequences of judgments that this is true and that is false are perturbation and disease. The skeptics warn us that "A pledge is a curse at one's elbow."[41] By suspending our judgments, we avoid disquietude. If we suspend judgments about the relation between reality and judgment, we can achieve imperturbability (*ataraxia*) and apathy (*apatheia*).

Aenesidemus is the next Pyrrhonian. We do not know the dates of his birth or death, but he seems to have lived in the first century BCE. He formalizes pyrrhonism in the 10 modes (*tropoi*). The modes function to produce to block an inference from a judgment about an object to the reality of that object. Suppose a person encounters a judgment about an object, such as "olive oil is beneficial for humans." Suppose that the judgment is employed as a premise to infer that olive oil is beneficial. The skeptic should counter the claim that olive oil is beneficial by deriving the contrary conclusion. The skeptic could assume the judgment that olive oil is not beneficial for bees. Then the skeptic may infer that olive oil is not beneficial. By granting the initial judgment and countering that judgment with a contrary judgment, the skeptic can put the conclusions together. The conjunction of the two conclusions is a contradiction, "Olive oil is beneficial and not beneficial."

---

[40] Diogenes Laertius, *Lives of Eminent Philosophers*, R.D. Hicks trans. (Cambridge: Harvard University Press, 1931), IX.61.

[41] Diogenes Laertius, *Lives of Eminent Philosophers*, R.D. Hicks trans. (Cambridge: Harvard University Press, 1931), IX.71.

This claim cannot be true. So, the skeptic suspends judgment (*epoche*). The skeptic can now say that olive oil is no more beneficial than it is not beneficial. Or simply say, "no more," for short. The 10 modes help the skeptic to develop, what we can call "no-more arguments." Indeed, the modes were also called arguments (*logoi*).[42]

The ancient skeptic can hold judgments stating that an object seems a certain way from a certain perspective. What the skeptic rejects is the judgment that the object is a certain way or has a certain feature. The skeptic blocks the move from the claim that an object seems to have a property at a certain perspective, to the claim that an object has a property:

	Proposed Position	*Skeptic's Response*
Premise: **Judgment**	Olive oil is beneficial to humans	Olive oil is not beneficial to bees
Sub-conclusion: **Reality**	Olive oil is beneficial	Olive oil is not beneficial
	Skeptic's Conclusion	
Conclusion: **Epoche**	Olive oil is beneficial and not beneficial	

The no-more argument referencing olive oil exemplifies the first mode, which is described as "the variety of animals."[43] Different animals have different sense impressions of the same object. Aenesidemus infers that different animals have different sensation of the same object because of the differences in their origins and their sensory organs. For some animals, an object is sweet, pleasant, or beneficial. For other animals the object is not. There are also variations within the same class of animals. The second mode refers to the differences among human beings. The third refers to the difference among sense organs. A person can get conflicting sensations of the same object. The fourth refers to differences in time or circumstances. An object can be pleasant at one time and not pleasant at another. The fourth mode notes the difference between waking and sleeping life, between youth and old age. There is a natural progression from birth to death. The fifth refers to variety in position, interval, and location. The sixth refers to

---

[42] Sextus Empiricus, *Outlines of Pyrrhonism*, R.G. Bury trans. (Cambridge: Harvard University Press, 1933), I.36.

[43] Sextus Empiricus, *Outlines of Pyrrhonism*, R.G. Bury trans. (Cambridge: Harvard University Press, 1933), I.36.

variety in "intermixtures," the elements through which we sense that objects mix in ways that alter the sensation of the object. The seventh refers to a variety of sensations due to the amount and form of an object. Scattered pebbles seem rough to sense, but when bundled together they seem soft. The eighth refers to the variety in relativity. A judgment is made in a certain relation to an object. Different relative perspectives afford different sensory impressions. Aenesidemus offers an additional application of the eight modes, when he applies it to the other modes. Different animals have different relative relations to the same object. Different human beings have different relative relations to the same object, and so on. The ninth mode refers to the frequency or rarity of occurrence. The sun is more impressive than a comet, but a comet is rarer than the sun. So, we are impressed more with the comet than with the sun. The tenth mode refers to variety in customs and laws. This mode focuses on ethics. A judgment about the good life, propriety, or law from one region is contradicted by a judgment from some other region.

Aenesidemus distinguishes a theme in the 10 modes. He applies one of the modes in two ways: the facts of relativity are a mode and they are also a theme applicable to the modes. We can also see that the first four modes follow from each other. No particular animal has a privileged perspective beyond sense and judgment. No human has a privileged perspective. No human sense has a privileged perspective. No circumstance has a privileged perspective on any other. When we consider circumstances, we can see that the fifth, sixth, and seventh modes are a deeper analysis of the fourth mode. They develop the various circumstances. The ninth mode distinguishes the influence of frequency and rarity of sense impressions on judgments. Again, we have relativity. The tenth mode argues that no cultural perspective is privileged. Aenesidemus places relativity as a theme or category over the seven modes he had mentioned, but the theme can encompass all the modes. The modes are instances of relativity. Does this make skeptics relativists? Absolutely not. Relativists hold that truth is relative to the individual person, the society, the age, or some other factor. Skeptics hold that truth is not intelligible. It is unknowable and unknown. Where the relativist knows that this is better than that for me or for us, the skeptic holds that this is no better than that.

8.2.3 The Academics

8.2.3.1 Arcesilaus

Arcesilaus (315/4–241/40 BCE) was from Pitane in Aeolis, Ionia. He left Pitane in defiance of his guardians and went to Athens to study at Aristotle's Lyceum when Theophrastus was the Scholarch. Then he moved to study at the Plato's Academy with Crantor, Polemo, and Crates. Arcesilaus became Scholarch of the Academy when Crates died (285 BCE). There are three periods in the leadership of Plato's Academy. The first period is called the Old Academy. It begins with Plato as Scholarch and goes to Crates the Cynic. The middle period begins with Arcesilaus. He initiates Academic skepticism, and he led the Academy for over 25 years until his death. Subsequent Scholarchs of the middle period include Lacydes of Cyrene, Evander and Telecles, and Hegesinus. The last period of the Academy is called the New Academy, and it begins with Carneades.

Arcesilaus thought that the Academy had strayed from Plato's founding vision. He had a particular interpretation of Plato's philosophy, by grounding it squarely in Socrates' approach to philosophy. Arcesilaus read Plato's dialogues as Socratic and aporetic. He thought that Plato was unceasingly searching for the truth, but never arrived at it. We might challenge this view by pointing to the *Republic* and Plato's theory of forms. Arcesilaus would counter with Plato's *Parmenides* and its critique of the theory of forms. He interpreted Plato as continuing in a thoroughly Socratic, or aporetic, method. Arcesilaus turned his attention to the Epicureans and the Stoics. As with Socrates, Arcesilaus did not author any texts. Also in the Socratic fashion, Arcesilaus does not claim to know the truth. With the Socratic Method and Plato's dialectic, Arcesilaus devotes his efforts to countering the claims of the rival philosophies.

It is difficult to reconcile a commitment to the Socratic method and a commitment to any particular claim. This is a challenge for all skeptics. How can one claim not to know, but search for knowledge, while also assenting to a proposition? It depends on what one claims not to know and what one claims to know. It is not as if Socrates knew nothing. He had to know enough to question the veracity of the proposed definitions he encountered. Arcesilaus claimed that even Socrates claimed too much.[44] We have already seen the Socratic method of refutation, the *elenchus*. The person who claims to know what x is, x being justice, temperance, courage, or even knowledge. There is no implication that the philosopher offering the counter-position assents to the counter-position in his philosophical commitments. The challenge for the skeptic is to adopt a philosophical perspective without assenting to a dogma or assenting to dogmatic propositions. The term dogma (*dogma*) in Greek means what seems true, a belief, an opinion or it can also mean a public decree or ordinance. Doubtless, it is expressed in a proposition to which one assents. We can apply the adjectival

---

A.A. Long *Hellenistic Philosophy* (Berkeley: University of California Press), 91.

form of "dogma" to the way that a person holds a belief or to the belief. We can say that a person holds a belief dogmatically or that a belief is dogmatic. These are different claims. One claim distinguishes different ways to hold a belief and the other distinguishes different types of beliefs. Arcesilaus does not turn to the different ways that we hold beliefs; he turns to the different beliefs that we hold.

Arcesilaus arrives at his commitments by countering the arguments of the Epicureans and the Stoics. Both schools claim that there are impressions to which we should assent. Arcesilaus counters this position by arguing that reality is hidden; it is not in any impression or any judgment.[45] So, no one should assent to any impression or judgment. We can express this position by holding that reality is not intelligible and the claim that we should suspend judgment. Arcesilaus' foremost concern is to avoid falsehood. We avoid falsehood and error by refusing to hold that reality is embodied in our impressions or in our judgments. It is not that we should achieve a knowledge of reality; rather we should avoid erroneous beliefs about reality. We can suspend judgments by following the Socratic method, counteracting claims with claims, deriving contraries, and suspending judgment. It seems that Arcesilaus is caught in a contradiction. The very sort of problem he generates for the Stoics, by means of the Socratic method. He seems to urge us to universally suspend assent and judgment, while also urging us to assent to a universal suspension of assent and judgment. He urges us to assent to the judgment that reality is not intelligible, but this is a judgment about reality.

Arcesilaus holds that we have no indication of reality and that we should suspend judgment (*epoche*). It is difficult to find a basis for action. Why do this instead of that, or why do anything at all, if we cannot know what to do? We need to add a third claim to Arcesilaus' philosophy. He claims that there is a practical criterion (*kriterion*) for action. The Stoics argued that action requires assent to impressions. They also argue that action requires assent to what is believed to be good. Arcesilaus rejects both of these views. He argues that action is possible without assent, since the Stoics hold that non-human animals act but do not assent. Secondly, he argues that a person can act without assent, by acting a "well-reasoned" or "reasonable" (*eulogos*) view. The substitution of "reasonable" for "assent" allows Arcesilaus to offer a basis for action that is not dogmatic. This would allow the skeptic to act much like other people act, with one big difference. Non-skeptics act by

---

[45] A.A. Long *Hellenistic Philosophy* (Berkeley: University of California Press), 92.

assenting to what they take to be true impressions or judgments that represent knowledge. The skeptic does not take true impressions or knowledge as expressed in assent as the basis for action. The skeptic acts from what seems reasonable, all the while admitting that there might be better alternatives or that the action might be misguided. There is humility in the skeptic's view. We act on what seems best, though we do not have access to reality and we do not know what is best. This view gives Arcesilaus the basis to reject the Stoic ideal of the wise man who assents only to true impressions and has knowledge. The wise man can suspend judgment and act without assent.

8.2.3.2 Carneades

Carneades (214–129/8 BCE) was born in Cyrene, a Greek colony in North Africa. When Carneades went to Athens, he studied at the Academy during the Middle period and with the Stoics under Diogenes of Babylon, who was a student of Chrysippus. Carneades became scholarch of the Academy sometime prior to 155 BCE. In that year, as Scholarch of the Academy he went to Rome on behalf of Athens. He was joined by Critolaus representing the Lyceum and Diogenes of Babylon representing the Stoics. When in Rome, Carneades is said to have argued for justice on one day and against justice on the next day. The pair of arguments functioned as a demonstration of the Socratic *elenchus*. By combining the argument and the counter-argument, the skeptics gave reason to suspend assent to either side. The last period of the Academy, the New Academy, begins when Carneades became Scholarch. Carneades and the Late Academy changed the direction of skepticism in two primary ways. He offered an account of probable impressions, which allowed for a preference of some impressions over others. He employed the account of probabilism to offer a novel basis for skepticism as applied to voluntary action and fate. We will take these topics in turn.

Carneades argued that some impressions are probable, a view that is called probabilism. This term comes from the Latin term "*probilis*," which refers to something that is likely or probable. The Latin term is a translation of the Greek term "*pithanos*," which refers to something persuasive or plausible. Putting the terms together, Carneades argues that some impressions are likely, probable, persuasive, or plausible. Whereas Arcesilaus argued for a criterion based on reasonableness (*eulogos*) and he applied this directly to a basis for action, Carneades argued for a criterion based on the probable (*probilis* or *pithanos*), and he applied this directly to impressions (*phantasmata*). To establish the criterion for probable impressions,

Carneades makes a series of distinctions among impressions. He distinguishes impressions related to the object from impressions related to the perceiver.[46] Though the impression related to the object can be true or false, Carneades argues that we have no access to the object or the relation between the impression and the object. We do have impressions as related to the perceiver. By taking this position, Carneades has rendered all of our impressions as subjective experiences of a perceiver. Carneades argues that there are two types of subjective impressions, the apparently true and the apparently false. The apparently true impressions are probable (*pithanos*), or they pull one to assent. The apparently false are not probable. There is a distinction between probable impressions; some are clear and distinct, but others are dim and confused. A dim probable impression is seen at a distance, not seen clearly, or is small in size. A clear and distinct probable impression is perceived close enough, under suitable conditions, and with sufficient function of the sensory organs. The pull to assent of the probable impression is due to its vividness, clarity, and distinctness.

Probable impressions come in degrees, some are clearer and more distinct than others. Some probable impressions are actually true of the object, some are actually false of the object, and some span both what is true and false. We cannot determine whether the apparently true probable impressions are true or false. So, we are left with probable impressions that span both truth and falsehood. There is no guarantee of truth among probable impressions that span truth and falsehood. So, even a clear and distinct probable impression of such a sort can turn out to be false, since they span both truth and falsehood. Still, Carneades holds that strong, clear, and distinct impressions turn out to be true more often than not.[47] He urges that we should not abandon all of the clear and distinct probable impressions that can be either true or false, even though some of them turn out to be false.

Within the category of probable impressions that can be true or false, Carneades distinguishes undiverted and diverted impressions. Carneades reminds us that impressions do not come in isolation. Impressions come in a sequence of impressions and in collocation with other impressions. When, for instance, we have the impression of a person, we also have impressions of size, color, shape, motion, dress, and other features. When we have

---

[46] Long and Sedley, *The Hellenistic Philosophers* (New York: Cambridge University Press, 1987), 69D.

[47] Long and Sedley, *The Hellenistic Philosophers* (New York: Cambridge University Press, 1987), 69D.

disagreement among these features of an impression, the impression is diverted. When we do not have disagreement among these features, we have an undiverted impression. Carneades argues that we can scrutinize, investigate, or judge undiverted impressions. This process allows us to thoroughly investigate and question the features of the impressions. We can now chart the path among the initial impressions to arrive at thoroughly investigated impressions:

Criterion for Impressions
Impression
In relation to the perceiver
Apparently true (probable)
Clear and distinct
Spanning truth and falsehood
Undiverted
Thoroughly investigated

Once we have thoroughly investigated the impression, we have an impression worthy of guiding our judgments. In this way, Carneades argues that we can prefer some impressions over others, and we can employ these impressions to guide our judgments and behaviors. These impressions do not make a claim about the reality of the object itself. They are preferable impressions among the impressions in relation to the perceiver.

We have conflicting reports about whether Carneades holds that thoroughly investigated impressions are worthy of assent. If we are to assent, then we are not suspending judgment. A close associate of Carneades, Clitomachus, reports that Carneades banishes assent.[48] This same source, Cicero, tells us that Clitomachus argues that Carneades distinguished two meanings for the claim "the wise man assents to nothing."[49] It can mean that (1) a wise person never assents to anything. Alternatively, it can mean that (2) a wise person never asserts or denies a claim. According to Clitomachus, Carneades adopts the first interpretation. We should never assent to anything. Carneades, however, allows the wise man to

---

[48] Long and Sedley, *The Hellenistic Philosophers* (New York: Cambridge University Press, 1987), 69J.

[49] Long and Sedley, *The Hellenistic Philosophers* (New York: Cambridge University Press, 1987), 69I.

assert or deny a claim. This distinction shows that Carneades distinguishes asserting or denying a proposition from assenting to the proposition. We can make sense of this distinction, if we take assent to mean holding a proposition as indubitably true. Carneades never holds an impression or proposition to be indubitably true. He does argue that some impressions or judgments are probable and thoroughly investigated. He does not claim that these impressions are true of the object or even true of the perception of the impression. They are apparently true, probable, and examined impressions that can be false.

Carneades innovates the skeptical approach to voluntary action and fate. If we accept that a proposition is either true or false and cannot be both, the bivalence of the true and false, then a proposition about the future must be either true or false. It seems that the propositions that are going to be true are going to be true because of a series of causes. When they become true, they are fated to have become true. Consider the proposition, "Cato will come into the senate."[50] Carneades counters this line of argument, by insisting that some things are up-to-us. Thereby he distinguishes different kinds of causes. The things that are up-to-us are contingent and can be otherwise. These things constitute *contingent* causes. Things that come to be from an "eternal chain of causes" are *necessary* causes. Whether Cato will come to the senate or not is not determined by necessary causes, but by contingent causes. No matter how much we know, we cannot know if Cato will enter the senate. The proposition that Cato will come into the senate is true or false. We cannot know whether it is true or false, not only due to our limited knowledge but also due to the contingent causes that will make it true or false. So, it is not fated that Cato will or will not enter the senate. The logical necessity in the bivalence of true and false does not entail fate or determinism.

---

[50] Long and Sedley, *The Hellenistic Philosophers* (New York: Cambridge University Press, 1987), 70G. The passage is from Cicero.

9

FATE AND THE GOOD LIFE

9.1 Historical Context

The Hellenistic philosophies focus on attaining a life of mental imperturbability. Though every major movement of the period seeks mental and physical tranquility, they chart different paths to differently specified goals. Some philosophies aim at imperturbability (*ataraxia*), apathy (*apatheia*), or at suspension of judgment (*epoche*). They all navigate the relations among the *Kosmos*, thought, and action. In doing so, they build on theories of the *Kosmos* from the early Greek philosophers. They build on theories of mind and theories of action from Plato to Aristotle. The early Greek philosophers focused on rational and material explanations of the *Kosmos*. One implication of the materialist approach is that the *Kosmos* is determined by physical matter, rational principles, material causes, and objective and determined events. In short, the *Kosmos* seems to be determined. Yet, Plato and Aristotle offer accounts of voluntary action. Here we are to think of the act as free. The Epicureans, for example, adopt atomism. It seems that if atomism is correct, then every event is determined by atoms and the *Kosmos* is determined. Yet, the Epicureans urge us to adopt a certain mental perspective that is not determined by atoms. They claim that this mental perspective is "up to us" (*hupo hemin*).

This Is Ancient Philosophy: An Introduction, First Edition. Kirk Fitzpatrick.
© 2024 John Wiley & Sons, Inc. Published 2024 by John Wiley & Sons, Inc.

The Hellenistic philosophers inherit positions, which when put together generate a puzzling dilemma:

A constructive dilemma	
Premise one	If events in the *Kosmos* are necessary, then there are no voluntary acts
Premise two	If there are voluntary acts, then events in the *Kosmos* are not necessary
Premise three	Either events in the *Kosmos* are necessary, or there are voluntary acts
Conclusion	Either there are no voluntary acts or events in the *Kosmos* are not necessary

The dilemma concludes that we can posit a necessary *Kosmos* or voluntary action, but not both. Yet, many of the Hellenistic philosophers aim to hold both propositions. Facing the puzzling inconsistency between a determined *Kosmos* and voluntary action, the Epicureans, for example, posit the "swerve." The Stoics hold that the *Kosmos* is a necessary being and that one can voluntarily act. The Hellenistic philosophers put the parts of the puzzle together. The resulting challenge remains with us today.

The relations that generate the puzzle are complicated and subtle. The impetus toward a consistent account of a material *Kosmos* and free action does not come from Aristotle. According to Plato, it comes from Socrates. In *Protagoras*, Socrates argues that a person always desires what is thought to be best and always acts according to what is thought to be best. All wrongdoing, for Socrates, is ignorance. If Socrates is right, then there is no moral weakness, and one cannot act against one's best judgment. Plato and Aristotle disagree with Socrates. They argue that one can act against one's better judgment. To explain such acts, they develop accounts of voluntary action. These acts are "up to us" from deliberation, decision, or choice. To understand the Hellenistic accounts of the good life, we need to trace the philosophical debates about freedom in action that inform them.

Different historical epochs conceive of moral weakness in different ways. Even within a historical epoch, philosophers disagree about the specifics of a morally weak act. In the classical period, they tended to refer to moral weakness with the term *akrasia*. In the modern period, they refer to *weakness of will.* In the contemporary period, they discuss *practical irrationality.*[1] The general features of a morally weak act are:

1. The person thinks, knows, or believes that act *x* is better than act *y*.
2. The person believes that both acts are possible or both acts are possible.
3. The person voluntarily does *y*.

In some epochs, "voluntarily" is not used; instead, they use "willingly" or "intentionally." In what follows, we will focus on moral weakness conceived of as *akrasia*. The term comes from an alpha privative, meaning not, plus *kratos* meaning strong. Morally weak acts contrast with morally strong acts. Morally strong acts are called *enkratos* (or *egkratos*), meaning strength. Just about everyone thinks that moral weakness occurs, despite a wide variety in the descriptions and explanations of the act. Almost every philosopher thinks it is obvious that such acts occur, everyone except Socrates.

9.2 Moral Weakness as *Akrasia*

In Plato's *Protagoras*, we encounter Socrates' position on moral weakness. He is discussing courage with Protagoras when the discussion turns to an analysis of the good life and its relation to pain and pleasure.[2] The analysis of pain and pleasure goes on at some length and it is not clear why until Socrates announces his concern. The majority of people, The Many (*hoi polloi*), hold that sometimes a person does a bad thing, knowing that it is a bad thing, when he believes the good act is possible for him. The Many explain this by saying that the person acts because he is overcome by something other than knowledge.[3] The Many argue that knowledge can be overcome by pleasure, pain, lust, fear, or any other passion. Socrates does not

---

[1] This chapter employs the term "moral weakness" to cover the range of phenomena named as "*akrasia*," "weakness of will," and "practical irrationality." *Akrasia* focuses on voluntary actions, weakness of will on willed actions, and practical irrationality on intentional actions. Since there are important differences among voluntary acts, willed acts, and intentional acts, there are important differences among the three classes of actions. Nonetheless, all three types of actions involve a failure of better judgment to guide action.

[2] *Protagoras*, 351b.

[3] *Protagoras*, 353a.

call this phenomenon *akrasia*; he calls it "being overcome." We can identify certain key features in the act and explanation of the act of being overcome:

	Being overcome
The phenomena	The person knows or believes that act x is better than act y
	The person believes that x and y are possible
	The person has the desire to do x and y
	The person voluntarily does y
The explanation	The person voluntarily acts because knowledge is overcome by a passion

The Many think that being overcome is a common occurrence, and they take their explanation to be accurate. They think that passion and desire are stronger than knowledge, since it can be overcome by just about any passion.

Socrates does not think that being overcome occurs. He rejects the phenomena by arguing that the explanation is incoherent. Socrates focuses on pain and pleasure as exemplars of the desires that can overcome knowledge, according to The Many. He notes that The Many think pleasure to be good and pain to be bad. Yet, they also take some pleasures to be bad and some pains to be good. Socrates distinguishes near pleasures from distant pleasures and near pains from distant pains. Socrates asks us to consider the pleasure and pain in an act by putting all the near and distant pleasures together, and all the near and distant pains together. We can then compare whether there is more total pleasure and more total pain in the act. Socrates treats pleasures as commensurate and pains as commensurate. Obviously, he treats near and distant pleasures as commensurate. Yet, he takes a more controversial position. He takes all pleasures to be commensurate. To commensurate value, there must be a single scale on which to place the two or more things. We tend to commensurate the value of objects by calculating the amount in money terms. Money, however, is just one aspect of the value of an object. Money does not capture all the value in an object. There are different kinds of pleasures, a cold drink on a hot day, a fine meal, victory in a competition, and studying philosophy. There is a cliché, "that is like comparing apples and oranges." The problem with the cliché is not that it is pithy or that there is a counterpoint cliché. It is worse. There is no problem in comparing apples and oranges, or apples and jumbo jets, or in comparing anything to anything else. There is a problem, however, with the commensuration of apples and oranges. There is no single scale of value that can commensurate the value of an apple and the value of an orange. We cannot accurately say that an apple is more valuable or better than an orange or vice versa. The apple gives apple value and the orange gives orange value. Socrates takes pleasures to be commensurate, pains to be commensurate, and pleasures and pains to be commensurate with each other. We are to pile up all the pleasures in an act, all the pains in the act, and determine which is more.

We can now understand why The Many take some pleasures to be bad and some pains to be good. They commensurate the pleasure and the pains, near and far, and determine which is more. If there is more pleasure than pain in an act, they call the pleasurable act good. If there is more pain than pleasure, they take the pleasure to be bad. If there is more pleasure than pain, they call the painful act good. If there is more pain than pleasure, they call the painful act bad. In this way, some pleasure they call bad, and some pains they call good. Overindulgence, for example, offers near pleasures, but overindulgence ruins health and involves more pain. The pleasures of overindulgence are bad. Going to the doctor for treatments involves near pains but engenders health and pleasure. The painful treatments at the doctor are good. We can see, Socrates argues, that The Many do not really think that pleasure is bad and they do not really think that pain is good. Calling a pleasure bad simply identifies more pain in the act than pleasure. The badness of the act is the predominance of pain in the act. The goodness of a painful act is the predominance of pleasure in the painful act. Socrates concludes that The Many hold pleasure to be good and pain to be bad. Socrates warns them about this conclusion.[4]

With this conclusion in hand, Socrates returns to the explanation of being overcome. He argues that The Many are confusing themselves and others by switching back and forth between two pairs of terms: pleasure and pain, good and bad. They say that a person does a bad thing knowing it is a bad thing, because he is overcome by pleasure. When we stop jumping from one pair of terms to the other pair, we get a clearer understanding of the explanation. Let us put the explanation in terms of pleasure and pain. Then we will put it in terms of good and bad.

---

[4] *Protagoras*, 354d–e.

	Being overcome in original form
Pleasure and bad	A person does a bad thing knowing it is a bad thing, because he is overcome by pleasure
	Being overcome reformulated
Pleasure and pain	A person does a painful thing knowing it is a painful thing, because he is overcome by pleasure
Good and bad	A person does a bad thing knowing that it is a bad thing, because he is overcome by a good thing

These explanations are incoherent and absurd. In one reformed version, a person acts for pain because he is overcome by pleasure. In the other, a person does something bad, because he is overcome by a good thing. The Many think that knowledge can be dragged around like a slave by any passion that arises. They do not think that knowledge is a powerful force capable of guiding action.

Socrates offers an alternative explanation of being overcome. No one does a bad thing knowing that it is a bad thing. This person thinks that he is doing a good thing, i.e., a pleasurable thing. What he fails to do is accurately calculate the amount of pleasure and pain. Near pleasure appears larger than distant pleasure. Distant pain appears smaller than near pain. The person incorrectly calculates the actual amount of pleasure and pain. A person who refuses a doctor's treatment, for example, does not calculate the distant pleasure of health to be more than the near pain of the treatment. He sees the near pain as larger than the distant pleasure. There is no such thing as being overcome; there is only miscalculation of pleasure and pain. Being overcome does not involve knowledge. It involves the ignorance of pleasure and pain. Socrates concludes that this explanation fails. In *Protagoras*, there is no such thing as moral weakness.

The Socratic denial of moral weakness is not isolated in *Protagoras*. We can see the Socratic position in a number of Socratic dialogues. In *Apology* he claims that he could not do the wrong of corrupting the youth voluntarily.[5] In *Gorgias*, Socrates argues that people who do wrong do what they think best, but act against their real wishes for themselves.[6] In *Meno*, Socrates argues that we desire only what we believe is good.[7] In *Lesser*

---

[5] *Apology*, 25d.
[6] *Gorgias*, 466c.
[7] *Meno*, 77a.

Hippias, Socrates offers an argument to the conclusion that no one voluntarily does wrong.[8] These positions run through the Socratic dialogues. Socrates holds that all wrongdoing is ignorance and that no one voluntarily does wrong. Socrates is committed to certain claims:

A Socratic rejection of being overcome	
Good and bad	Good and bad things are commensurate
Judgment and desire	Only things thought to be good are desired
Desire and action	One acts only for what is most desired

Suppose that a person values and desires only one thing, money. Someone offers you two options to do one and the same task. One option offers one dollar and one option offers two dollars. There is no difference between the two options other than the dollar amount. We cannot explain a person taking one dollar instead of two. To explain the act, we need to explain that the person acted for some object to secure some value. Socrates' claims taken together leave no room for desiring what one does not think is good, let alone desiring what one thinks is bad. They leave no room for voluntarily acting for anything other than what the person thinks best. The necessary tie between good and bad things, the tie from judgments about good things to desires for them, and the tie from desires for good things to actions leave no room for a morally weak break between thought and action. For Socrates, the relation between judging best and voluntarily acting for what is judged best is necessary.

The Many might have informed their position about being overcome from going to the theater. Euripides (c. 480–406 BCE) wrote two plays that portray what appears to be acts of moral weakness. In *Medea*, Medea accompanies Jason when he returns to Greece after his heroic feats. Medea helped him accomplish these heroic deeds, even killing her brother to aid Jason's return to Greece. Medea is a barbarian, a non-Greek foreigner, and she has children with Jason. When Jason returns to Greece, he has the opportunity to marry a princess and join a kingly family line. Jason puts Medea to the side, dishonoring her and her children. Medea understands that she can take her children and go. She understands that Jason will take care of her and her children, though they cannot stay at the royal palace. Yet, Medea has been dishonored. She is very angry (*thumos*) and she wants

---

[8] *Lesser Hippias*, 370e.

to hurt Jason.[9] Her anger drives her to kill the king, the princess, and Jason's children. Though she vacillates about what she ought to do, she does not think that killing these people is good. Yet, she does not want to endure the dishonor without a response. Medea suffers a conflict between her rational desires and her spirited desires of anger. Her rational desires are overcome by her spirited desires. This appears to be a vivid illustration of just the sort of moral weakness that Socrates rejects, being overcome by anger.

Euripides returns to the topic of moral weakness in *Hippolytus*. In this play, Phaedra falls in love (*eros*) with her stepson Hippolytus. This is shameful for her and for her husband's house. Her spirited desires urge her not to shamefully fall in love with Hippolytus. Yet, her appetitive and erotic desires are too strong. She cannot hide her love or keep her mouth shut about it. Phaedra is overt about her conflicting desires. She tells us that her wits are fine, and she understands what she is doing.[10] She says that she tried to overcome her appetitive desires by means of self-control. This failed and she could not overcome Aphrodite (aka Cypris). After her shameful lust is discovered, Phaedra kills herself. She suffers a conflict between her spirited desires and her appetitive desires. Her spirited desires represent her better desires and her view of the good thing to do. Her appetitive desires represent her worse desires. Her better desires overcame her worse desires. This appears to be a vivid illustration of just the sort of moral weakness that Socrates rejects, being overcome by lust.

Plato returns to the topic of moral weakness in *Republic*, albeit indirectly. Plato divides the three parts, distinguishing rational desires, irrational desires, and partly rational desires. The rational desires are tied to a person's judgment of all things considered good. Reason desires only what it thinks to be good. The irrational desires are not grounded in judgments about goodness. These appetitive desires go after objects regardless of them being thought to be good. Consider the first division of the soul between reason and appetite. Plato points out that a person can desire to drink, even though the person does not think that the drink is good. Indeed, this can happen when dying of thirst while adrift at sea. The desire to drink drives the person as if he were a beast. Plato does not tell us whether the person drinks or not. He does not need to tell us the outcome in order to make the distinction between the two parts of the soul. Yet, for the distinction to function, it must be possible for the person to drink or not to drink. Plato has made

---

[9] Euripides' *Medea*, line 1013.
[10] Euripides' *Hippolytus*, line 343.

room for a break between judgments about goodness and desires. Appetite can desire something that the person does not think is good. The person can act on the desire for an object that he does not think to be good, even when there is a counteracting desire for what the person does think to be good. The conflict between reason and appetite, rational and irrational desire, is the paradigmatic setting for moral weakness.

Plato makes room for other cases of moral weakness. Recall the distinction between reason and spirit in *Republic* Book IV. This was the example from the *Odyssey* Book XX. As the story goes, Odysseus returns home incognito. As he sits in his great hall, dressed as a beggar, he sees the suitors eating his food, trying to bed his wife, and readying for sex with his female slaves. Odysseus is responsible for his slaves and he cannot protect them from being exploited. He is angry with the suitors. He is also angry with the slaves for behaving in a way that dishonors his house. He wants to kill them all, both the suitors and the slaves. He is furious and his anger keeps him up all night. Homer describes Odysseus trying to sleep. He is like a fatty sausage thrown into a hot pan. Just as the sausage bounces around the pan from the exploding fat, Odysseus turned this way and that through the night. Odysseus knows that if he tries to kill them, all right then they will kill him. His better judgment and Athena urge him to wait for a plan. The desire to kill the suitors is not irrational. It is a desire of righteous indignation, based on a judgment about justice. The timing of his spirited desire is not opportune, but the desire is partly rational. Odysseus controls himself, abides by his reason, and kills them all later. So Odysseus demonstrates a morally strong act. Yet, the framework allows for, and the drama of the scene demands, that Odysseus could have done otherwise. The scenes imply that when a person suffers a conflict between reason and spirit, it is possible for the person to act on the spirited desires. Plato employs Homer's illustration to show that our rational judgments about all things considered goodness can conflict with judgments about goodness in part. If the person acts on spirited desires at the expense of the rational desires, then the worse desires overcome the better desires. In such a case, we have Euripides' illustration in *Medea*. We also have a counterexample to Socrates' claim in *Protagoras* that knowledge cannot be overcome by anger.

In another vignette, Plato describes Leontius walking along the wall that runs from Athens to Piraeus. Along the way, Leontius sees some beheaded corpses. He has an appetitive desire to look at the corpses. Plato tells us that the primary desires of appetite are for food, sex, and drink. He also tells us that appetites are the largest part of the soul and the only part that is liable to fracturing into parts. Though some interpreters speculate that Leontius had a sexual desire for the corpses, Plato does not specify the appetitive desire. Possibly the desire is what we would call "morbid curiosity," such as the desire to look at the aftermath of a gruesome car accident. We do not know the particular appetitive desire. Leontius also has a spirited desire not to look, because he was disgusted by the sight of the corpses. We can add to this that gawking at the beheaded corpses is shameful and the road is well traveled. His spirited desire leads him to cover his eyes. In the end, the appetitive desire is too strong, and he throws back his hands to look at the corpses. This is the only vignette of the three where Plato gives us an illustration of moral weakness. Here the spirited desires are the better desires and they are overcome by the worse appetitive desires. Though it is not the paradigmatic case of reason against appetite, it is a case of better desires being overcome by worse desires. The Leontius case has the same kind of opposition that we see in Euripides' *Hippolytus*. The Leontius case is a counterexample to Socrates' position in the *Protagoras*. There he tells us that The Many think that the desires for food, sex, and drink, namely the appetitive desires, overcome knowledge or the rational desires.

The Socratic position in the *Protagoras* denies that there are cases of moral weakness. This view is at odds with the convictions of The Many. Euripides offers two vivid cases of moral weakness that focus on the psychological drama of the conflict of desires but does not confront the philosophical problems in explaining moral weakness. Socrates brings the philosophical problem of moral weakness to the fore by establishing a necessary tie running from judgment to action. Suppose we take all of what a person values and determine that act x offers the most of what he values. If only what he values counts as a reason to act, what reason can he have to do some lesser alternative act y instead of x? He cannot have a reason. Socrates' position is not popular; it was not then and it is not now. Almost all philosophers and nonphilosophers think that moral weakness occurs. Socrates' rejection of moral weakness was as instructive then as it remains today. At least he shows us what we cannot hold when explaining moral weakness. We need to challenge one of Socrates' claims about the commensuration of good things, judgment, desire, or action. Plato does this in *Republic*. He rejects the claim that we desire only what we think to be good. The irrational desires go after objects without reference to goodness or despite judgments about goodness. The spirited desires consider goodness in part. They are capable of functioning as the worse desires, when set in relation to reason, and as the better desires, when functioning in relation to appetite. By rejecting the tie between judgments about goodness and desire, Plato makes room for the cases of moral weakness in the *Republic*.

Aristotle offers an account of moral weakness in Book VII, Chapter 3 of the *Nicomachean Ethics*. He also discusses the topic in the *Eudemian Ethics*, since Book VI of the *Eudemian Ethics* is Book VII of the *Nicomachean Ethics*. Aristotle's account of moral weakness is technical, subtle, and complex. We do well to switch terminology when discussing Aristotle's account. Rather than referring to the phenomena as moral weakness, we will refer to them as moral incontinence or *akrasia*. There are many reasons to refer to the phenomena in Aristotle's account as *akrasia*. As we will see, Aristotle distinguishes two types of *akrasia*, weakness and impetuosity. By referring to *akrasia*, we avoid having a general category of moral weakness with one subtype being moral weakness. Another reason is that as we specify Aristotle's account, we can use the term "*akrasia*" to reference his particular conception of the phenomena. I will refer to the morally strong person as "*enkratic*" and the class of actions as "*enkratia*."

Aristotle holds that the virtuous person deliberates well, ends his deliberation with a choice, chooses well, and acts according to his choice without facing conflicting desires. The vicious person does not deliberate or choose well, and he acts according to his choice without facing conflicting desires. The virtuous person does what he thinks is best and it is actually the best. The vicious person does what he thinks is best but it is not the best. The enkratic person deliberates and chooses well, and he acts according to his choice while facing conflicting desires. There are two types of *akrasia*. The *weak akratic* person deliberates and chooses well, but he does not act according to his choice while facing conflicting desires. The akratic person does not abandon his choice or change his choice, though he voluntarily acts against it. The impetuous akratic person does not deliberate and choose, but had he deliberated and chosen he would have deliberated and chosen well. The *impetuous akratic* person acts against what he would have chosen and faces desires to act against what would have been his choice. Impetuosity is often found in keen or excitable people.[11] Weak akratic people are done in by the strength of their passions, but impetuous akratic people are done in by the quickness of their passions. In what follows, we will discuss Aristotle's account of the weak akratic person. I will continue to use the term "*akrasia*" to refer to weak *akrasia*.

Aristotle distinguishes unqualified *akrasia* from qualified *akrasia*. *Unqualified akrasia*, or *akrasia* without qualification, involves a conflict of desires between reason and appetite. This type of *akrasia* is concerned with

---

[11] *Nicomachean Ethics*, VII.7.1150b20.

the same objects as the virtue of temperance, the objects of taste and touch. These are the objects of the appetitive desires for food, sex, and drink. *Qualified akrasia* involves a conflict of desires between reason and spirit.[12] Here the person is akratic with respect to anger, honor, gain, victory, or some other object of a spirited desire. The desires of appetite are not worthy of choice, but in the right contexts, the objects of spirited desires are worthy of choice. The spirited part listens to reason but mishears it. Aristotle tells us that anger is like a slave that hears part of the directive and rushes out to fulfill what he takes the directive to be. In this way, qualified *akrasia* is not as bad and is less shameful than unqualified *akrasia*.[13] This form of *akrasia* is not simply bad but bad with qualification. No form of *akrasia* is good.

In Chapter 2 of Book VII, Aristotle refers to Socrates' position on moral weakness in *Protagoras*.[14] He reminds us that Socrates did not believe that moral weakness occurs. It is clear that Aristotle takes himself to be talking about the same phenomena that Socrates rejected in *Protagoras*. So we can say that Aristotle takes Socrates to have rejected the possibility of *akrasia*. Socrates holds that knowledge is a powerful force in human life and that no desires are more powerful than knowledge. Knowledge cannot be dragged around like a slave, according to Socrates. Aristotle says that Socrates' rejection of *akrasia* contradicts the plain and obvious facts. He focuses on the knowledge and ignorance involved in *akrasia*. The problem of *akrasia* does not turn on a distinction between knowing and believing, since some people are equally convinced of what they opine as what they know. For Aristotle, it does not matter whether we say that the akratic person acts against knowledge, belief, or thought. All that matters is that the person is convinced that the act is better and that he understands that what he is doing is wrong. Though Aristotle will talk about the akratic person knowing what he should do and knowing that the act is wrong, his account applies to belief and opinion.[15]

Nonetheless, Aristotle does have a lot to say about the way in which the akratic person knows. He reminds us of a distinction that he made in *On the Soul*.[16] There he discusses potentiality and actuality, and then he applies them to three ways that we refer to a person as a knower. As human animals

---

[12] *Nicomachean Ethics*, VII.4.1148b10.

[13] *Nicomachean Ethics*, VII.6.1149a25.

[14] *Nicomachean Ethics*, VII.2.1145b25.

[15] *Nicomachean Ethics*, VII.3.1146b25.

[16] *De Anima*, II.5.417a25.

we have the potential to learn grammar. Other animals do not have this potential. Through education we can actualize the potential to learn grammar and come to know grammar. Now the person actually knows grammar. This way of knowing is also a potentiality, since the person can use the knowledge when he wants. This person *has* knowledge, but he is not *using* his knowledge. When a person is *using* his knowledge of grammar, he actualizes the potential in the knowledge that he *had* but was not *using*. When we put the distinctions of potentiality, actuality, having knowledge, and using knowledge together, we get the following:

Knowledge	Potentiality and actuality		Having and using knowledge
Knower$_1$		Actuality$_1$ (*entelekheia*)	Has and uses knowledge
Knower$_2$	Actuality$_2$ (*energeia*)	Potentiality (*dunamis*)	Has and does not use knowledge
Knower$_3$	Potentiality (*dunamis*)		Does not have knowledge

In *Nicomachean Ethics*, Aristotle says that it would be strange to say that the akratic person is using his knowledge, knower$_1$, when he acts against his knowledge.[17] It would not be strange to find that he has but is not using his knowledge, knower$_2$, when he acts against his knowledge. Though this person is not using his knowledge, he does actually know (actuality$_2$).

Aristotle turns to the practical syllogism and applies the different ways of knowing to the premises in the syllogism. The syllogism employs a universal premise and a particular premise. He argues that a person could have knowledge of both the universal premise and the particular premise when he acts against his knowledge. There is no way that the akratic person is using his knowledge of both the universal and the particular premises. Yet, he could use his knowledge of the universal premise, but either not have (knower$_3$) or have and not use (knower$_2$) his knowledge of the particular premise. Aristotle distinguishes two ways of having and not using knowledge. One person is not using his knowledge, because he does not want to use it or he is not in applicable circumstances to use his knowledge. Another person is not using his knowledge, because he is mad, asleep, or drunk. The akratic person is in a similar state, because he is in a fit of passion. The sexual appetites cause changes in the body and some people under the

---

[17] *Nicomachean Ethics*, VII.3.1146b31.

influence of these desires act as if they are in a fit of madness. The akratic person knows$_2$ the particular premise in like fashion with a drunk person. Though the akratic person might use the language that comes from knowledge, when he is in this state, he does not understand the meaning of the words that come out of his mouth. He is like an actor on a stage or a student who can recite a formula without understanding how to use it. Saying the words of knowledge does not necessitate that the person is a knower$_1$.

With these preliminaries in hand, Aristotle turns to his account of *akrasia* according to nature (*phusis*).[18] The universal premise is the akratic person's choice. The particular premise is a perception. When a person is using his knowledge of both premises, he must act for the conclusion. The rational syllogism has a universal premise that restrains the person from tasting. The appetitive syllogism urges the person to taste. Aristotle explicitly mentions the universal premise in the appetitive syllogism, "All Sweets are to be tasted." He also mentions the particular premise in the appetitive syllogism, "this is sweet."[19] He tells us that the universal premise in the rational syllogism urges the akratic person to avoid the object, but the universal premise in the appetitive syllogism urges the akratic person to pursue the sweet.

Though Aristotle tells us that a particular premise refers to a sweet object, he does not tell us what feature of the object is mentioned in the rational syllogism. It is possible that the rational syllogism mentions sweetness, but it is also possible that it does not. There is a big difference between the two possibilities. If the syllogisms mention the same feature, sweetness, then one particular premise could function in either or both of the syllogisms. In this case, the forbidden feature is the same as the attractive feature. If they mention different features of the object, then the particular premises in the two syllogisms are different. In this case, it is possible for the appetitive syllogism to mention sweetness and the rational syllogism to mention some other feature such as desserts. On this interpretation, the universal premise in the rational syllogism would be something such as "All desserts are not to be tasted." Aristotle could be referring to either a common feature between the two syllogisms or to different features in the two syllogisms. If we think it must be the latter possibility, then we restrict Aristotle's account with the constraint that the forbidden and attractive features in the syllogisms must differ. We will interpret Aristotle as allowing the two syllogisms to refer to the same feature, sweetness.

---

[18] *Nicomachean Ethics*, VII.3.1147a24.
[19] *Nicomachean Ethics*, VII.3.1147a33.

We can now see enough detail in Aristotle's account of the conflicting syllogisms in the explanation of akratic action. Aristotle applies the distinction between having and using knowledge to the akratic agent's syllogism. In reason's syllogism, he tells us that the agent uses the universal premise. He has and does not use the particular premise:

The rational syllogism			
Syllogism	Having and using	Knowing	Example
Universal premise	Uses knowledge: Actuality$_1$ (entelekheia)	Knowing$_1$	All sweets are not to be eaten
Particular premise	Has and does not use knowledge: Actuality$_2$ (energeia)	Knowing$_2$	This is a sweet
Conclusion			Do not eat this

In contrast to the rational syllogism, the appetitive syllogism goes through to the conclusion. Aristotle does not tell us that either of the premises in appetite's syllogism is used, an actuality$_1$ (entelekheia). He does not employ his technical terminology in reference to appetite's universal premise. He simply says that the universal opinion (doksa) is present (1147a32). The particular premise is active (energeia) (1147a34):

The appetitive syllogism			
Syllogism	Having/using knowledge	Knowing	Example
Universal premise	Appetite is present: Opinion (doksa)		All sweets are to be eaten
Particular premise	Has and does not use knowledge: Actuality$_2$ (energeia)	Knowing$_2$	This is a sweet
Conclusion			Eat this

Aristotle does not apply *having* or *using* knowledge to the universal premise. Since Aristotle holds that appetite can move the body and since appetitive acts are voluntary, it is appetite and not knowledge that explains eating the sweet (1147a34). If we think of using knowledge, actuality$_1$, as using it as it should be used, then the agent does not use knowledge. Aristotle says that the agent has a particular premise, actuality$_2$, and does not use his knowledge. This is an accurate description, since the agent does not use knowledge as it should be used. Eating the sweet is not a demonstration of knowledge in action. Aristotle is not focused on explaining the success of the appetitive syllogism. He is focused on explaining the failure of knowledge in the rational syllogism.

Aristotle returns to Socrates' account in the *Protagoras* to close his discussion of *akrasia* in *Nicomachean Ethics* VII.3. He distinguishes knowledge proper from perceptual knowledge. *Knowledge proper* concerns the universal premise in a practical syllogism. The universal premise in the rational syllogism represents the end of deliberation, a choice. Virtuous, enkratic, and akratic persons choose well. This rational universal premise is the best that reason can do on its own. From there it will need to encounter an object to be moved into action. *Perceptual knowledge* concerns the use of the senses, thought, and imagination. The particular premise is not *essentially* contrary to reason. It is *accidentally* contrary to reason.[20] The particular premise of appetite's syllogism is not essentially contrary to the major premise of reason's syllogism. It is an appetitive desire that causes action.[21] Appetitive desire is contrary to reason. Subsequently, he says that the particular premise is about perceptions. When a person has a universal premise and sees an object, or thinks of an object, or images that there is an object, straightaway he acts. Aristotle says that a particular premise determines action. So the perception, the particular premise, is the proximate efficient cause of action. Suppose a person has and uses the universal premise. As he goes about, he might see a particular object and go after it. Then again, he might think that a particular object is in a certain place and go after it. Alternatively, he might imagine that there is a particular object and go after it. The particular premise is not just in the domain of perception; it is also in the domain of thought and imagination. The particular premise is perceptual knowledge, which is not knowledge proper. Aristotle charitably interprets Socrates. Socrates holds that knowledge cannot be overcome by passions. Aristotle says that Socrates must have meant that knowledge proper cannot be overcome by passions. It is not the universal premise in reason's syllogism that is overcome; it is the particular premise that is overcome. It is perception, thought, or imagination that overcomes used knowledge of reason's universal premise. So Aristotle argues that Socrates was half right. He was wrong to think that no sort of knowledge can be overcome, since the rational universal knowledge is overcome by

---

[20] *Nicomachean Ethics*, VII.3.1147b2.
[21] *Nicomachean Ethics*, VII.3.1147a34–35.

perceptual knowledge of the particular premise. Aristotle argues that, in *akrasia*, appetite with perception can overcome reason. Socrates was right, however, to think that knowledge proper is not dragged around like a slave. The universal premise in the rational syllogism is not dragged anywhere. It is a standing choice awaiting perception.

Plato's position in *Republic* is noticeably absent from Aristotle's discussion of *akrasia*. Regardless, both accounts make room for *akrasia* by holding that the appetites are irrational. Both accounts hold that it is possible to desire something without thinking that it is good. Aristotle argues that appetites are irrational and that they go after objects regardless of goodness. Appetites can go after objects that are thought to be bad. Aristotle's explanation is subtle and complex, but Aristotle solves Socrates' problem of *akrasia* in the same way that Plato does in *Republic*. He breaks the ties between judging good and desiring. Aristotle explains *akrasia* without qualification, and Plato explains *akrasia* without qualification. Aristotle and Plato attempt to explain *akrasia* with qualification. Aristotle makes the formal distinction. Plato offers an example in the Leontius case and the Odysseus case. Euripides only attempts to illustrate *akrasia* with qualification. In *Medea*, he illustrated Medea's conflict between reason and spirit. In *Hippolytus*, he illustrated Phaedra's conflict between spirit and appetite. Aristotle owes more to Plato than he admits, since he takes the solution as Plato does in *Republic* to breaking the necessary tie between judgment of value and desire.

Amélie Oskenberg Rorty offers an insightful interpretation of Aristotle's theory by showing that his account can function as a framework with broader implications.[22] Accordingly, the practical syllogism can be interpreted as marking different stages on the path from thought to action. In the first stage, a person deliberates. In deliberation a person considers his most general beliefs about living well. If a person wants to lose weight, for example, he will consider different means to achieve that end. The person might deliberate about options, such as going for a walk every day, eating healthy foods, and avoiding desserts. These are some of the means that a person might consider to lose weight. Deliberation ends with choice. To choose one of the means is to commit to realizing those means in action. Suppose that this person chooses to avoid desserts. He has committed to the choice, and we can represent the choice with a universal proposition in

---

[22] See "Where Does the Akratic Break Take Place," Amélie Oskenberg Rorty. *Australian Journal of Philosophy*, Vol. 58. No. 94 December 1980. 333, fn. 1.

a practical syllogism, "All desserts are to be avoided." Stage one is the move through deliberation, and it ends in choice. Sometimes it happens that a person deliberates and identifies certain means to achieve his goals, but he does not bring himself to commit to the choice. In this case, the person does not end deliberation with a choice. It might be that the person finds that he just will not get out of bed for the day. This sort of phenomenon was called *melancholia* in the ancient and medieval historical epochs. We call this form of akrasia "depression." The first stage of moral weakness is called *akrasia of direction or aim.*

In the second stage, the person moves toward perception and the particular premise. Suppose that the person does choose and he commits to the universal premise, "All desserts are to be avoided." He now has a choice standing at the ready to become grounded in circumstances. To enact the choice, the person needs to identify appropriate objects or circumstances. To do this, he uses perception, thought, or imagination. The appropriate perception is represented by the particular premise in the practical syllogism, "This is a dessert." Sometimes it happens that a person is in applicable circumstances but fails to commit to the particular premise. In Aristotle's account, the person does not have, or has and does not use, the particular premise. This person does not interpret the circumstances appropriately. He does not pay heed to the relevant features in the world around him. He does not use his perceptual faculties in the service of his choice. Possibly he redescribes the object as a cake or a pie, without committing that the object is a dessert. All the information is there for him to identify circumstances or objects that allow him to make progress in implementing his choice. Yet, he fails to do so. This represents a failure to commit to the particular premise. This form of moral weakness is Aristotelian *akrasia* and it is called *interpretive akrasia.*

In the third stage, the person moves toward a decision or intention and the conclusion of the practical syllogism. Suppose that the person commits to the choice and to the appropriate perception. In this case, we can say that the person commits to the universal premise and to the particular premise. The person needs to put the premises together and draw the inference. It may be that we are out to dinner and the person has announced his choice to avoid desserts, and then, after dinner, the dessert cart comes around. The person might say, "there are the desserts." As the cart goes around the table and people pick the desserts they want, the cart comes to the person committed to avoiding desserts. The desserts smell delicious and he finds his mouth salivating. He can almost taste the dessert. Sometimes it happens that a person in such a state reaches out and grabs a dessert. As strange as this is, it does seem that it sometimes happens. Even after committing to the universal and the particular, the person fails to come to a conclusion. This form of moral weakness is called *akrasia of irrationality.*

In the fourth stage, the person commits to the choice, the perception, the conclusion, and tries to move to the act. Suppose that the person does not take the dessert off the cart and sits while others enjoy their desserts. He sits watching them, seeing their enjoyment, and smelling their delicious selections. He can feel stronger and stronger desires for the desserts. This is difficult for him to endure and the longer it goes on, the harder it gets. Suppose a person at the table takes a bite or two of the dessert and finds that he is full. The dessert is just sitting there, largely untouched, and unloved. Sometimes it happens that he takes the neglected dessert and eats it. He has failed to act on his decision. This form of moral weakness is called *akrasia of character.*

Rorty's four types of moral weakness	The parts of the syllogism	An example
	Deliberation	
Akrasia of direction or aim		
	Universal premise	All desserts are to be avoided
Interpretive *akrasia*		
	Particular premise	This is a dessert
Akrasia of irrationality		
	Conclusion	Avoid this
Akrasia of character		
	Action	The act of refraining

The akratic break is a failure to move from one stage in the process to the next stage in the process. So the four types of *akrasia* are placed between the steps from thought to action. In stage one, the person fails to move from deliberation to choice. In stage two, the person fails to move from the universal premise to the particular premise. In stage three, the person fails to move from the particular premise to the conclusion. In stage four, the person fails to move from the conclusion to the action.

Aristotle's account of *akrasia* focuses on the failure of the particular premise in the rational syllogism. Yet, the framework that he offers is a valuable tool for considering other possible failures. The explanation that he offers for interpretive *akrasia* explains, if successful, one type of *akrasia*.

It cannot function as an explanation for the other three types of *akrasia*. It is not clear that Aristotle would count the failure to end deliberation with a choice as a form of *akrasia*. In this case, the person would not have deliberated and chosen well, which are requirements for Aristotelian *akrasia*. Also, as I interpret his account of the practical syllogism, he would not think that *akrasia* of character is possible, since he holds that the conclusion of a practical syllogism is an action. Not all interpreters of Aristotle agree with this position. Some interpreters hold that action is an additional step after drawing the conclusion. It does not seem that Aristotle would accept either of these types of akrasia.

Aristotle takes Socrates' account of being overcome in *Protagoras* as an attempt to reject the possibility of interpretive *akrasia*, since he thinks that they are talking about the same phenomena. It is not clear that this interpretation of Socrates' position is accurate. Socrates does not refer to the practical syllogism. So we cannot be sure where The Many take the akratic break to occur. Socrates seems focused on knowing the good in such a way that the person draws the conclusion, if we assimilate his account into the practical syllogism. It is more likely then that Socrates is rejecting the possibility of *akrasia* of character. An explanation of interpretive *akrasia* cannot function as an account of *akrasia* of character. So, even if Aristotle explains interpretive *akrasia*, he has not thereby shown that there are cases of *akrasia* of character. As far as the arguments go, Aristotle and Socrates can be right. When we consider Euripides' illustrations, it is even clearer than Socrates' discussion that his characters draw the inference and arrive at the conclusion. Medea laments to her children the deed that she eventually commits. Phaedra admits her lust for Hippolytus. Medea does not lament, "All killing of my children is to be avoided." She laments killing these particular children, and she says that the killing should be avoided. Phaedra does not just lament, "All lusting for stepsons is to be avoided." Phaedra laments lusting for her stepson, Hippolytus. These illustrations give us reason to think that they reference what would be the particular premise(s) and the conclusions of the practical syllogisms. If this interpretation is correct, then Euripides discusses *akrasia* of character. Analyzing where the akratic break takes place among the various discussions amplifies our understanding of each account.[23]

---

[23] Every form of government, other than the aristocratic state, is acting against better judgment. The reasons for their failure to act according to reason are many: coming from the military class, the wealthy, The Many, or the lawless.

9.3 Fate and Voluntary Action

If nothing is up to us, then there is no point in urging anyone to do anything. The person will do it or not, despite any of our efforts. If all actions are involuntary, then what in the *Kosmos* could we be addressing through ethics? Ethics would simply become a *descriptive* task and it would lose all *prescriptive* features. We can describe what happens, but to prescribe is to urge the person to action. It may be that determinism is true. It is of the utmost importance to find out whether it is true or not. Otherwise, all prescriptive ethics is pointless, and we will suffer under the illusion that there is something that we can do about our circumstances through decisions, habits, and behavior that alter the outcomes in our lives. It may be that there is tranquility in holding that all things are determined, but pointing it out is pointless. If there is no voluntary action, then there is no justification for prescriptive ethics. There are at least three positions on determinism and voluntarism: hard determinism, soft determinism, and compatibilism.

Plato approached freedom of action by examining desires. Usually, he examined rational desires (reason) and irrational desires (appetite). In a couple of places, he examined tripartite desires: rational (reason), partly rational (spirit), and irrational (appetite). Plato has these three desires as flowing like streams such that a person can use reason or judgment to alter the strength of the flows. By enhancing reason, through education, habituation, and practice, a person can enhance the flow of the rational stream and train, or constrain, the flow of the appetitive desires. The spirited desires, the natural allies of reason, are aligned with reason unless a person has a bad upbringing. The rational desires, supplemented by the spirited desire, can constrain appetite. It might seem that Plato thinks people are simply subject to their desires. He does not. Judgment always plays a role in determining action. If it is weak, it plays a subordinate role. If it is strong, it plays a directive role. Plato holds that there is a faculty of judgment that can direct action and modify the streams of desire. He names the rational stream as the logical part (*logistikos*), or more specifically in the divided line as thought (*dianoia*) and understanding (*noesis*). As these streams contract or enlarge through the judgment or lack of judgment by the person, the character of the person is enlivened.

Aristotle approached freedom of action by determining voluntariness and choice (*prohairesis*). A voluntary action is not compelled; the moving principle is in the agent, the act is up to us to do or not to do, and it is done with knowledge of the circumstances. He holds that the agent must know what he is doing. Aristotle distinguishes actions done in ignorance and actions done through ignorance. An example of a person acting *in ignorance* is a drunk person acting the fool and behaving thoughtlessly. If this person consumed the drink, not knowing that it contained alcohol, and possibly someone spiked the drink without him knowing, then he acted *through ignorance*. Actions done through ignorance and in ignorance are not voluntary. Actions done in ignorance but not through ignorance are voluntary. Aristotle distinguishes choice from action. A person makes a choice when he ends deliberation. Subsequently, he can voluntarily act either according to his choice or against his choice. There are two types of involuntary acts. An involuntary act comes with regret at the moment of action. Nonvoluntary acts do not come with regret. The division between a voluntary and an involuntary act is subtle. There are mixed actions, as when circumstances pressure a person to behave in a way that he otherwise would not behave. For example, a person might do dishonorable things to free a family member from captivity. A person might do things because he is being coerced, as when there is a gun held to his head. These acts tend to be voluntary, but Aristotle admits that there are limits to the amount of coercion that we can endure. At some point, the act becomes compelled and thereby is involuntary.

Plato and Aristotle do not refer to freedom of the "will." They refer to actions that are voluntary (*hekousion*) or "up to us" (*hupo hemin*) to do or not to do. These acts come to be called "voluntary" (*voluntarius*) in Latin. The will, or "free will," is a subsequent invention of Christians to address the problem of evil.[24] It is anachronistic to apply the concept of freedom of the will to Plato or Aristotle. Contemporary discussions of action tend not to employ the concept of the will or the free will. They tend to employ the concepts of intention and intentional action. When we turn to the Hellenistic philosophers, it is common for interpreters to frame their discussions in terms of the free will vs. determinism debate. This application is anachronistic, since the concept of "free will" was not conceived until after the Hellenistic period.

The Hellenistic philosophers worried about determinism through an analysis of Fatalism. *Fatalism* is the view that whatever is must be, or whatever will be necessarily will be, and there is nothing that one can do about it. *Freedom of action* is the view that our acts are up to us to do or not to do. Fatalism and freedom of action have implications for moral responsibility.

---

[24] Arthur Schopenhauer, Gunter Zoller ed., Eric F.J. Payne trans., *Prize Essay on the Freedom of the Will* (Cambridge, Cambridge University Press, 1990), Chapter IV, 59.

If fatalism is true, then moral responsibility is an illusion. If freedom of action is true, then moral responsibility is possible. We can distinguish three forms of determinism that each in their own way support fatalism. *Logical determinism* holds that a proposition referring to a future event is true or false before the event. Logical determinism comes from bivalence: every proposition is either true or false. *Causal determinism* holds that all events are caused by prior sufficient conditions. Causal determinism comes from a view of physical causality; every event is caused by sufficient physical events. *Epistemic determinism* holds that all events are already known by some being. Epistemic determinism comes from the view that future events can be foreseen and are thereby inevitable. For instance, a god might be all knowing or an oracle might know the future. These forms of determinism, each in their own way, threaten the freedom of action. If any of these forms of determinism are true, then it seems that the past, present, and future are fated to happen. We can place the three forms of determinism under the general heading of fatalism.

Epicurus (Epicurean) and Chrysippus (Stoic) hold that causal and logical determinism are inter-entailing, or entail each other. So they hold that causal and logical determinism stand or fall together. They both hold that epistemic determinism entails either or both causal and logical determinism. Despite their common view of the relation between causal and logical determinism, the two hold diametrically opposed views on the two forms of causation. Epicurus rejects both forms of determinism. Since Epicureanism holds that atoms happen (*tukhe*) to become entangled or that they swerve in their motion, there is no causal or logical determinism. Though it is clear that the swerve is meant to account for voluntary acts, up to us to do or not to do, it is not clear how the swerve does account for voluntary acts. If the swerve is a motion that happens at no determined time, place, or way, then it seems that voluntary action happens at no determined time, place, or way. The finest atoms, the soul atoms, account for the swerve and thereby for voluntary action. It seems, however, that all atoms are subject to the swerve. When the soul atoms swerve, they transmit the motion through the larger atoms in the body. Yet these larger atoms swerve too. It would seem then that the motion of the larger atoms occurs at no determined time, place, or way. This would undermine the Epicurean account of how the soul atoms impart motion to the larger atoms in a way that determines the motion of the larger atoms. So, although the swerve may account for the voluntary motion of the soul atoms and thereby the larger atoms, the swerve undermines the account of the soul atoms moving the larger atoms in a determined way. We cannot expect to have a causal account of voluntary action, though the Epicureans hold that once a voluntary act is instigated by the soul atoms there is a causal account of it imparting motion to the other bodily parts. The difficulty that remains is that we are left wanting an account of the transmission of that motion that is not itself subject to the swerve. Carneades argues that the Epicureans can offer a preferable account of voluntary action without positing the swerve.[25] The Epicureans, Carneades suggests, should have held that the mind can move the body through voluntary motion. The motion would be caused by volition. This position would allow the Epicureans to maintain that all motion is causally determined and attribute the cause to volition. Volition, in turn, is up to us to do or not to do.

Chrysippus (Stoic) accepts both forms of determinism.[26] The epistemic determinism comes from the belief that the *Kosmos* is a physical-rational living organism. So he thinks that the physical organism entails causal determinism and the rational aspect of the organism entails epistemic determinism. His account of causal determinism entails epistemic determinism, since matter is imbued with *logos*. We have a *logos* just as the *Kosmos* has a *logos*. In this way, one's actions are co-fated. The view is termed *compatibilism*. As we encounter impressions, they push us. One can exercise choice (*prohairesis*) in relation to impressions. The choice is up to us to make or not to make. One can choose to act (*hairesis*) or not act. The options one has are not limitless. One cannot choose not to have impressions. One cannot choose to be 20-feet tall. Different people have different propensities, strengths, and weaknesses. Within nature, there is a human nature, and each individual has a nature. All people are limited by human nature. Each individual is limited by one's own nature. Within these bounds, one can choose to act or not to act. Almost all people are not virtuous. Recall that for the Stoics, virtue is not a matter of degree. There is one sort of virtuous person, the wise Stoic. Since the wise Stoic is virtuous, the wise Stoic always chooses rightly. The wise Stoic has a "firm and fixed disposition toward virtue," to borrow a description from Aristotle: In like fashion, the wise Stoic cannot act otherwise. After all, otherwise, the person would not be the wise Stoic. Although the Stoics hold that almost every person can choose to act or not to act, the wise Stoic does not have alternate

---

[25] Cicero, *De Fato*, 23.

[26] For a detailed and insightful discussion of freedom and determinism in Stoicism, see Susanne Bobzien, *Determinism and Freedom in Stoic Philosophy* (New York, Oxford University Press, 2001).

possibilities. The wise Stoic could choose to do or not to do acts that are up to us before becoming a wise Stoic.

Whence does the wise Stoic come? It does not seem that the Stoics hold that the wise Stoic comes fully formed as such from birth or from nature. Since every person has a human nature and a particular nature, these endowments come with certain propensities, not all of which are virtuous. In addition, each of us grows through childhood, adolescence, and adulthood. The Stoics do not claim that the wise Stoic is that way as a child. Quite the opposite, the Stoics stress the need for training ourselves toward virtue. When one achieves virtue, one is a wise Stoic. Recognizing the import of training through the stages of life allows us to appreciate the context of the Stoic claim that not every act is such that one could do otherwise. The context is the framework of training disposition, assent, and judgment. They are referring to an ideal toward which all Stoics, or all but the wise Stoic, endeavor.

Carneades (skeptic) treats the three forms of fatalism as distinct: logical, causal, and epistemic. He holds that the epistemic entails both causal and logical. Logical determinism, he holds, does not entail either causal or epistemic determinism. He makes an astute point when he argues that logical determinism does not entail either causal or epistemic determinism. Bivalence is a logical feature of language. The reason that a claim about the future is true or false is that the *truth making* causal determiners occur. Yet, the causal determiners do not come about because of the logical determination as true or false. To put it another way, the causes of the causal determinants are not caused by logical determinism. Along similar lines, logical determinism does not entail epistemic determinism. The bivalence of propositions is not known beforehand, not even by the gods. The skeptics hold that there are non-determined acts, *contingent* acts. These acts are up to us to do or not. Actions are caused by volitions, but volitions are self-caused. Volition functions as an uncaused cause of actions.

9.4 The Good Life

The Cynics embraced nature (*phusis*) and rejected convention (*nomos*). They aimed to reduce their dependence on material goods to a minimum. The desire for material goods and the demands they place on a person to maintain them are the primary inducements for a lack of tranquility and vicious action. Though they worked to reduce their desires for, and dependence on, material goods, they did indulge in basic natural desires. They ate simple food, lived on the streets, defecated wherever they happened to be, and had sex when and where it was available. They did not spend their time in dialectic arguments; they spent their time in pursuing their way of living. By avoiding the entrapments of material goods, they had more time for leisure. By reducing their material desires and needs, they were easily able to remove pain from their lives. Their goal was not to amass pleasure. They embraced hardship, even seeking it out. This was not in an effort to cause themselves discomfort and pain, but to learn how to accept discomfort as a fact of life. By accepting it and not fighting against it, they sought to achieve freedom from the causes of unhappiness. Happiness for them is found in virtue. By removing the material inducements to vice, not fighting against hardships, accepting them as a necessary part of life, and accepting that life involves difficulties, the Cynics claim to achieve happiness. True wealth and happiness are found in the soul, not in striving for or acquiring material things.

The Epicureans removed themselves from the consternations of politics, both philosophically and physically. Epicurus placed his school, The Garden, away from the city center. The Epicureans offer metaphysics, epistemology, and ethics. They take sensations, preconceptions, and feelings as true. In addition to sensations, we have opinions and judgments. All of these factors inform choice. We can choose to pursue pleasure and avoid pain. Not all pleasures are to be pursued, since some pleasures involve more pain than pleasure. They hold that mental pleasures and pains are more important than physical pleasures and pains. Their goal is not to amass as much pleasure as possible. Instead, they seek to avoid pain. Pleasure for them is not a positive state. Pleasure is simply the removal of pain. They achieve the removal of pain. The Epicureans keep their desires to a minimum. They focus on natural necessary desires. Once the desire for other sorts of pleasures is removed, they argue that the desires that we must satisfy to avoid pain are easily satisfied. Hunger is painful and we need to eat. We do not need to eat exotic foods that are expensive and difficult to procure. Hunger and thirst are easily satiated. In this way, physical pleasure is easy to achieve. There are two main sources of mental pains. The fear of Kosmic events is often expressed through a fear of the gods and the fear of death. After removing the causes of these fears through their metaphysics, the Epicureans claim to achieve mental pleasure. They call this state imperturbability or *ataraxia*.

The Stoics make ethics one of the three main parts of their philosophy, physics and logic being the other two. Physics is an account of matter and *logos* as the basic features of the *Kosmos*. Human beings also have the basic features of matter and *logos*. Logic is an account of *logos* in the *Kosmos* and in human beings. The aim of ethics is to live life in accord with the *logos*, both in the *Kosmos* and in ourselves. The Stoic desire for a comprehensive, systematic, and consistent system is demonstrated partly in their subcategories of ethics. We collected the eight subcategories under three headings: desire, duty, and assent. The account of desire includes accounts of impulse and passion. Our first impulses are for survival and pleasure. Over time, they develop into desires for our personal benefit, the benefit of our family, and the benefit of our community. Passion is an excessive impulse, usually as the result of frustrated desires. There are physical and mental passions; the latter include jealousy, envy, and confusion. The passions, both physical and mental, interfere with our ability to follow reason. Yet, the good life is a life in agreement with the *logos*. Passion is to be avoided, since it detours us from reason. Reason sets our duties as indicated in our proper functions. These functions are first grounded in our natural desire for survival and expand from there to include obligations that we take on in the family and in society. Assent is the acceptance or endorsement of a desire, duty, or judgment. Assenting at the wrong time or in the wrong way leads us to be unhappy. In place of passions, the Stoics urge us to adopt apathy (*apatheia*). In place of fighting against nature, the Stoics urge us to adopt imperturbability (*ataraxia*). This leads to a life that avoids the tumult of passions and the perturbations of life's apparent misfortunes. The result is the aim of life: happiness (*eudaimonia*), virtue, or Stoic wisdom.

The skeptics distinguish reality, judgment, and the consequences of judgment. They hold that we do not know the nature of reality. They block the inference from our judgments based on our impressions of judgments that hold the reality of this way or that. They offer a process that allows us to suspend judgment and pronounce that reality is no more this than that. The method of producing contrary arguments is developed through the Modes. When we judge that olive oil is beneficial to humans and infer that olive oil is beneficial, we are to produce a contrary argument. For instance, olive oil is not beneficial to bees, so olive oil is not beneficial. We now can make an inference to a conjunction, "olive oil is beneficial and not beneficial." From this we conclude that olive oil is no more beneficial than not beneficial. To put it another way, it is no more this than that or "no more" for short. Arriving at this position allows us to suspend judgment. Later skeptics allow us to hold probable impressions. These impressions are thoroughly investigated. These impressions allow us to act this way or that, but they do not involve a claim about the nature of reality. In addition, they do not lead us to assent to any assertion or deny a judgment. The skeptics hold that the wise person gives assent to nothing. To put it another way, the wise person suspends judgment. When a person is able to achieve this result, the person achieves happiness (*eudaimonia*).

There are four main philosophical movements in the Hellenistic period: Cynicism, Epicureanism, Stoicism, and Skepticism. Every movement, except Epicureanism, traces its philosophical inspiration to Socrates. In the shadow of the great philosophical systems developed by Plato and Aristotle, they find light in establishing Socrates as their touchstone. In this way, they are kindred with Plato and less like Aristotle. Epicurus is the exception, since he did not trace his philosophical roots to Socrates. The aim of each of the four Hellenistic movements, whether inspired by Socrates or not, is to find tranquility in thought, assent, judgment, and action. In this way, even the Epicurean school is Socratic. Socrates was well known for his ability to face hardship without complaint, even going into death with a calm demeanor and a happy countenance. The Hellenistic movements are unlike Socrates, since Socrates did not spend time investigating metaphysics. The Cynics are an exception, since they avoided dialectic and metaphysics. The other Hellenistic philosophical systems develop robust accounts of metaphysics and physics. In this way, the Cynics are alone in possessing the Socratic exclusion of metaphysics and the sole focus on the good life. Regardless, each of the Hellenistic schools is focused on ethics, virtue, happiness, and the good life in action.

INDEX

This Is Ancient Philosophy: An Introduction, First Edition. Kirk Fitzpatrick.
© 2024 John Wiley & Sons, Inc. Published 2024 by John Wiley & Sons, Inc.

Printed and bound by CPI Group (UK) Ltd, Croydon, CR0 4YY

09/06/2025

14685911-0001